How Does Foster Care Work?

also in the series

How Does Foster Care Work?

International Evidence on Outcomes

Edited by Elizabeth Fernandez
and Richard P. Barth

Foreword by James K. Whittaker

Jessica Kingsley Publishers
London and Philadelphia

Tables 5.1–5.3 are reprinted from *Children and Youth Services Review* 31 (8), Jorge F.
Valle, Mónica López, Carme Monstserrat and Amaia Bravo, *Twenty Years of Foster Care
in Spain: Profiles, patterns and outcomes,* 2009, with permission from Elsevier.
Figure 12.1 is reprinted with permission from Statistics Denmark

First published in 2010
by Jessica Kingsley Publishers
116 Pentonville Road
London N1 9JB, UK
and
400 Market Street, Suite 400
Philadelphia, PA 19106, USA

www.jkp.com

Library of Congress Cataloging in Publication Data
How does foster care work? : international evidence on outcomes/edited by
Elizabeth Fernandez and Richard P. Barth ; foreword by James K. Whittaker.
p. cm.
Includes bibliographical references and index.
ISBN 978-1-84905-812-4 (alk. paper)
1. Foster home care. 2. Foster children. 3. Children--Institutional
care. I. Fernandez, Elizabeth. II. Barth, Richard P. 1952-
HV873.H67 2010
362.73'3--dc22
2010006972

British Library Cataloguing in Publication Data
A CIP catalogue record for this book is available from the British Library

ISBN 978 1 84905 812 4

Printed and bound in Great Britain by
MPG Books Group

Acknowledgments

Our thanks are due to Professor James Whittaker for writing the Foreword to this book with insights based on his international understandings of research, practice developments and challenges in this field. We would like to acknowledge all the authors for contributing their valuable and committed work to this collection. We appreciate their patience and cooperation in responding to the editorial process and to our request to extend their expertise in providing commentaries on individual chapters.

Included in our thanks are members of the International Association for Outcome Research and Evaluation in Child and Family Services (iaOBER fcs) led by Professors Tony Maluccio and Tiziano Vechiato. During the period when the book was conceived it was invaluable to exchange ideas with a wide range of skilled and experienced international researchers who are members of this network.

We thank Professor Harriet Ward, Series Editor for her insights and encouragement through the process. We also thank Stephen Jones, Commissioning Editor and Caroline Walton, Editorial Assistant, Jessica Kingsley Publishers for their helpful feedback and for guiding this work to completion.

We would like to acknowledge the University of Maryland Dean's Research Fund and Janice Carver for assistance. Thanks are also due to Jessica Rojas, University of New South Wales for formatting and producing the manuscript with exceptional care.

Special thanks go out to workers, carers and service users – children and young people. We hope you feel that that we have done justice to your aspirations for better outcomes and best practice.

Elizabeth Fernandez,
Richard P. Barth

Contents

List of Tables

List of Figures

Part One:
Introduction

Foreword

> What the best and wisest parent wants for his own child, that must the community want for all of its children. Any other ideal for our schools is narrow and unlovely; acted upon, it destroys our democracy.
>
> *John Dewey from School and Society, 1907*

This timely and substantive volume produced by Elizabeth Fernandez and Richard P. Barth and their distinguished international contributors extends Dewey's oft quoted challenge from the sphere of public education to the very core of the lived experience of children in out-of-home state care. It is perhaps fitting that the present volume appears barely a decade into the 21st century and slightly more than a century later than Dewey's original exhortation. As Fernandez and Barth note, family foster care in many countries has pushed beyond its original goals of safety, stability and permanency to include a focus on *well-being* which encompasses developmental, health, and educational outcomes, familial and social relationships along with emotional development. This broadened focus on a wide range of developmental outcomes required in turn, critical examination of a deeper empirical and theoretical knowledge-base –including longitudinal research on factors which positively influence children and families in achieving healthy developmental outcomes, as well as factors that blunt and divert the effect of known risk factors. As with education, for researchers and reformers alike, the net effect of this present effort underscores the critical linkage between empirical research and public policy and the need for research designs, methods of analysis and rapid and coherent dissemination of key findings to match the increasing complexities of the foster family care services enterprise. *Foster family care* as the editors and their contributors faithfully note has expanded to include a wide range of shared and kinship-care variations along with a variety of purposefully designed intensive treatment interventions using the foster family as an integral platform for service delivery, often as an alternative to residential placement. Moreover, as the population of children entering care increasingly reflects the harmful effects of child maltreatment – in one or several of its forms – service arrangements must take into account factors such as childhood trauma in forward planning along with the traditional goals of safety, continuity and nurture. The overall task is daunting as witnessed by the erratic progress of educational reform and the difficulties inherent in reaching consensus on what, indeed, *the best and wisest parent wants for his own child.*

Without diminishing the enormity of foster care reform, the contributors to the present volume refreshingly provide numerous examples of how cross-national perspectives on findings, methodology, service populations and emergent reform initiatives can both enhance local efforts and realize incremental improvements through the insights of others. In fact, it is heartening to experience the ease with which the reader can transition from Australia, to the US, UK, Sweden, Denmark, Ireland, Spain and Canada in examining the contours of the out-of-home care system viewed in cross-national perspective. This is indeed a coherent volume, owing perhaps primarily to the central focus on understanding *how does foster care work?* This central theme of the book (and its title) is explicated and carried through in virtually every chapter. It is also a tribute to Fernandez and Barth – both senior and well recognized foster care researchers in their respective countries – and their contributors who are also well-respected child welfare researchers whose work is known internationally. The net effect for this reader stops perhaps just a bit short of a "common language," but that clearly is the goal both in policy reform and methodological understanding to which these pioneering investigators are committed and which, in large measure because of their efforts including this present work, appears now within reach. Networks of child welfare researchers and policy scholars such as EUSARF (The European Scientific Association on Residential and Foster Care for Children and Adolescents), IAOBER

(The International Association for Outcome-Based Evaluation and Research on Family and Children's Services) and INTRAC (The International Research Network on Transitions to Adulthood from Care) provide important forums for cross-national exchange. In addition, a growing cross-national literature on topics as diverse as residential care (Courtney and Iwaniec 2009), child welfare research influences on policy and practice (Lindsey and Shlonsky 2008), the integration of evidence-based practices into existing services (McAuley, Pecora and Whittaker, 2009), and transitions to adulthood (Stein and Munro 2008) complements detailed within-country studies of foster care dynamics such as the recently published study on the Casey Family Services in the US (Pecora *et al.* 2010) and focused research on infants and very young children in the care system in the UK (Ward, Munro and Dearden 2006).

Taken as a whole, the contributors to this volume provide hope that the child welfare field indeed has made solid progress in fulfilling the promise implicit in its title: *How Does Foster Care Work?* Much work remains including: the refinement of promising analytic techniques such as propensity score modelling which Barth and Fernandez reference as well as the further refinement of methodologies for systematically analyzing administrative data sets in the manner pioneered by the Chapin Hall Center for Children at the University of Chicago (see the contribution by Wulczyn and Chen in this present volume) so that practice and policy are continuously informed by the systematic analysis of routinely gathered data in a given local authority, state or country. Beyond analysis of administrative data, child welfare research seems greatly in need of models for partnership between public authorities, university-based researchers, and private philanthropy which can work collaboratively to develop and evaluate service innovations as well as continue to refine and improve what are typically referred to as "usual services." Research spearheaded by Mark Courtney and colleagues in the *Partners for Our Children* project at the University of Washington and Washington State Department of Social and Health Services would seem to come closest to this model and is worth critical examination.

A final area for future development is suggested both by Fernandez and Barth's note of foster care's shift toward *child well being* in practices and outcomes, as well as by Dewey's challenging criterion for the crafting of any public programs for children. At least it seems to this writer that following the data on child well-being and discerning *what the best and wisest parent wants* will lead, ineluctably, to a closer interface between child welfare research and policy and child development research including longitudinal studies of child development in a wide variety of contexts. The seminal studies of Emmy Werner on the island of Kauai in Hawai'i, the Isle of Wight Studies in the UK, the critical re-examination of maternal deprivation by Michael Rutter as well as scores of empirical studies by Rutter and associates including David Quinton, the life-course research of sociologist Glen Elder and the pioneering work on family and kinship networks in east London by Michael Young and Peter Willmott and others come to mind. At centres of excellence, as for example, the Institute of Child Development, University of Minnesota more recent longitudinal studies on child development from L. Alan Sroufe, Byron Egeland and W. Andrew Collins, as well as longitudinal studies of risk and resilience by investigators such as Ann S. Masten and associates and critical work on developmental psychopathology by Dante Cicchetti and others provide additional rich examples. Such linkages with child development research – particularly when the study cohort involves more than service populations – are perhaps rarer and more difficult to forge, yet they seem critical if one sets *child well-being* as a primary outcome of interest: what is learned from the life-course experience of "normal" children and families may contribute greatly to the crafting of particular service responses to meet the needs of children presently served in foster care. Conversely, the lived experience of children in out-of-home care settings viewed over time may contribute important information about risk and resiliency to our understanding of basic child development.

We are in debt to Elizabeth Fernandez and Richard P. Barth for compiling this richly detailed view of foster care viewed in cross-national perspective. With their international contributors and critical commentaries they have answered many questions while uncovering many others. *How Does Foster Care Work?* stimulates a critical conversation among child welfare researchers, policy makers, and practitioners that one hopes will not only continue but expand.

James K. Whittaker, Charles O. Cressey Endowed Professor
Emeritus, School of Social Work, University of Washington, Seattle

References

Courtney, M.E. and Iwaniec, D. (eds) (2009) *Residential Care of Children: Comparative Perspectives.* New York: Oxford University Press.

Elder, G.H. (1974) *Children of the Great Depression.* Chicago, IL: University of Chicago Press.

Institute for Child Development. Minneapolis, MN: University of Minnesota. Available at www.cehd.umn.edu/icd/

Lindsey, D. and Shlonsky, A. (eds) (2008) *Child Welfare Research: Advances for Policy and Practice.* New York: Oxford University Press.

McAuley, C. Pecora, P.J. and Whittaker, J.K. (eds) (2009) 'High risk youth: evidence on characteristics, needs and promising interventions'. special issue of *Child and Family Social Work 14,* 2, 129–242.

Partners for our Children Project. Seattle, WA: University of Washington. Available at www.partnersforourchildren.org.

Pecora, P.J. Kessler, R.C. Williams, J. Downs, A.C. English, D.J. White, J. and O'Brien, K. (2010) *What Works in Foster Care?: Key Components of Success from the Northwest Foster Care Alumni Study.* New York: Oxford University Press.

Quinton, D. Rutter, M. and Gulliver, L. (1990) 'Continuities in Psychiatric Disorders from Childhood to Adulthood in the Children of Psychiatric Patients' in Robins, L.N and Rutler, M. *Straight and Devious Pathways form Childhood to Adulthood.* Cambridge: Cambridge University Press, 259–279.

Rutter, M. (1981) *Maternal Deprivation Reassessed.* London: Penguin Books.

Stein, M. and Munro, E.R. (eds) (2008) *Young People's Transitions from Care to Adulthood: International Research and Practice.* London: Jessica Kingsley Publishers.

Ward, H. Munro, H.R. and Dearden, C. (eds) (2006). *Babies and Young Children in Care: Life Pathways, Decision-making and Practice.* London: Jessica Kingsley Publishers.

Werner, E. and Smith, R.S. (1992) *Overcoming the Odds: High Risk Children from Birth to Adulthood.* New York: Cornell University Press.

Young, M. and Willmott, P. (1962) *Family and Kinship in East London.* London: Pelican.

Introduction

Reviewing International Evidence to Inform Foster Care Policy and Practice

By Elizabeth Fernandez and Richard P. Barth

National and international initiatives to monitor and improve children's wellbeing abound. The United Nations Convention on the Rights of the Child has long called for attention to child wellbeing and recent advancements in developmental theory and research methods offer new opportunities to understand the need for and outcomes of, foster care. Initiatives to monitor children's wellbeing also stem from accountability and outcome oriented public policy schemes that require accurate representations of situations of children and interventions designed to address their needs. Understanding of child wellbeing and what raises or lowers it, has become more inclusive of protective factors and adversities, current and future wellbeing, placement types and the incorporation of children's perspectives in addition to adult evaluations (Bradshaw, Hoscher and Richardson 2007). All these can, then, be loosely tied to children's outcomes.

It is expectable that these developments should be extended to the wellbeing of children in out-of-home care. As out-of-home care policy has evolved over time, the goals of safety, stability and permanency have assumed priority. Broadening this focus to include child wellbeing and developmental outcomes including health, education, family and social relationships and emotional development has become an evolving agenda in child welfare policy and research (Courtney, 2009; Parker *et al.* 1991; Wulczyn *et al.* 2005)

This book is an edited volume of empirical studies from many of the world's foremost scholars on the progress and outcomes of children in foster care. The volume is fundamentally about out of home care and what we know of how it works. The outcomes for children in care are rightfully the focus of research scrutiny and continuing efforts to build a knowledge base of how child welfare interventions such as foster care work to benefit children and young people are needed. Yet, the research in this area has not, until recently, had anywhere near the level of resources needed to arrive at plausibly definitive ideas about which children benefit in what way from what types of placement experiences.

Empirical studies on children in care have emerged over time to capture their needs and trajectories and the operation of systems of care. In particular the seminal works of Maas and Engler (1959), Fanshel and Shinn (1978), Rowe and Lambert (1973), Berridge and Cleaver (1987), Millham *et al.* (1986), Stein and Carey (1986) and Stein, Gambrill and Wiltse (1978) have contributed significant insights. However, since these landmark studies the profile and typologies of children and young people entering care may have changed. The care system has become increasingly concentrated on maltreated children. Children ostensibly may be less likely to enter care because of parental hardship. There is reason to believe that many children enter care for emotional and behavioral problems (Barth, Wildfire and Green 2006; McDonald and Brook 2009). Challenges to the foster care system are also posed by the changing availability of residential care provision (Courtney and Iwaniec 2009) resulting in children and young people who would have previously been served by residential care—which is being reduced in many jurisdictions—now being fostered. Different kinds of care provision have also emerged based on purpose and provider such as kinship care, treatment foster care and shared family care; outcomes from these different kinds of care can be expected to be varied and the research is confirming that they do—sometimes in unexpected ways.

Increasing recognition of the challenges posed by foster care has led to a spate of research in the last two decades focusing on different facets of process and outcome. While an exhaustive portrayal of the burgeoning research in foster care internationally is beyond the scope of this volume we set out to feature some major new studies as an attempt to bring together ideas, evidence, and lessons learned from a range of countries.

Family based foster care remains the dominant form of out of home care for maltreated and dependent children in the developed countries represented in this volume. Policy makers have begun drawing on different initiatives to reduce the use of group care by using alternative forms of care including treatment foster care, to lessen the use of foster care by placing children with relatives in kinship care and to reduce all forms of out of home care by expanding intensive placement prevention services. The proliferation of these service responses, their organization and delivery will be of substantial interest to the international child welfare practice and research community as will be the outcomes being achieved. This volume offers much information that allows for a better understanding of how each of these programs perform and offers a basis for comparisons between them.

Just as program models have expanded so too have methods for evaluating outcomes. Large and longitudinal administrative data sets permit us to follow the trajectories of children and youth through child welfare services over substantial periods of time. National probability surveys of child welfare services in the US and Canada provide detailed case information and longitudinal follow up that generate findings not previously available. In addition, greater sophistication in measurement, statistical methods, analytical tools and scientific models allow us to estimate durations of time in care when there are incomplete and ongoing episodes of care. New causal modelling methods such as propensity score modelling enable us to better estimate the impact of various treatments when there is a likelihood of biased selection into different types of care. This volume will inform readers of the outcomes of foster care as well as the methods to estimate such outcomes.

Further developments of note are the national longitudinal studies that assemble outcome data on samples to represent the national population of children and youth. Authors in this collection draw on a range of evidence including administrative data sets, survey data, views of children and young people, carers and caseworkers, data from developmental and clinical assessments, experimental manipulation, statistical analyses, and judgments of practitioners and researchers. All of these sources of evidence have vital contributions to make to developing a knowledge base in this crucial area while at the same time carrying inherent limitations.

In order to achieve comparability between chapters each author attempts to address the legislative and policy context of the care system in their country or jurisdiction, rationale and methodology of their research, theoretical underpinnings, key findings and implications for policy, practice, and service delivery.

Contributors to this collection are internationally recognized researchers who have played a significant role in building knowledge in this field in their respective countries. In inviting their contributions for inclusion in this volume we were conscious of having omitted other significant studies. It is beyond the scope of this book to examine the wide range of international research available in this field and to represent all countries. Another limitation to be acknowledged in the studies reported is the absence of the views of parents. This omission is to be noted in considering the evidence. A further caveat is that while we have included selected studies from different countries we have not considered in detail the extent to which research findings and conclusions are transferable. We anticipate readers will bring to bear their discretionary judgments about applicability and adaptability that may be needed. We have endeavoured to aid them in that process by having authors from other countries provide a brief commentary about each study.

Turning to the contents of this book the first of the chapters offers a succinct overview of the international out of home care scene. June Thoburn examines the challenging subject of how definitions and uses of care vary across countries and signals the complexities of cross national comparisons. This chapter uses administrative data on children in out of home care in 14 countries as the starting point for a cross national comparison of the context, polices, and outcomes of foster family placements. Her analysis of the differential use of foster family placements draws attention to the varying social and cultural contexts and attitudes that underpin the use of specific forms of care and how these differences may in part explain reported outcomes in different countries.

In Chapter 2 Richard Barth and Christopher Lloyd draw on the US National Survey of Child and Adolescent Wellbeing to estimate outcomes from a comparative, prospective follow up of young children who remained in care, were adopted, or returned home. The first prospective study that follows children through these different pathways, the analysis draws on baseline and follow up data from three waves of data collection over six years using a battery of measures to capture developmental and clinical outcomes. A noteworthy finding is that returning to the home of the biological parent and adoption were associated with generally similar positive outcomes compared to remaining in foster care.

Placement stability for children in foster care is a continuing concern for practitioners and policy makers. Multiple placements are thought to have a pernicious effect on the development of attachment to primary caregivers, an early developmental milestone considered to be essential for achievement of later developmental tasks. In Chapter 3 Fred Wulczyn and Lijun Chen expand previous approaches to the study of placement stability through an analysis of the timing of moves within placements and types of placements used. They draw on multivariate models to analyze the placement trajectories of children to illuminate the dynamics of placement changes.

Continuing the theme of placement stability Johan Strijker from the Netherlands draws on a retrospective longitudinal study with a sample of 419 children in long term foster care, to analyze child, family and system variables and their relationship to fostering outcomes with particular reference to breakdown. The chapter sheds light on how factors of age, behaviors, replacement, parental visiting, and attachment problems are implicated in a casual explanatory model of placement breakdown.

In Chapter 5 Jorge F. del Valle and Mónica López provide an overview and analysis of the profile of foster care in Spain. Drawing on research commissioned by the Ministry of Social Welfare they use survey data from several communities to profile the scope of foster care provision, the differences between kinship and other types of foster care and the nature and extent of residential care. They analyze a sample of 292 children in kinship and non kinship care and highlight unique characteristics of the out of home care landscape in Spain where nearly half of the children are in residential care and there is a preponderance of kinship care.

Attention turns to reunification or restoration of children from care to birth families in Chapter 6. A system that is able to return children home will be better able to maintain an adequate supply of placements for new children entering care, but also assist in maintaining the attachments between children and their biological parents. In this chapter, Elizabeth Fernandez and Paul Delfabbro provide evidence from two

Australian studies that have used a longitudinal approach to examine the process and nature of family reunification in different jurisdictions (South Australia and New South Wales). As well as identifying the factors that appear to influence reunification rates, both studies provide detailed insights into the complexities associated with conceptualizing the process of reunification, conducting research in this area and how reunification data might be most effectively analyzed.

The next chapter by Harriet Ward and Emily R. Munro offers an in-depth look at the vulnerabilities of babies and young children in care and illustrates the particular impact of the legal and policy frameworks on their wellbeing. The chapter tracks the experiences of 42 babies from birth till six years and analyzes their circumstances, characteristics, and experiences before, during, and after care and highlights impact of delayed decision making on the children's pathways. The authors' messages for practice with children, carers, and birth parents are compelling.

In Chapter 8 Elaine Farmer turns our attention to adolescents in care whose difficulties and needs require concerted attention from foster carers. Farmer analyzes results from a UK study examining how supports for foster carers and their parenting approaches relate to outcomes for fostered adolescents. Based on this one year prospective study using interviews with 68 young people and their carers, Farmer argues for proactive approaches to enhancing parenting skills and supports for foster carers and specialist help for fostered teenagers.

What happens to young people who "age out" of the system has been the focus of a growing body of research. In Chapter 9, Peter J. Pecora and his team of researchers draw on the US North West Foster Care Alumni Study to examine outcomes for alumni who were placed in family foster care over a ten year period and who were served by Casey Family Programs and Oregon and Washington State foster care agencies. The study, focusing on how alumni were faring and what foster care experiences resulted in positive outcomes, is based on reviews of case records for 659 alumni and interviews with 479 of them. Key findings reflect that despite challenges including maltreatment and placement instability one fifth of the alumni were doing well in terms of educational achievement, income and other major outcomes. The majority however faced significant challenges in the areas of mental health, education, employment and finances, trends which resonate with the experience of care leavers in many countries.

In Chapter 10 Ian Sinclair focuses on the roles of carers in the English care system. Drawing on a large scale study the chapter profiles characteristics of the children involved, the rate at which they enter and leave care and the nature of placements. Through a cohort study of 596 children followed over three years Sinclair examines in depth the chemistry between carers and children, the attributes of carers and the dynamics of contact between children and birth parents to identify their relative contribution to success or failure of placements. Importantly the key to successful outcomes appears to be in the qualities of foster carers, relations with birth families and the schooling experience.

In Chapter 11 Bo Vinnerljung and his team analyze results from a series of national cohort studies on children in Swedish foster care to examine a range of outcomes during adolescence and young adulthood including suicide, attempted suicide, psychiatric morbidity, teenage child bearing and indicators of educational and self support problems. Based on the striking over risks for negative long term outcomes, the authors call for a rights based and partnership model in European child welfare to benefit young people transitioning from care.

The use of kinship care within the range of options for children and young people needing care is an increasing focus for outcome research. In Chapter 12, Lajla Knudsen, Tine Egelund and Anne-Dorthe Hestbæk compare the profiles of children and carers in kinship and non kinship care in Denmark and highlight ways in which kin and non kin samples differ. The broad spectrum of outcomes for children in these different types of care is informative.

Next Fiona Daly and Robbie Gilligan report on the Irish experience. Chapter 13 reports on the second phase of an ongoing study on the educational histories, economic status and social support experiences of 168 young people who were transitioning out of care. Based on interviews with carers the study explores the nature of social supports available to young people beyond the foster family; social supports being measured in terms of contact with birth family, friendship networks and participation in leisure and social activities. The research strongly supports the care for giving priority to children and young people's education and stresses the value of involving children's wider social networks in assessment and intervention.

Research in a number of countries indicates that young people in care are often at a disadvantage relative to their general-population age peers with respect to educational performance and attainment. Given the widely acknowledged importance of the problem of low educational achievement among young people in care, it is surprising that few interventions appear to have been created and evaluated to date to address the problem. In Chapter 14 Robert J. Flynn, Marie-Pierre Paquet and Robyn A. Marquis provide a detailed review of the international literature on education and care and analyze data on the academic achievement of young people in care, showing that the problem of low educational outcomes poses itself in many countries. The chapter also examines strategies for improving the academic achievement of young people in care, with a focus both on foster home based interventions, in which foster parents have a major role and school based interventions, in which teachers and other school personnel are important players. This chapter discusses a randomized foster-parent tutoring intervention that the three co-authors of the chapter are currently conducting in collaboration with nine Children's Aid Societies in Ontario, Canada.

In Chapter 15 Elizabeth Fernandez offers an in-depth examination of developmental outcomes for children in long term care from an eight year longitudinal study of 59 children in foster care. Data from interviews with children and their respective carers and caseworkers and developmental and clinical measures illuminate outcomes in the spheres of attachment, emotional and behavioral development, identity and self esteem. Overall findings from the study indicate that alongside concerns related to placement instability and academic performance children reflected resilient outcomes in family and social relationships and prosocial behaviors as they progressed over time in their care placements. The voices of children and young people add an important dimension to the study bringing into the research their lived experience and their conceptions of present wellbeing.

As an innovative feature and integrative mechanism each of the above chapters is followed by an invited commentary from a different contributing author from another nation. These commentaries highlight significant themes stemming from the chapter bringing particular reflective insights to the findings and introducing at times a cross national perspective.

Countries differ in their culture, policies and programs, their values and knowledge and the priorities underpinning child welfare interventions. Acknowledging, these differences is crucial in evaluating the evidence from each country and comparing trends and findings. It is hoped this empirical collection will provide useful and easily accessible evidence and the opportunity to compare trends across countries in advancing our knowledge in this challenging field.

References

Barth, R.P. Wildfire, J. and Green, R.L. (2006) 'Placement into foster care and the interplay of urbanicity, child behaviour problems and poverty.' *American Journal of Orthopsychiatry, 76,* 358–366.

Berridge, D. and Cleaver, H. (1987) *Foster Home Breakdown.* Oxford: Basil Blackwell Ltd.

Bradshaw, J. Hoscher, P. and Richardson, D. (2007) 'An index of child well-being in the European Union.' *Social Indicators Research 80,* 1, 133–177.

Courtney, M.E (2009) 'Beyond safety and permanency: making well-being a focus of policy and practice for children in state care.' *Children Australia 34,* Special Edition, 1, 15–21

Courtney, M.E. and Iwaniec, D. (eds) (2009) *Residential Care of Children: Comparative Perspectives.* Oxford: Oxford University Press.

Fanshel, D. and Shinn, E.B. (1978) *Children in Foster Care: A Longitudinal Investigation.* New York: Columbia University Press.

Maas, H.S. and Engler, R.E. (1959) *Children in Need of Parents.* New York: Columbia University Press.

McDonald, T. and Brook, J. 'Typologies of children in foster care for reasons other than abuse or neglect.' *Journal of Public Child Welfare 3,* 391–408.

Millham, S. Bullock, R. Hosie, K. and Haak, M. 1986 *Lost in Care: The Problems of Maintaining Links between Children in Care and Their Families,'* Aldershot: Gower.

Parker, R. Ward, H. Jackson, S. Aldgate, J. and Wedge, P. (1991) *Assessing Outcomes in Child Care.* London : Her Majesty's Stationery Office (HMSO)

Rowe, J. and Lambert, L. (1973) *Children Who Wait. A Study of Children Needing Substitute Families.* London: Association of British Adoption Agencies.

Stein, M. and Carey, K. (1986) *Leaving Care.* London: Blackwell.

Stein, T.J. Gambrill, E.D. and Wiltse, K.T. (1978) *Children in Foster Homes: Achieving Continuity of Care.* New York: Praeger Press.

Wulczyn, F. Barth, R.P. Yuan, Y.T. Jones-Harden, B. and Landsverk, J. (2005) *Beyond Common Sense: Child Welfare, Child Well-Being and the Evidence for Policy Reform.* Piscataway, NJ: Aldine Transaction.

CHAPTER 1

International Perspectives on Foster Care

June Thoburn

Introduction

In the search for improved outcomes for children in foster care, policy makers appropriately look across national boundaries to see if other jurisdictions 'get it right' and if so, what aspects of the foster care service are contributing to improved outcomes. Important though it is to learn from each other, it is equally important first to gain an understanding of the different contexts, circumstances and reporting conventions for children in out-of-home care in different jurisdictions.

This discussion of outcomes for children in foster care in different jurisdictions draws on a study of administrative and contextual data on children in care in 21 states in 14 countries (Thoburn 2008 and in press). I also draw on collaborative work with USA and UK colleagues that led to the publication of an edited collection of seminal English language articles on child welfare (Courtney and Thoburn 2009) and an overview of the international research on outcomes for children in care (Bullock *et al.* 2006).

The nature of the evidence on foster care outcomes in different jurisdictions

Reliable statistics on children in out-of-home care are most readily available via routinely collected administrative data on total populations. However, in order to ensure high completion rates, these are based on minimum data sets. To gain a fuller picture of the processes associated with more or less positive outcomes, these minimum data sets have to be complemented by more detailed information on sub-samples. In some European jurisdictions, whilst there is a strong research tradition (represented by the national Observatories in France, Italy and Spain), there has been less emphasis on the routine collection of administrative data to inform policy. Where available, data are often reported separately for children in group care and foster care (Flanders and Italy for example) or for children in legally mandated care and voluntary care (France). It is also important to note that in the USA and Canada it is not always clear whether children in group care as well as foster family care are included in a particular 'foster care' research sample. As will be discussed below, in some countries, data on some children in mental health service sectors (USA) or juvenile justice facilities (USA and UK) are reported separately, whereas child welfare statistics from Nordic countries include almost all children and young people in public out-of-home care.

Inter-country differences in the characteristics of children in foster care

Rates in care and entering care

From the available administrative data, a picture can be built up of differences between countries in terms of the 'stock' of children in care and the 'flow' of those entering and leaving care. Rates entering care are influenced by the degree of deprivation in a jurisdiction and also by the resources spent on universal and targeted child and family welfare services.

The most obvious difference is with respect to absolute numbers of children in the population. In my study, numbers in the under 18 population varied between around a million or fewer in eight jurisdictions to 74 million in the USA. With respect to the 'stock' of children in care, the range was between fewer than 3000 in Northern Ireland and nearly half a million in the USA. In order to make comparisons, therefore, rates per 10,000 children under 18 are used in this chapter. Table 1.1 shows that some countries make more use of the care system than others. Alberta (111 per 10,000), Denmark and France (each with 102 per 10,000) were, in the mid-2000s, the countries with the highest rates in care; Japan and Italy (11 and 30 per 10,000 respectively) had the lowest rates and the others spread between around 50 (Australia and New Zealand) and the mid 60s (Germany, Norway, Sweden and the USA). This does not necessarily translate into rates in foster family care as different proportions of those in care are in residential and family care. Table 1.2 shows that generally those with high rates in care have high rates in foster family care and the converse. However, high usage of group care in some European countries means that high rates in care are not invariably translated into high rates in foster family care.

TABLE 1.1 Rates per 10,000 children under 18 in care and entering care in a given year (in most cases obtained from administrative data for 2003–2004 or 2004–2005)*

COUNTRY/ STATE	RATE IN CARE	RATE ENTERING CARE	RATIO OF ENTRANTS TO 'IN CARE' RATES
Australia	49	26	1:1.9
Alberta**	111	***	
Denmark	102	30	1:3.4
France	102	***	
Germany	74	30	1:2.5
Ireland	50	***	
Italy	38	***	
Japan	17	6	1:2.8
New Zealand	49	24	1:2
Norway	68	13	1:5.2
Spain	51	18	1:2.8
Sweden	63	32	1:2
England****	55	23	1:2.4
USA	66	42	1:1.6

*For detail on sources see Thoburn 2008
**National data not available for Canada as a whole because of different provincial legislation.
***Data not routinely collected.
****These are slight underestimates as children entering care in England for a series of short term placements are omitted from the 'looked after' statistics, but similar placements would be included in statistics of other countries.

TABLE 1.2 Children in kin and non-kin family foster care at a given date (% of all in care) and rate per 10,000 of all children under 18 in a family foster care placement*

COUNTRY/STATE	KINSHIP CARE	UN-RELATED FOSTER FAMILY CARE	RATE IN FOSTER FAMILY CARE PER 10,000 UNDER 18
Australia	40%	54%	46
Alberta	8%	66%	81
Denmark**		48%	50
France	7%	46%	54
Germany	9%	38%	35
Ireland **		84%	42
Italy	26%	24%	19
Japan	0.6%	7%	<1
New Zealand	35%	40%	37
Norway	17%	61%	53
Spain**		62%	31
Sweden	12%	65%	49
England	18%	47%	36
USA	23%	46%	45

*To facilitate comparisons, where possible only those in care aged 0–17 are included in the per centages in this table.

**Not differentiated in national statistics between kin and non-kin placements

Equally important to an understanding of any differences between outcomes for children in foster care in different countries is a comparison of rates entering care. Table 1.1 shows that the USA had the highest rate of entrants to care (42 per 10,000) and Japan was again the 'low outlier' with six per 10,000. Of the three with high rates in care, 'flow' data were only available for Denmark, which had an average rate for entrants (30 per 10,000). Norway, with a fairly high 'in care' rate, had one of the lowest rates for entrants (13 per 10,000).

Differences in age profiles and length of stay

Rates in care are also influenced by the ages of children entering care and length of stay (those entering young can potentially stay longer and increase the 'in care' rate, although, in all countries, it is the youngest entrants who are most likely to stay for the shortest periods). Table 1.3 gives information on age groups for care entrants (not available for all jurisdictions in the study) and shows that a larger per centage of entrants in the USA, Canada and the UK are in the youngest age groups than is the case in Sweden, for example, where almost 50 per cent of entrants were aged 15 or over (compared to 20% in the USA and only 4% in England). The difference between the comparatively low 'flow' rate and the high 'stock' rate in Germany, Denmark and Norway is largely explained by the fact that more children in these countries remain in care for longer periods than is the case, for example, for USA care entrants (Thoburn, 2008). Table 1.1 shows that ratios of entrants rates to in care rates varies between 1:1.6 in the USA and 1:5.2 in Norway.

TABLE 1.3 Age at entry to out-of-home care

COUNTRY/ STATE	0–4 (<12 MTHS IN BRACKETS)	5–9	10–14	15–17	18–20
Australia	38% (*13%*)	27%	27%	8%	
Canada*	27% (0–3)	12% (4–7)	20% (8–11)	42% (12–15)	
Germany	!5% (0–5) (*4%*)	28% (6–11)	23% (12–14)	28%	5%
Italy (foster care)	34% (*13%*)	37%	29% (10–17)		
Italy (res. care)	30% (0–5)	20% (6–11)		20%(12–17)	
Japan	49% (*7%*)	28%	20%	3%	
New Zealand	34% (*14%*)	19%	47% were aged 10–17		
Norway	23% (0–5)	18% (6–12)		51% (13–17)	8%
Sweden	12% (0–3)	15% (4–9)	24%	34%	15%
UK/England	34% (*16%*)	18%	42%	4%	
USA	38% (*15%*)	20%	23%	20%	

*Figures from 2001 Incidence Study, Child protection cases only (Trocme *et al.* 2003)

Reasons for entering care and legal status

All large scale outcome studies have pointed to correlations between ages of children entering foster placements, the reasons for needing to come into care, any characteristics that may make them 'hard to care for' and outcomes. Children in different countries enter care through different legal routes (in Australia, Canada and the USA most enter care via the courts, whilst in most European countries and Japan the majority enter care at the request of parents or without their active opposition). However, the literature on child welfare services in different countries indicates that the children entering care do so for broadly similar reasons, with child maltreatment, various forms of neglect and parenting issues, especially intimate partner violence and addictions, being important reasons in all countries. The different age profiles indicate that larger proportions of those entering care in Europe do so because of the child's emotional or behavioural problems. In particular, whilst more children in the UK and the USA who commit offences will be in the juvenile justice systems (and therefore not in the out-of-home care statistics) similar young people in other European jurisdictions are likely to be in the care system.

Legislation, influenced as it is by attitudes towards the family and the willingness of the state to intervene through either family support or more coercive child protection measures, impacts also on the service provided when children are in care. In mainland Europe, the Nordic countries, Ireland and New Zealand there is a strong emphasis on entry into care (sometimes for prolonged periods) as part of the family support services. Especially with respect to troubled older children, there is a shared care ethos, with family contact being an integral part of the foster care service. Permanent severance of parental rights and responsibilities is rare in these countries. In the USA and to a lesser extent Canada and the UK nations, severance of parental contact in order to achieve legal adoption and sometimes for children in long term foster care, is more common. The dimension of birth family contact is therefore another variable to be considered when looking at outcomes across national boundaries, with some countries more than others emphasizing continuing birth family links as an outcome measure.

The ethnic background of children in care is an important issue for all countries with diverse populations and must be considered as a further possible explanatory variable with respect to rates in foster care and outcomes. Several studies have highlighted higher rates in care of some ethnic minority populations. Children of indigenous heritage are especially likely to enter care in numbers which are disproportionate to their numbers in the community (Tilbury and Thoburn 2009). In Australia, Canada, New Zealand and the UK nations, legislation requires that children should, wherever possible, retain links with their ethnic group and linguistic and cultural heritage. Whilst there is evidence that children of minority ethnic heritage tend to remain longer in care, the evidence on differential child welfare outcomes for children of different ethnicities is not clear, so it cannot be predicted (when other variables are held constant) that a higher proportion of children of ethnic minority heritage in foster care in a particular country will contribute to better or worse overall child/adult welfare outcomes.

The aims of the foster care service in different countries

Outcome research which can lead to reliable inter-country comparisons has to be specific, not only about the characteristics of the children being served, but also about the aims of the foster care systems being compared. For example, there are similarities across jurisdictions in the treatment foster care services provided for older children who enter care because of challenging or criminal behaviour, which make for more robust comparisons of outcomes. In contrast, short or intermediate term foster care provided as part of a family support service (sometimes referred to as 'respite' or 'support' foster care) is an important part of the foster care service in mainland Europe and the Nordic countries, used to a lesser extent in the UK nations, some Australian states and New Zealand and much less frequently present in samples of children entering care in the USA and Canada.

At one end of the continuum, foster carers aim to help families over a difficult period (which may be prolonged) by caring for their children wherever possible through collaborative arrangements At the other end of the continuum, foster care is generally conceptualized as a short or intermediate term service for maltreated children, with the aim of assisting the move out of care to the appropriate permanence option.

Whatever the predominant approach, some children will remain in long term foster care. There are differences, however, in the extent to which it is recognized (in law or through administrative or professional practice) as a 'permanence' option (more likely in the UK nations, Australia and New Zealand). Schofield (2009) uses the term 'part of the family' to identify the aim of these placements, which have much in common with open adoption placements of older children from care. In some European countries long term foster care just 'evolves' out of a short term placement and little distinction is made in research studies between 'mainstream' and 'family for life' foster families.

Rowe, Hundleby and Garnett, (1989) listed the purposes of care, the proportions of children in each category and the success in achieving these aims with respect to 3554 foster family placements of English children. Whilst 15 per cent of placements were for 'care and upbringing' outside the family, 85 per cent had short or intermediate term aims. Other 'short term' aims in the Rowe *et al.* research were: temporary care (46%); emergency care (14%); preparation for long-term placement (14%); assessment (13%); treatment (9%); 'bridge to independence' (4%). Sinclair *et al.* (2007) used these categories more recently. As a cross sectional sample, their study contained a larger proportion of 'care and upbringing' placements (52%) but even allowing for this there appears to have been a shift in England towards more foster family placements having this aim. Looking only at placements with a short term aim in the Sinclair *et al.* sample, a larger proportion than in the Rowe *et al.* study (29%) were for 'preparation for permanence' outside the family.

Outcome data from different jurisdictions

It can be hypothesized (although the evidence is weak since few outcome studies provide data on placement aims) that the balance of aims in different jurisdictions impacts on the output or outcome measures selected by researchers and on reported 'success' rates. Rowe *et al.* (1989) reported higher success rates (around 80%) for placements with the aims of 'temporary care', 'emergency care' and 'preparation for long term placement' than for 'assessment' (57%), 'bridge to independence' (53%) or 'treatment' (46%). Other chapters in this book will provide detailed data on outcomes in different countries. What follows is a broad overview.

Comparisons of placements with short term / intermediate / task centred aims

Few studies reporting on general populations of children in short or intermediate term foster care provide outcome data on children's wellbeing and/or changes over time although the large data sets of Vinnerljung, Hjern and Linblad (2005) and Doyle (2007) provide long term data on children the majority of whom will have been in placements which were not (at least at the time of placement) intended to be for care and upbringing. The most robust studies providing output data are the USA longitudinal studies which evaluate foster care in terms of its success in moving children out of care into legally permanent family placements, usually defined as return to a member of the birth family or adoption (Barth and Lloyd 2010; Wulczyn 2004). Some examples of per centages of those leaving care to return to parents or relatives in a given year in a country or state wide population are: Germany, 40 per cent, England , 42 per cent; Sweden, 56 per cent; Western Australia, 63 per cent; USA, 64 per cent (see Thoburn 2008 for sources). Those with lower rates returning to parents have higher rates in 'care and upbringing' placements (see next section) and therefore higher per centages who 'age out' of care in a given year.

More useful are data which record the proportions who enter care and leave through reunification within specific time scales, but these are less readily available. The consensus from USA studies is that between 50 per cent and 60 per cent of children entering care will have returned to birth parents within three years (though some will have gone back into care, sometimes more than once) (Doyle 2007; Wulczyn 2004). In England, somewhere between 55 per cent and 58 per cent will have left care to live with a birth parent or relative within two years (Dickens *et al.* 2007; Rowe *et al.* 1989). This compares with between 25 per cent and 30 per cent leaving care via adoption over a 10 year time scale in the USA (Wulczyn 2004) and around 10 per cent in the UK.

Given the generally young age of children placed for adoption, most of these will have been in foster family care and a substantial proportion will have been adopted by their (initially short term) foster carers. The difference in adoption rates between the UK and the USA is in large part explained by the fact that adoption by kin foster carers is very unusual in the UK but an important minority of foster care adopters in the USA are kinship carers (a quarter of the USA children who left care through adoption in 2005 were adopted by relatives). These studies mostly indicate that children in kinship foster care placements are less likely to leave care to return to birth parents than those in group care or non-kin foster family care. However, del Valle *et al.* (2009) found that those in kinship foster care who left care in a planned way (neither following a disruption nor 'ageing out') were more likely to return to parents and (as in England) less likely to be adopted by their foster carers than those placed with non-kin foster families. .

Data on outputs and outcomes of task-centred care can more readily be compared across national boundaries if both the age and characteristics of the child placed and the purpose of the placement, are held constant. Sallnas, Vinnerljung and Westermark (2004), reviewing the international literature on new placement of teenagers in foster care concluded that somewhere between 30 per cent and 50 per cent of placements end prematurely, the wide range being explained by the range of placement types (some but not all included kinship placements) and the range of problems of the young people at the time of placement. Doyle (2007) concluded that children aged 5 to 15 on the margins of care because of concerns about parental physical abuse or neglect did as well in terms of employment and avoidance of delinquency and teen pregnancy if they remained at home. Where aim and duration are specified (as with treatment foster care) a smaller proportion of placements are prematurely terminated but there are wider differences between studies when aspects of wellbeing or behavioural change are the outcomes used (Reddy and Pfeiffer 1997).

Research on outcomes of 'short term' or 'task-centred' foster care in several countries uses the extent (and less often the quality) of continuing links with birth family members as an output measure, since several studies going back over a long time frame have found an association between contact arrangements that are comfortable for the child and birth parents and a planned return home. A key element of treatment foster care programmes is work with the birth parents to ensure continuity of parenting and treatment when young people return home.

Outcomes when the aim is 'care and upbringing'

Outcome studies for children in care are most helpful if comparisons are made with alternative possible placements for similar children. As has been noted earlier, the major difference between jurisdictions for children needing 'care and upbringing' in alternative families is the extent to which adoption and other forms of legal guardianship are used as routes out of formal care. There are no data sets or recent large scale longitudinal studies on outcomes for children placed from care for adoption or with the intention of permanence in foster family care. There is therefore no robust way of comparing outcomes for children adopted from care with similar children who join 'permanent' foster families or leave care through guardianship orders. Within-country comparisons are not feasible for young children since national policy means that, for example, in some jurisdictions almost all young entrants who do not return home leave care through adoption, whilst in others, similar children are placed in kin or non-kin foster family care and few are placed from care for adoption.

Small scale foster care or 'leaving care' studies in several countries indicate that a proportion of children growing up in foster care become 'part of the family' into adult life, including some who joined their foster families in their teenage years (Moffatt and Thoburn 2001; Schofield 2009; Sinclair *et al.* 2007; Stein and Munro 2008). Although data on living arrangements for cohorts of young people leaving care as young adults may be reported (Courtney *et al.* 2001; National Statistics and DCSF 2008) the fact that an 18 year old is not actually resident in the foster or adoptive family cannot be taken to mean that he or she is not a 'family member'. Conversely residence in a foster family home could mean that the young person is merely a temporary lodger (Sinclair *et al.* 2007).

A major difficulty in making comparisons between long term welfare outcomes in different countries is sample loss and this is especially the case with respect to adoption and guardianship. A small number of (usually small scale) longitudinal studies have retained adopted children within 'in care' research samples, or have specifically studied longer term outcomes of children adopted from care (Fernandez 2007; Lahti 1982; Neil 2009; Simmel, Barth and Brooks 2006; Sinclair *et al.* 2007; Thoburn *et al.* 2000). It is therefore becoming more possible to look across national boundaries at the outcomes for children in different age groups remaining in foster family care and those placed for adoption. For example del Valle's (2009) large Spanish sample of children of all ages placed in kin and non-kin foster care, or the Australian sample of Fernandez (2006), can be compared with UK and USA research on children placed from care for adoption.

Comparisons between countries are more possible for children placed in long term foster care past infancy, since samples of these children in all countries are larger, but the fact that research samples rarely provide information on whether the placement was intended to be a 'part of the family' placement impede reliable comparisons (Schofield 2009). Comparisons between outcomes of long term kinship care placements in different countries have fewer confounding variables, but even here context and differing characteristics of the children in kinship placements, have to be carefully considered. The comparatively low use of this placement option in Sweden and France, for example, is linked to the fact that financial and practical support and casework services are more readily available to support family members taking on the care of their young relatives outside the care system than is the case in some other countries.

Putting together the available data, the studies cited above provide growing evidence from across national boundaries that – irrespective of legal status, the key variables impacting on long term child and adult welfare outcomes are age at placement, the emotional and behavioural characteristics of the child at the time of placement, whether or not the child was maltreated prior to placement and whether the carers and child have a 'sense of permanence' – their family will not be arbitrarily disrupted. For children growing up in foster family care, this is related to whether agency practice can ensure that they are freed from anxiety about unplanned removal back to the birth parents or to another placement in care and especially that they will not have to 'move on' when they reach 18 or the official care leaving age (Cashmore and Paxman 2006; Moffatt and Thoburn 2001; Sinclair *et al.* 2007).

The generally more positive reported outcomes of kinship care (even though material circumstances are usually lower than for non-kin care) are likely to be associated with a stronger sense of family membership. Bullock *et al.* (2006) review the international evidence as to whether the State can be an effective 'corporate parent' for children in longer term care and conclude that for the *majority* of children who cannot return safely home, the outcomes will be broadly positive or neutral (depending on the characteristics of the sample and the care experience): most of those who enter care because of proven serious or prolonged maltreatment or neglect will do as well or better than if returned to the families from whom they entered care. The groups who do badly in long term care are those who enter when older because they have serious problems and those who enter care when young but have multiple moves, or experience the disruption of a placement (whether the intention was adoption or a 'foster family for life') after several years and are not successfully placed with a new family with whom they put down roots (Courtney *et al.* 2001; Pecora *et al.* 2005; Stein and Munro, 2008).

Concluding comments on comparing outcomes across jurisdictions

It has been argued in this chapter that different attitudes to the family and the place of out-of-home care in child welfare services impact on the characteristics of children in care, their length of stay and the pattern of placements used. These differences can be expected to impact differently on outcomes. In particular, note must be taken of the growing evidence that children who enter care when fairly young and who stay long in care are likely to have a more stable care experience and (on average) better outcomes than those who enter when older and/or stay less long (Bullock *et al.* 2006; Cashmore and Paxman 2006; del Valle *et al.* 2009).

A higher proportion of children entering when older (as in Nordic countries) may result in poorer overall outcomes as their problems may be more entrenched. On the other hand, if placement stability is the output measure used, less time in care means less time to experience multiple moves. If, in the USA and the UK, most of the young entrants exit care via adoption, those remaining in care and eventually becoming part of 'leaving care' cohorts are likely to have more problems than those remaining long in care in countries which only rarely use adoption as a route out of care.

The large scale total cohort studies described in this volume, supplemented by 'drilling down' records searches and interviews with children, carers, birth relatives and workers, will allow for more meaningful comparisons. This will especially be the case if those leaving care through adoption or guardianship can be retained in the samples until adulthood. The smaller scale process and outcome studies being conducted in many countries, focusing on specific foster care programmes for specific groups of children in care, can and should (suitably modified to take on board different contexts) be replicated across national boundaries. To date, most of these have concerned troubled adolescents and have concentrated on short term interventions. More research programmes are needed to aid our understanding of the complex service needs of children who join foster families on a long term basis.

This volume evidences the determination of researchers in different countries to work to overcome some of the barriers to learning from each other how to improve outcomes for the different groups who need foster care services.

References

Barth, R. and Lloyd, C. (2010) 'Five-Year Developmental Outcomes for Young Children Remaining in Foster Care, Returned Home or Adopted.' In E. Fernandez and R.P. Barth (eds) *How Does Foster Care Work? International Evidence on Outcomes.* London: Jessica Kingsley Publishers.

Bullock, R. Courtney, M. Parker, R. Sinclair, I. and Thoburn, J. (2006) 'Can the corporate state parent?' *Children and Youth Services Review 28,* 11, 1344–1358.

Cashmore, J. and Paxman, M. (2006) 'Predicting after-care outcomes: the importance of "felt" security.' *Child and Family Social Work 11,* 3, 232–241.

Courtney, M. Piliavin, I. Grogan-Kaylor, A. and Nesmith, A. (2001) 'Foster youth transitions to adulthood: a longitudinal view of youth leaving care.' *Child Welfare 80,* 6, 685–717.

Courtney, M. and Thoburn, J. (2009) 'An overview of the knowledge-base on children in out-of-home care'. In M. Courtney and J. Thoburn (eds) *Children in State Care.* Aldershot: Ashgate. pp xv–xxx.

del Valle, J.F. López, M. Montserrat, C. and Bravo, A. (2009) 'Twenty years of foster care in Spain: profiles, patterns and outcomes.' *Children and Youth Services Review 31,* 847–853.

Dickens, J. Howell, D. Thoburn, J. and Schofield, G. (2007) 'Children starting to be looked after by local authorities in England: an analysis of inter-authority variation and case-centred decision-making.' *British Journal of Social Work 37,* 597–617.

Doyle, J.J. (2007). 'Child protection and child outcomes: measuring the effects of foster care.' *American Economic Review 97,* 5, 1583–1610.

Fernandez, E. (2007) 'How children experience fostering outcomes: participatory research with children.' *Child and Family Social Work 12,* 4, 349–359.

Lahti, J. (1982). 'A follow-up study of foster children in permanent placements.' *Social Service Review 56,* 556–571.

Moffatt, P. and Thoburn, J. (2001) 'Outcomes of permanent family placement for children of minority ethnic origin.' *Child and Family Social Work 6,* 1, 13–22.

National Statistics and DCSF (2008) *Children Looked After by Local Authorities in England.* London: Office of National Statistics. Available from www.dcsf.gov.uk/rsgateway/DB/SFR/s000810/SFR23-2008Textv1oct.pdf, accessed on 8 April 2010.

Neil, E. (2009) 'Post adoption contact and openness in adoptive parents' minds: consequences for children's development.' *British Journal of Social Work 39* 1, 5–23.

Pecora, P.J. Kessler, R.C. Williams, J. O'Brien, K. *et al* (2005) *Improving Family Foster Care: Findings from the Northwest Foster Care Alumni Study.* Seattle, WA: Seattle Casey Family Programmes.

Rowe, J. Hundleby, M. and Garnett, L. (1989) *Child Care Now. A Survey of Placement Patterns.* London: British Agencies for Adoption and Fostering.

Reddy, L.A. and Pfeiffer, S.I. (1997) 'Effectiveness of treatment foster care with children and adolescents: A review of outcomes.' *Journal of the Americal Academy of Child and Adolescent Psychiatry, 36,* 581–588.

Sallnas, M. Vinnerljung, B. and Westermark, P.K. (2004) 'Breakdown of teenage placements in Swedish foster and residential care.' *Child and Family Social Work 9,* 141–152.

Schofield, G. (2009) 'Permanence in Foster Care.' In G. Schofield and J. Simmonds (eds) *The Child Placement Handbook: Research, Policy and Practice.* London: BAAF.

Simmel, C. Barth, R.P. and Brooks, D. (2006) 'Adopted foster youths' psychosocial functioning: a longitudinal perspective.' *Child and Family Social Work 12,* 4, 336–348.

Sinclair, I. Baker, C. Lee, J. and Gibbs, I. (2007) *The Pursuit of Permanence: A Study of the English Care System.* London: Jessica Kingsley Publishers.

Stein, M. (2009) 'Young People Leaving Care.' In G. Schofield and J. Simmonds (eds) *The Child Placement Handbook: Research, Policy and Practice.* London: BAAF.

Stein, M. and Munro, E.R. (2008) *Young People's Transitions from Care to Adulthood.* London: Jessica Kingsley Publishers.

Thoburn, J. (in press) 'Achieving safety, stability and belonging for children in out-of-home care: the search for "what works" across national boundaries.' *International Journal of Child and Family Welfare.*

Thoburn, J. Norford, L. and Rashied, S.P. (2000) *Permanent Family Placement for Children of Minority Ethnic Origin.* London: Jessica Kingsley Publishers.

Tilbury, C. and Thoburn, J. (2009) 'Racial disproportionality and disparity: using disproportionality and disparity indicators to measure child welfare outcomes.' *Children and Youth Services Review* 31, 10, 1101–1106.

Trocme, N. Fallon, B. MacLaurin, B. and Daciuk, J. *et al.* (2003) *Canadian Incidence Study of Reported Child Abuse and Neglect.* Ottawa: Public Health Agency of Canada.

Vinnerljung, B. Hjern, A. and Lindblad, F. (2005) 'Suicide attempts and severe psychiatric morbidity among former child welfare clients – a national cohort study.' *Journal of Child Psychology and Psychiatry 47,* 7, pp 723–733.

Wulczyn, F. (2004) 'Family Reunification.' *The Future of Children 14,* 1, 95–113.

Commentary by Richard P. Barth on:
International Perspectives on Foster Care

June Thoburn

I commend June Thoburn for looking beneath the largely misleading per capita rates of children in foster care in order to bring additional meaning to them. By detailing variations in the ways that we define foster care and the way that our strategies for describing the ebb and flow of children in care makes on the conclusions we first might draw, she helps clarify the options that are available to improve comparisons between countries. She offers much more than that, however, by providing keen insight about the differing rationales for placement and about the programme goals that countries have embraced in developing and delivering out-of-home care services.

Her conclusion that 'there is growing evidence that children who enter care fairly young and stay long in care are likely to have a more stable care experience and (on average) better outcomes than those who enter when older and/or stay less long' is an intriguing conclusion. If this is as sturdy a cross-national result as she claims, this finding deserves more consideration in policy making, which seems to be heading toward shorter stays. But her conclusions finds little support in Barth and Lloyd (this volume) which indicates that those children who are young when they enter care do more poorly than those who exit and go home or are adopted – at least during the first six years. So, this is one of the intriguing places that Thoburn shines a light and that may be worth testing further when there are better data to understand just what is going on and how placement stability factors into the outcomes. From this very American perspective it appears that long stays in foster care are most often not characterized by placement stability unless it is kinship care. Research on how to increase the placement stability of *non*-kinship foster care would be much help and is slowly emerging (e.g. Price *et al.* 2008).

Nor is it necessarily, or even likely to be, the case that countries that have more adolescents entering care (as in Nordic countries) are more likely to have worse outcomes because their problems may be more entrenched. Indeed, they may have entered for very different reasons. In the US, at least, these children are more likely to enter because of mental health problems and parent child conflict – conditions that may not be more resistant to change than would problems that might arise from substantial amounts of prenatal alcohol exposure, early childhood neglect and deprivation. What we lack in almost all administrative data systems is a way to know how severe the maltreatment or behavioural problems have been prior to entrance into care. Without this background, comparing the quality of the outcomes should be done very gingerly (unless 'outcomes' only refers to their status, not to their progress during the service programme). In all, this is a major contribution to understanding the entrants, stays and dispositions of children who enter out-of-home care in a substantial proportion of the world.

References

Price, J.M. Chamberlain, P. Landsverk, J. Reid, J.B. Leve, L.D. and Laurent, H. (2008) 'Effects of a foster parent training intervention on placement changes of children in foster care.' *Child Maltreatment, 13*, 1, 64–75.

Part Two:
Placement Movements
and Destinations

CHAPTER 2

Five-Year Developmental Outcomes for Young Children Remaining in Foster Care, Returned Home, or Adopted

Richard P. Barth and Christopher Lloyd

US foster care policy for young children in foster care

Foster care in the United States is considered to be a last resort and temporary. The United States has relatively strong federal leadership in child welfare services (CWS) and over foster care because the federal government pays for nearly half of the cost of foster care, group care and adoption subsidies. This totals to about $7,000,000,000 dollars a year. Federal law also has some sway over the way that child abuse and neglect—which are, with a few exceptions, the defining event for entrance into foster care—are reported (all states have mandated reporting) and responded to by local CWS agencies. Federal policy—going back as far as the seminal policy of 1980, the Adoption Assistance and Child Welfare Act and to the present—makes relatively little differentiation between young children in foster care and older children (see the pleas for a developmentally sensitive child welfare policy in Berrick *et al.* 1998 and Wulczyn *et al.* 2005).

In concept, the expectation of the Adoption and Safe Families Act (1997) is that all (or almost all) children will be reunified to the home of the parent—within 12 months—if it is possible given reasonable efforts. Although some of the children who receive foster care could be placed there voluntarily by their parents—under US law states can get federal reimbursement for up to six months for voluntary placements—almost all young children who are placed are placed by court order. Termination of parental rights is supposed to take place for children who cannot go home, even if they do not have a clear alternative permanent placement, such as adoption or living with relatives. If they cannot be reunified, then adoption is the first option. Failing the availability of adoption, legal guardianship is considered the next best option with a future of preparation for independent living being least favored.

In the US the federal law generally sets low standards that any of the 50 state legislatures can modify. So, Colorado has shortened the time for decision making for children younger than six years old to six months (with possible extensions to 12 months), with the first hearings about making plans for adoption coming as early as six months in order to be sure that children who have already been observed to have almost no chance of reunification can be moved on to adoption.

The US has an extraordinarily active adoption program. More than 50,000 children are adopted from foster care, each year—about 20 percent of all children leaving foster care. Another 20,000, or so, have parental rights terminated—usually in an adversarial court proceeding—so that they will not be reunified and have the option of being adopted (assuming that an adoptive family is located). The likelihood of adoption is much higher for young children than for older children although in 2006, as many as one-third of all children younger than three who enter foster care will leave via adoption (Wulczyn 2003). The group that is most likely to be adopted is children who are removed at or near birth and placed with their adoptive families when they were between zero and six months of age—this comprises about 40 percent of all the young children who are adopted (Wulczyn 2003). Although about 2 percent of children are identified in the US's federal statistics (called AFCARS) as being adopted as younger than one year old, many young children are placed with their adoptive parents for several months or years before their adoption is legally formalized—this occurs because there are often court challenges by the mother or by putative fathers. Indeed, about one quarter of all foster children who are adopted are no older than three years of age and more than half of all foster children are adopted before five years of age in the US; the median age of adoption from foster care is now 5.4 years and the mean is 6.6 years (AFCARS 2006). New evidence suggests that the amount of time that children wait for adoption seems to be independent of the race or gender of the child (NSCAW n.d.).

In terms of prior risk, the children who were adopted were often protected from severe harm (about 28% were identified as having experienced severe harm) while the level of risk was much higher (60%). The children often had special health care needs (about 70%). The rate of adoption did not vary significantly by race.

According to the National Survey of Child and Adolescent Well-being, described below and the basis for the analyses featured in this paper, among all children who came to the attention of CWS, 28 percent were considered eligible for adoption because they were placed out of the home and not reunified with their birth parent (NSCAW n.d.). Among this group, 61 percent were finally adopted by the five- to six-year follow up, 30 percent were not adopted but living with relatives and just 9 percent were in foster care with unrelated parents.

The reasons that these young children came into foster care had to do with child welfare workers' (CWWs) determination that there was going to be or, in fact, was parental incapacity to provide safely for the child. The child welfare workers' risk assessment showed that about 56 percent of the primary caregivers were misusing drugs. In each of the following areas, at least half of the caregivers were reported to have problems: serious mental health conditions, poor parenting skills and a history of having being abused or neglected during childhood. CWWs reported that more than two-thirds of the families did receive efforts to reunify the children—services that ultimately did not succeed.

Relatively little is known about the outcomes of foster care for young children although there is a smattering of studies about placement into foster care for children between the ages of 6–12. The best two of those (Doyle 2008 and Taussig, Clyman and Landsverk 2001) contradict each other—the earlier study indicating that children reunified from foster care do worse than those who remain and the more recent study indicating that among neglected children who go into foster care the rates of problems in adolescence and young adulthood are greater than those who remain at home.

This study addresses the short-term developmental outcomes for young children who have entered CWS at a very young age and have been adopted, who have remained in foster care, or have, primarily, lived at home. Although there are now a substantial number of longitudinal adoption studies that compare adopted children to other populations of unadopted children, there is no other US study that examines this question, per se. Longitudinal American studies tend to compare children who were adopted to other children in a general survey population (see review in Barth 2002). These studies tend to indicate that adopted children fare less well than non-adopted children although the differences tend to be minimized as children approach and move through adulthood, as long as the family environment in which they were raised is supportive (e.g. Feigelman 1997; Riggins-Caspers *et al.* 2003).

A French study, completed by Duyme, Dumaret and Tomkiewicz (1999), examines the development of children adopted from foster care as older children (between the ages of four and six) but does not compare them to other children who remained in foster care. The intent of this study was to study the malleability of IQ and its relationship to social class. In this study, 65 abused and neglected children who were later adopted children with moderately low IQs (< 86) at the time of adoption were selected from a sampling frame of 5003 files of adopted children. The results show a significant gain in IQ following adoption, with larger gains among high SES (social-economic status) adoptive families.

The closest American study is the Maternal Life Style (MLS) study which is a large multi-site study of infants born drug-exposed or not drug-exposed and followed to early school age. Henrietta Bada and colleagues (2008) used the MLS data to discover that the family environment—especially ongoing family violence and maternal depression—is an important correlate of developmental progress. This is an indication that continuing to live in the home of the birth parent—where we know there is often ongoing violence (Kohl 2007) and maternal depression (Burns *et al.* 2010)—may result in worse developmental outcomes.

In a related longitudinal analysis of prenatally drug-exposed and not drug-exposed newborns, Bada *et al.* (2008) evaluated how living arrangements of children would be associated with their behavior outcomes and adaptive functioning. A total of 1388 children with or without prenatal cocaine or opiate exposure were enrolled in a longitudinal cohort study at birth and, then, tracked over time for their living situation and evaluated for behavior problems and adaptive functioning at three years of age. Behavior problem scores worsened 2.3 and 1.3 points, respectively, with each move per year and each caretaker change was associated with a worsening of 2.65 and 2.19 points, respectively, in communication and daily living scores. They conclude that, "While family preservation continues to be the goal of the child welfare system, expediting decision toward permanency remains paramount once children are placed in foster care" (p. 173). This study predicts that adoption would be an antidote to continued placement instability and likely to be more beneficial than foster care.

Other studies from around the globe reflect on either outcomes of adoption or outcomes of foster care, with almost no studies comparing the two. Fernandez (2008) recently compared outcomes after three years (on average) among children in foster care and found that their high rates of behavior problems at admission to care were reduced by the second assessment—more closely approximating those of a randomly selected classmate. (Yet, the small sample size means that there was only power to detect a very large difference between the foster youth and non-foster youth, a difference present at intake but not later.)

Rushton and Dance (2006) followed the adoption of children from foster care who were placed between the ages of 5 and 11 but had no comparison to children not placed into foster care or who remain at home. The study outcomes showed substantial difficulty for a significant proportion (approaching half) of children who were adopted. Most other adoption follow up studies are of children adopted internationally so there is no appropriate non-adoptive foster care comparison group (e.g. Colvert *et al.* 2008; Hjern *et al.* 2004; van der Vegt *et al.* 2009).

The current study

This analysis focuses on levels of change in singular measures of child wellbeing outcomes for children who became involved with CWS during their first year of life and were placed into foster care (more detailed analyses with additional measures are available in Lloyd and Barth, in preparation).

Methods

SAMPLE

The NSCAW study is a federally funded study intended to explain the pathways of children through child welfare services. The sample design was a stratified cluster sample of all children in the United States with a report of maltreatment. Children ranged in age from infancy to 14[1] years of age, at the time of sampling. All analyses were conducted with weights to address the sampling design and allow for inferences about the population of children investigated as victims of child maltreatment in the US. There is a sample of children entering "CPS" (Child Protective Services) and one of children sampled after already being in foster care for a year. The "CPS" sample, on which this study draws, includes 5501 children interviewed from those entering child welfare services from October 1999 to December 2000. Methods are further described in Barth *et al.* (2002).

Interviews or assessments were conducted with the child and current caregiver (e.g. biological parent, foster parent, or adoptive parent). In this study, children had to be younger than 13 months at time of baseline sampling; the achieved sample size (unweighted) was 353 children. Characteristics of the sample group may be found in Table 2.1.

TABLE 2.1 Demographic characteristics at baseline (BL) by group status at 66 months

CHARACTERISTIC	ADOPTED	FOSTER CARE	IN-HOME	TOTAL
Demographic characteristics				
Male	43 (5.6)	46 (7.3)	68 (8.4)	49 (3.7)
Female	57 (5.6)	54 (7.3)	32 (8.4)	51 (3.7)
White	33 (6.2)	49 (9.1)	42 (8.9)	40 (5.5)
Black	32 (7.3)	23 (6.1)	41 (10.0)	31 (5.4)
Hispanic	21 (6.2)	25 (7.7)	14 (7.1)	21 (4.2)
Other	14 (6.1)	3 (2.1)	3 (1.5)	9 (3.3)
0–4 months	40 (6.2)	48 (9.6)	38 (8.7)	42 (4.9)
5–8 months	44 (6.7)	30 (9.1)	33 (9.6)	37 (4.8)
9–12 months	16 (5.9)	22 (7.7)	29 (6.5)	20 (3.8)

---

1   A small number of youth turned 15 between the time of sampling and the initial interview (n=99).

Case characteristics				
High Risk BINS Score at BL*	79 (4.4)	45 (9.3)	50 (9.0)	63 (4.3)
Poor at BL^	50 (7.3)	69 (7.2)	42 (7.6)	54 (4.5)
Poor at 66 mos.*	58 (5.5)	58 (8.3)	80 (7.1)	62 (4.1)
Failure to Thrive at BL	1 (0.6)	~0 (0.2)	~0 (0.1)	1 (0.3)
Birth Mother < 20 Years Old	10 (11.0)	25 (14.5)	26 (8.4)	24 (6.9)
Maltreatment Type				
Physical or Emotional Abuse	16 (4.1)	10 (3.2)	11 (4.5)	13 (2.5)
Failure to Provide Neglect	38 (5.5)	33 (9.1)	53 (7.6)	39 (4.1)
Failure to Supervise Neglect	18 (5.2)	16 (5.0)	14 (5.3)	17 (3.1)
Abandonment	8 (2.6)	17 (10.0)	8 (6.1)	11 (3.2)
All Other Types	20 (7.3)	24 (9.9)	14 (8.4)	20 (4.7)
Severity of Maltreatment				
None/Minimal	18 (6.1)	10 (4.6)	11 (4.5)	14 (3.7)
Minor	10 (4.7)	13 (5.0)	29 (7.3)	15 (3.7)
Moderate	24 (7.1)	36 (8.4)	23 (7.0)	28 (4.0)
Severe	48 (7.7)	41 (9.3)	38 (8.6)	44 (4.8)

^p<.07; *p<.05.

Four full waves of data collection were completed at baseline and approximately 18, 36 and 66 months post-baseline. An additional, reduced wave of data was collected, primarily over the telephone from caregivers, at 12 months post-baseline (Research Triangle Institute (RTI) 2008). Legal substantiation of maltreatment was not used as a criterion for inclusion in the present study, so not all participants had a legal finding that maltreatment had taken place (i.e. substantiation of maltreatment). Overall, most cases did not receive ongoing services (76%) although the cases that did receive ongoing services were over-sampled to understand better the receipt of services and its relationship to outcomes (although this was not a program evaluation study, it was a panel study).

Measures
DEMOGRAPHICAL CHARACTERISTICS
Gender was coded as male or female. Race was coded as white, African-American, Hispanic (any race) and other race/ethnicity. Age was measured in months.

MALTREATMENT TYPE
Maltreatment type was classified as physical or emotional abuse, neglect subtype failure to supervise, neglect subtype failure to provide necessities, abandonment, or other.

MALTREATMENT SEVERITY
Child welfare workers classified the harm resulting from the maltreatment at time of baseline data collection. Harm was classified as none or minimal, minor, moderate, or severe.

BIRTH MOTHER
A dummy variable was created to indicate if the child was born to a mother less than 20 years old.

FAILURE TO THRIVE
A dummy variable was created to indicate whether the child was diagnosed with failure to thrive at time of baseline data collection.

HIGH-RISK BINS
All infants were given the Bailey Infant Neurodevelopmental Screener (Aylward 1995) at baseline. A dummy variable was created to indicate whether the infant was classified as being at high risk for developmental problems.

POOR AT BASELINE/POOR AT 66 MONTH FOLLOW-UP
Household income, size and year were used to identify the poverty threshold for the child's household of residence using US Census Bureau tables. Children were identified as living in a poor home if the household had a total income less than 200 percent of the poverty line for that year.

VINELAND ADAPTIVE BEHAVIOR SCALES SCREENER—DAILY LIVING
A brief instrument used to screen children for problems in the domain of adaptive behavior and daily living skills. The Vineland Screener (Sparrow, Carter and Cicchetti 1993) is completed by a caregiver or other person knowledgeable about the child. The version for child ages zero to two was used at baseline with the three to five year old version used at subsequent waves as the cohort aged. The Vineland Screener strongly correlates (r=.87 to .98) with the full Vineland instrument.

PRE-SCHOOL LANGUAGE SCALES
The PLS-3 was used to assess the developmental domain of language. It produces two sub-scales, expressive communication and auditory comprehension and a total scale in children younger than six years old (Zimmerman, Steiner and Pond 1992). The scores are based on observations of the child. Interrater reliability is .98.

KAUFMAN BRIEF INTELLIGENCE TEST
The K-BIT was used to assess cognitive development in children older than four years. The K-BIT assesses 4 sub-domains as well as provides a total score. It is a self-administered, paper and pencil instrument. The test–retest reliability of the K-BIT varies by construct considered, but ranges from .74 to .95 (Kaufman and Kaufman 1990).

WOODCOCK-JOHNSON III TESTS OF ACHIEVEMENT
The Woodcock-Johnson (WJ; Woodcock, McGrew and Mather 2004) was used to assess educational outcomes of all children at least five years old. The exception is the calculation scale, which is only calculated for children at least six years old. All four WJ scales were used: applied problems (WJA), calculation (WJC), letter-identification (WJL), and passage comprehension (WJP). The WJA scale assesses a child's ability to use math to solve problems. The WJP scale assesses a child's ability to read a passage and understand what they've read. The WJC assesses a child's math skills. The WJL assess a child's basic reading skills. It is reported to have acceptable concurrent validity and reliability (RTI 2008).

CHILD BEHAVIOR CHECKLIST (CBCL)
Behavior problems were assessed using the CBCL, a well-validated measure of child emotional and behavior problems (Achenbach 1991). The CBCL was administered to caregivers of children ages two and older, with slightly different versions for two- and three-year-old children and children ages four and older. For internalizing, externalizing and total problem score dimensions, T-scores above 63 are considered clinical-level problems, scores of 60–63 are considered borderline-level and scores below 60 are considered normal. The decision to group borderline and normal scores (rather than borderline and clinical scores) was based on previous results from the NSCAW study that more children with borderline total problem behavior move into the normal category over 18 months than into the clinical-range category. The CBCL shows moderate reliability ($\alpha=.50-.70$) among children in the NSCAW study.

SETTING
Setting is the type of residence or status the child is in. In this analysis all the children were in out-of-home care at baseline but some changed setting to be in the home of origin (not with relatives), adopted, or remaining in foster care.

TIME IN PLACEMENT
Time in placement was reported in the data files. It indicates time in the current household of residence *not* time in the current child welfare setting (e.g. foster or kinship care).

NSCAW ANALYSIS WEIGHT FOR WAVE 5
This variable is unique for each case and is designed to produce results which are representative of almost all American children involved with child welfare systems. The details of its creation are given by the Data File Users Manual (RTI 2008).

STRATUM
This indicates which of the nine strata in NSCAW the data came from. Each of the first eight strata is a single, large population state while the ninth stratum includes data from several smaller states. It is part

of the complex survey sample data necessary to account correctly for clustering in NSCAW data (RTI 2008).

PRIMARY SAMPLING UNIT
This indicates which primary sampling unit (PSU) the data came from. Each PSU was typically a child welfare agency serving a geographical locale (normally a county). It is also part of the complex survey sample data necessary to account correctly for clustering in NSCAW data (RTI 2008).

Analytic methods
The CBCL and BINS were coded as dummy variables (clinical vs. sub-clinical and high vs. lower risk, respectively) and cross tabulated with outcome group (adopted, foster care and in-home) using PROC CROSSTAB in SUDAAN 10.0 (RTI 2008). Demographical, maltreatment and other key characteristics were also cross tabulated with outcome groups. Chi-square difference tests were completed for all cross tabulations.

Developmental and clinical measures produced continuous variables as did the time in placement variable. Means, standard errors and pair wise contrasts of means (using t-tests) were obtained. All analyses included weights and complex sample design variables. Sample size was 353 when complete data were available. Missing data resulted in modest pair wise deletion.

Results
BASELINE
The backgrounds of the children who later ended up in these three groups—(1) returned home from foster care (in-home), (2) remained in foster care, (3) adopted—were reasonably similar. There were, at least, no significant differences by race, gender, age at time of measurement following CWS investigation, maltreatment characteristics, having failure to thrive at entry to the study, or having been born to a teen-aged mother.

At baseline significantly fewer (79% vs. 49% and 50%) children in the adopted group had been classified as at high developmental risk (on the BINS) compared to their peers in the foster care and in-home groups ($\chi 2=4.04$ (2); p<.01). Mean contrast tests between the three groups demonstrated significant (t=2.4, p<.05) differences between the adopted group and the in-home group indicating the adopted group had been in their current home significantly longer than the in-home group and that the children in the adopted and foster care groups were somewhat more likely to be poor at BL (p<.07).

MEASURES AT 66 MONTHS

Mean contrast testing of the HOME scales indicated the adopted group had significantly higher scores on both the cognitive stimulation (t=5.1, p<.001) and caregiver responsiveness (t=1.9, p=.059). In addition, the adopted group score had a higher mean cognitive stimulation score than their peers in the foster care group (t=3.6, p<.001).

TABLE 2.2 Developmental and clinical measures at 66 months

CHARACTERISTIC	ADOPTED (1)	FOSTER CARE (2)	IN-HOME (3)	TOTAL
CBCL clinical (%)	24 (5.8)	32 (9.0)	21 (7.7)	26 (4.6)
CBCL subclinical (%)	76 (5.8)	68 (9.0)	79 (7.7)	74 (4.6)
Mean time in current home*** (years)[13]	4.7 (0.1)	4.3 (0.4)	3.6 (0.5)	4.4 (0.2)
HOME				
Cognitive stimulation***[12,13]	12.6 (0.1)	11.2 (0.4)	10.6 (0.4)	11.7 (0.2)
Caregiver responsiveness*[13]	9.9 (0.2)	9.6 (0.3)	9.2 (0.3)	9.6 (0.1)
Developmental outcomes at 66 month follow-up	Adopted	Foster care	In-home	Total
Mean VABS***[21,31]	79 (2.4)	90 (4.4)	87 (2.7)	84 (2.2)
Mean PLS-3**[12]	96 (1.3)	88 (4.2)	97 (4.4)	94 (1.7)
Mean K-BIT*	95 (1.2)	91 (2.4)	96 (2.2)	94 (1.2)
Mean WJ Basic Math***[12,32]	100 (2.8)	87 (2.5)	103 (4.8)	93 (2.4)
Mean WJ Letter-Word***[12,]	104 (1.2)	99 (1.8)	97 (2.5)	101 (1.1)
Mean WJ Reading***[12,32]	102 (1.8)	95 (1.2)	99 (1.7)	99 (1.1)
Mean WJ Applied Math***[12,32]	94 (1.8)	86 (2.3)	93 (2.7)	91 (1.1)

*p<.05; **p<.01; ***p<.001, for 3-way analysis of variance (ANOVA). Superscripts show significant bivariate comparisons.

The adopted group had significantly higher mean scores than their peers in foster care on the VABS (t=2.6, p=.01), the PLS-3 (t=1.8, p=.07), as well as all four Woodcock-Johnson scales; Basic Math (t=3.3, p<.001), Letter-Word Identification (t=2.0, p<.05), Reading Comprehension (t=3.1, p<.01) and Applied Math (t=2.3, p<.05). The in-home group also had significantly higher scores than the foster care group on the Woodcock-Johnson scales: Basic Math (t=3.1, p<.01), Reading Comprehension (t=1.9, p=.06) and Applied Math (t=1.8, p=.07). Finally the adopted group scored significantly less highly on the VABS (t=2.5, p=.01) than the in-home group while the reverse was true on the Woodcock-Johnson Letter Word Identification (t=2.6, p=.01).

Overall, the foster group had the lowest means in cognitive and language skills (but also the highest in adaptive behavior). The adopted and in-home groups were very close to each other on these measures (and to the normative mean for language skills) although there were significant advantages for the adopted children. There were also no significant differences on the CBCL at W5 with more than 90 per cent of children in the non-clinical range in all three index groups on the internalizing scale and about 80 percent in the non-clinical on the externalizing scales.

LIMITATIONS

The analysis would be stronger if it could have overcome these short-comings: the lack of change in placements, lack of long enough time to understand the impact of subtle differences, limited school data, measures done by field representatives not expertly trained psychometricians and no measures of what foster care workers or in-home service workers provided to families. Also, large by adoption study standards, there were nonetheless relatively few infants in NSCAW who met criteria for inclusion into this study. This results in a lack of precision in the estimates and is reflected in some large standard errors. The result is that Type II errors are more likely.

FUTURE RESEARCH

Understand the impact on all measures (cumulative effects), endeavor to get an estimate of placement instability, add information from teachers, and employ analyses that consider change over time.

Implications for policy and practice

Returning to the home of the biological parent and adoption were associated with the most similar and, generally, positive outcomes. Children in foster care had the poorest development on many measures even though the children in the in-home condition had less responsive parents and much greater poverty. The findings, like Bada *et al.* (2008), suggest that placement stability and parental commitment are major forces in development (unfortunately, we do not have credible placement move data for the entire 5–6 years), apparently at least as much of a force than the type of placement, per se.

Given the greater exposure to poverty in the in-home group the impact on development could be delayed or may never arise. Magnuson and Duncan (2006) conclude that there are many reasons why socioeconomic circumstances may not be as consequential for children's achievement as one might think. Maybe what really matters is a collection of psychological dispositions of parents—for example depression—and thus the association between socioeconomic status and achievement for children may merely reflect the fact that both are higher in the case of better-adjusted parents. Or maybe the association between socioeconomic status and achievement stems from the poor health and developmental problems of the children themselves which can lower a child's academic achievement and reduce a family's resources by limiting parents' employment.

The study adds to much American and international literature indicating the risks associated with prolonged stays in non-kinship foster care (e.g. Doyle 2007; Newton, Litrownik and Landsverk 2000; Rubin *et al.* 2007; Sinclair *et al.* 2005; Vinnerljung *et al.* 2010). Although the adopted children were faring the best, on many measures, they still had elevated rates of problem behaviors, according to their parents' reports on the CBCL, suggesting that their development was not optimal in their parents' eyes. On the positive side, all three groups have language, intelligence and academic achievement scores that are in the average range. Although we have no comparison group of abused and unserved children, it is highly plausible that their wellbeing would be more compromised.

References

Achenbach, T. (1991) *Manual for the Child Behaviour Checklist 4–18 and 1991 profile.* Burlington, VT: Department of Psychiatry, University of Vermont.

AFCARS (2006) *The AFCARS Report.* Available from www.acf.hhs.gov/programs/cb/stats_research/afcars/tar/report14.htm, accessed on 15 March 2009.

Aylward, G.P. (1995) *The Bayley Infant Neurodevelopmental Screener Manual.* San Antonio: The Psychological Corporation (Standardization manual published 1992).

Bada, H.S. Langer, J. Twomey, J. Bursi, C. *et al.* (2008) 'Importance of stability of early living arrangements on behaviour outcomes of children with and without prenatal drug exposure.' *Journal of Developmental and Behavioural Paediatrics 29*, 3, 173–182.

Barth, R.P. (2002) 'Outcomes of adoption and what they tell us about designing adoption services.' *Adoption Quarterly 6*, 45–60.

Barth, R.P. Biemer, P. Runyan, D. Webb, M.B. *et al.* (2002) 'Methodological lessons from the National Survey of Child and Adolescent Well-Being: the first three years of the USA's first national probability study of children and families investigated for abuse and neglect.' *Children and Youth Services Review 24*, 6–7, 513–541.

Berrick, J. Needell, B. Barth, R.P. and Jonson-Reid, M. (1998) *The Tender Years: Toward Developmentally Sensitive Child Welfare Services.* New York, NY: Oxford University Press.

Burns, B.J. Mustillo, S.A. Farmer, E.M.Z. Kolko, D.J. McCrae, J. Libby, A.M. and Webb, M. (2010) 'Caregiver depression, mental health service use and child outcomes.' In M. Webb, K. Dowd, B. Jones-Harden, J. Landsverk and M.F. Testa (eds) *Child Welfare and Child Wellbeing: New Perspectives from the National Surbey of Child and Adolescent Well Being.* Oxford: Oxford University Press.

Colvert, E. Rutter, M. Beckett, C. Castle, J. Groothues, C. Hawkins, A. *et al.* (2008) 'Emotional difficulties in early adolescence following severe deprivation: Findings form the English and Romanian adoptees study.' *Development and Psychopathology, 20*, 2, 547–567.

Doyle, J.J. (2008) 'Child protection and child outcomes: measuring the effects of foster care.' *American Economic Review 97*, 5, 1583–1610.

Duyme, M. Dumaret, A.C. and Tomkiewicz, S. (1999) 'How can we boost IQs of "dull children"?: A late adoption study.' *Proceeding of the National Academy of Sciences of the United States of America, 96*, 15, 8790–8794.

Feigelman, W. (1997) 'Adopted adults: comparisons with persons raised in conventional families.' *Marriage and Family Review 25*, 199–223.

Fernandez, E. (2008) 'Unravelling emotional, behavioural and educational outcomes in a longitudinal study of children in foster-care.' *British Journal of Social Work 38*, 7, 1283–1301.

Hjern, A. Vinnerljung, B. and Lindblad, F. (2004) Avoidable mortality among child welfare recipients and intercountry adoptees: a national cohort study. *Journal of Epidemiology and Community Health, 58*, 5, 412–417.

Kaufman, A. and Kaufman, N. (1990). *Kaufman Brief Intelligence Test.* Circle Pines, MN: American Guidance Services, Inc.

Kohl, P.L. (2007) *Unsuccessful In-Home Child Welfare Service Plans Following a Maltreatment Investigation: Racial and Ethnic Disparities.* Baltimore, MD: Annie E. Casey Foundation.

Magnuson, K.A. and Duncan, G.J. (2006) 'The role of family socioeconomic resources in the black-white test score gap among young children.' *Developmental Review 26*, 4, 365–399.

National Survey of Child and Adolescent Well-Being (NSCAW) (n.d.) *Research Brief No. 14: Need for Adoption among Infants Investigated for Child Maltreatment and Adoption Status 5 to 6 Years Later.* Available at: National Data Archive on Child Abuse and Neglect (NDACAN), Cornell University, ndacan@cornell.edu.

Newton, R.R. Litrownik, A.J. and Landsverk, J.A. (2000) 'Children and youth in foster care: Disentangling the relationship between problem behaviours and number of placements.' *Child Abuse and Neglect 24*, 1363–1374.

Research Triangle Institute (RTI) (2008) *Data File User's Manual.* Cary, NC: RTI.

Riggins-Caspers, K.M. Cadoret, R.J. Knutson, J.F. and Langbehn, D. (2003) 'Biology-environment interaction and evocative biology-environment correlation: contributions of harsh discipline and parental psychopathology to problem adolescent behaviours.' *Behaviour Genetics 33*, 3, 205–220.

Rubin, D.M. O'Reilly, A.L.R. Luan, X.Q. and Localio, A.R. (2007) 'The impact of placement stability on behavioural well-being for children in foster care.' *Paediatrics 119*, 2, 336–344.

Rushton, A. and Dance, C. (2006) 'The adoption of children from public care: a prospective study of outcome in adolescence.' *Journal of the American Academy of Child and Adolescent Psychiatry 45*, 7, 877–883.

Sinclair, I. Barker, C. Wilson, K. and Gibbs, I. (2005) *Foster Children: Where They Go and How They Get On.* London: Jessica Kingsley Publishers.

Sparrow, S.S. Carter, A.S. and Cicchetti, D.V. (1993) *Vineland Screener: Overview, Reliability, Validity, Administration and Scoring.* New Haven, CT: Yale University Child Study Centre.

Taussig, H.N. Clyman, R.B. and Landsverk, J. (2001) 'Children who return home from foster care: a 6-year prospective study of behavioural health outcomes in adolescence.' *Paediatrics 108*, 62–68.

Van der Vegt, E.J.M. Tieman, W. van der Ende, J. Ferdinand, R.F. Verhulst, F.C. and Tiemeier, H. (2009) 'Impact of early childhood adversities on adult psychiatric disorders. *Social Psychiatry and Psychiatric Epidemiology, 44*, 9, 724–731.

Vinnerljung, B. Franzén, E. Hjern, A. and Lindlblad, F. (2010) 'Long-Term Outcomes of Foster Care: Lessons from Swedish National Cohort Studies. In E. Fernandez and R. Barth (eds) *How Does Foster Care Work?* London: Jessica Kingsley Publishers..

Wulczyn, F. (2003) 'Closing the gap: are changing exit patterns reducing the time African American children spend in foster care relative to Caucasian children?' *Children and Youth Services Review 25*, 5–6, 431–462.

Wulczyn, F. Barth, R.P. Yuan, Y.Y. Jones Harden, B. and Landsverk, J. (2005) *Beyond Common Sense: Evidence for Child Welfare Policy Reform.* New York, NY: Transaction De Gruyter.

Woodcock, R.W. McGrew, K.S and Mather, N. (2004) *Woodcock-Johnson III Tests of Achievement.* Itasca, IL: Riverside Publishing Company.

Zimmerman, I.L. Steiner, V.G. and Pond, E.P. (1992) *Preschool Language Scale-3.* San Antonio, TX: The Psychological Corporation.

Commentary by Bo Vinnerljung on:

Five-Year Developmental Outcomes for Young Children Remaining in Foster Care, Returned Home, or Adopted

Richard P. Barth and Christopher Lloyd

In the US, "permanency planning" has for decades been the guiding policy for providing long term substitute care to neglected and abused children who enter the child welfare system. Considering the commitment to this principle from policymakers, professionals and researchers, it is (from a European perspective) somewhat surprising that the research base for this consensus contains few sound US comparative follow-up studies, estimating the impact of adoption compared to long-term foster care.

Richard P. Barth's and Christopher Lloyd's study is therefore a very valuable contribution to this anthology, but also to international child welfare research. It is based on baseline and follow-up data from a large battery of standardized instruments. Follow-up data has been collected in three waves, the last more than five years after baseline. This distinguishes their work from most other studies in this field. They have also created a solid base for future comparative follow-ups, e.g. of academic performance and development of antisocial behaviour in adolescence.

The results clearly point in the same direction as important European studies, for example the groundbreaking work of Michael Bohman and Soren Sigvardsson. They followed around 600 Stockholm children, originally left for adoption by their birth mothers, from birth to 22 years of age (e.g. Bohman and Sigvardsson 1990). Roughly, a third were adopted in infancy, a third returned home to their mothers and a third grew up in foster care. Follow-up data was collected at age 11, 15, 18 and 22. At age 11 – and even more pronounced at age 15 – the foster children had more behaviour problems and poorer school performance than their adopted peers. At age 15, the adopted group was not significantly different than a control group of peers from the same schools as the study groups. At age 22, far more foster children had official records of criminality and alcohol abuse than both adopted peers and the group who grew up in their mother's care. A small French study of birth siblings from multi-problem families compared school outcomes for siblings who were either adopted by middle-class families, grew up with their parents, or grew up in foster care. The outcomes for the foster children were dismal (all were "school failures"), worse than for their siblings who remained in their birth homes, while their adopted sisters on brothers did fine in school (Dumaret 1985).

In international child welfare research, there are far too few examples of trans-Atlantic replications. In my view, it would be a great service to European policy-making and practice if Barth's and Lloyd's study was replicated in the UK, where child welfare legislation has more common ground with the US than most other European countries.

References

Bohman, M. and Sigvardsson, S. (1990) 'Outcomes in Adoption: Lessons from Longitudinal studies.' In D. Brodzinsky and M. Schecter (eds) *The Psychology of Adoption*. New York, NY: Oxford University Press, pp.93–106.

Dumaret, A. (1985) 'IQ, scholastic performance and behaviour in sibs raised in contrasting environments'. *Journal of Child Psychology and Psychiatry 26*, 553–555.

CHAPTER 3

Placement Stability and Movement Trajectories

Fred Wulczyn and Lijun Chen

The impact of multiple placements on children in foster care has been a salient topic in child welfare policy and programmatic debates for decades. Legislative initiatives to promote permanency for foster children (e.g. Adoption Assistance and Child Welfare Act, Adoption and Safe Families Act) have increased emphasis on shorter lengths of stay in foster care and greater placement stability. The US Department of Health and Human Services (USDHHS) now monitors the number of movements recorded for children in foster care as part of the national outcomes standards (US Department of Health and Human Services 2002).

The reasons for concern about frequent movement in foster care are clear. The clinical literature documents the negative effects of placement instability on children, including attachment difficulties to primary caregivers and externalizing behaviour problems (e.g. Newton, Litrownik and Landsverk 2000; Rubin *et al.* 2007; Stovall and Dozier 1998). Generally, researchers report that between one-third and two-thirds of traditional foster care placements are disrupted within the first 1–2 years in different states (Wulczyn, Kogan and Harden 2003; Wulczyn, Hislop and Chen 2007). Factors identified to be associated with placement disruption include child characteristics such as older age and behaviour or emotional problems (e.g. Barth *et al.* 2007; Chamberlain *et al.* 2006; James 2004; Leathers 2006; Smith *et al.* 2001). However, foster family attachment and sense of belonging by the children will serve to reduce the effect of behavioural problems on placement disruption (Leathers 2006). Research has also consistently shown that kinship foster homes tend to be more stable than traditional foster homes (Chamberlain *et al.* 2006; James 2004; Wulczyn *et al.* 2007). Placement with siblings is also found to reduce placement instability (Zinn *et al.* 2006).

It should be noted that many placement changes, especially initial placement moves after entering foster care, are not induced by children's behaviour but are instead related to policy and procedural requirements, such as moving a child from an emergency placement into more family-like setting and placing a child with a sibling (James 2004; Zinn *et al.* 2006).

Placement stability and change

Most studies reviewed above generally investigate the attributes and characteristics of children, searching for an explanation of variation in the number and pace of placement movements. However, relatively little work focuses on the movements themselves, such as patterns in the timing of moves. A study of children entering foster care during 1997 and 1998 in New York City indicates that, although a majority of children leave care without any placement change, the changes that do happen tend to occur early, during the first six months of a foster care spell (Wulczyn *et al.* 2003). Among children in care for more than six months, the rate of placement change, measured by the number of moves per child for those still in care during that period, gradually decreases.

In the present study, we adopt a largely similar approach to the study by Wulczyn *et al.* (2003). However, we expand our scope beyond New York City to include children in foster care in 11 states. Our goal is to describe the timing of moves relative to the start of placement in order to ascertain when movement is most likely. In addition we are interested in determining the extent to which certain child characteristics (e.g. age at placement) and placement type influence the number and timing of movement from one placement to another.

Data and methods

We present our empirical work in three parts. The first part examines the number of moves and the timing of the moves, using the negative binomial regression model and the Cox regression model. The second part examines movement trajectories using the period-specific rate of movement for all children as well as for children of different race, age groups and of different initial placement settings. The third part of the study examines the patterns of transition between different placement settings from the first to second placement and the second to third placement.

Data

The data include children who first entered foster care during 2000, 2001 and 2002.[1] Each observed foster care spell is followed through December 31, 2005 or until the child exited care.[2] Only the first foster care spell of each child is examined (i.e. subsequent spells in foster care are not included). A foster care spell is a continuous period of time in out-of-home care and may consist of one or more movements between placement settings. Included in this study are 176,905 children whose first foster care spells started during 2000 to 2002. These children experienced a total of 227,418 placement changes. The duration of the foster care spells range from five days to six years. It should be noted that a destination of a placement move or change can be and often is, the same type of placement, such as moving from one family foster home to another foster home.

Movement counts

Data analyses are conducted as follows. First, we construct two major measures of placement stability: the average number of movements per child and the average number of movements per 100 days in care. The number of movements per child is calculated as the ratio of the total number of moves to the total number of children in the sample. The number of movements per 100 days is calculated as the total number of moves divided by the total spell duration in units of 100 days. The number of moves per 100 days captures movement stability more accurately because it takes into account the length of stay for each child in care.

---

1   The data are maintained by the Center for State Foster Care and Adoption Data at Chapin Hall at the University of Chicago.

2   Exit destinations from substitute care include reunification, adoption, guardianship, death, independence, runaway and detention.

The movement count data are further used in a multiple regression analysis to obtain the effect of each covariate on movement rate while controlling for the other covariates. Efficient estimates are obtained by using the negative binomial distribution (Allison 2005). To study the effect of the covariates on the timing and speed of first placement, the proportional hazard regression analysis is adopted. Results of the two models can be compared to see whether the effect of a covariate on the average movement rate diverges from its effect on the risk of a first move.

The covariates examined include year of entry to foster care, initial placement setting and child characteristics such as age at entry to foster care, gender and ethnicity. Four initial placement settings are differentiated: foster family care, kinship/relative care, congregate care and other type of settings. Congregate care includes group homes, group residential care and institutions.

Movement trajectories

The next section of the analysis considers the issue of movement trajectories more specifically. To study the trajectory of placement moves, we calculate the period-specific measures of placement stability. Placement duration is divided into six-month intervals, for a total of 12 intervals (six years, two intervals per year). During each interval, the number of children in care at the start of the interval is identified; a count of moves for each child as well as their length of stay during the interval are recorded. For each interval, both the average number of moves per child and the average number of moves per 100 days in care are calculated to examine the temporal trends. Finally, we examine the transition between different types of placement, when a child makes the first and second placement changes.

Results

Movement counts

Table 3.1 is a summary of sample sizes and measures of placement stability for children with different characteristics and initial placement types and movement frequencies. Three summary measures of placement stability are provided: per cent of children with any move, movements per child and movements per 100 days. Of the 176,905 children under study, 46 per cent have never moved and just over a quarter of the children move only once. Together they constitute over 72 per cent of the children in foster care.

It is obvious that infants have greater placement stability than children of older age groups since their movement rate per 100 days is much lower and median time to first placement move is longer. However, largely due to their longer stay in care, a somewhat higher proportion of infants have eventually moved, reflected by their long median time to exit. For children of different ethnic groups, white children seem to have more placement disruptions than either black or Hispanic children, although white children may not differ from black children in the average number of moves experienced per child.[3] There is no discernible difference between males and females. All measures indicate that children in kinship care experience better stability than children in foster homes or congregate care. Although a smaller per centage of children in congregate care than in family foster care have ever moved, they tend to experience more placement disruptions (more moves per child and per 100 days).

Multivariate event count regression

Results from the binomial regression model on movement counts and the Cox regression model on time to first placement change are presented in Table 3.2. The coefficient in the negative binomial model gives the ratio of placement moves per unit time for children in a given category relative to that of the reference category. For black and Hispanic children placed in care, their movement rates are only 88 per cent of the movement rate of white children after taking into account differences in age, gender and first placement settings. This is largely consistent with the unadjusted measure of moves per 100 days for children of different ethnic groups as shown in Table 3.1. The results of the model for entry age and first placement setting are also consistent with the moves per 100 days in Table 3.1. Although children in congregate care generally have higher rate of placement movement than children in foster care, an analysis of the interaction between placement setting and child age (not shown here) indicates that teenagers placed in foster homes experience the highest level of disruption – higher than the rate for children of any age group in congregate care.

---

3   This seeming inconsistency between moves per child and moves per 100 days is caused largely by the shorter spell duration of white children than black children.

TABLE 3.1 Summary measures of placement stability and time to discharge for children with various sttributes

COVARIATES	TOTAL SPELLS	PER CENT MOVED	MOVES PER PERSON	MOVES PER 100 DAYS	PER CENT EXIT CARE	MEDIAN TIME TO EXIT
Entry year						
2000	58,764	54	1.34	0.24	95	350
2001	59,983	54	1.30	0.25	92	348
2002	58,158	53	1.22	0.25	87	356
Entry age						
0 to 1	32,619	57	1.05	0.16	91	553
1 to 5	45,410	55	0.96	0.21	91	388
6 to 12	50,584	55	1.70	0.26	88	367
13 to 17	48,292	49	1.33	0.35	96	211
Race						
White	82,201	54	1.29	0.28	94	311
Black	67,964	55	1.35	0.22	88	429
Hispanic	16,018	49	1.13	0.22	91	331
Other	10,722	44	1.02	0.21	93	302
Gender						
Female	86,976	54	1.29	0.25	92	340
Male	89,929	53	1.28	0.24	91	360
First placement						
Congregate care	37,655	53	1.44	0.34	93	250
Foster care	10,1193	57	1.32	0.25	91	354
Kinship care	33,061	40	0.89	0.15	89	447
Other	4996	86	2.06	0.30	88	586
Number of moves*						
0	81,983	46.3	0	0	96	145
1	44,590	25.2	1	0.19	93	391
2 plus	50,332	28.5	3.63	0.42	81	808
Total	176,905	54	1.29	0.24	91	351

For the 'number of moves' covariate, the data in the 'per cent moved' column is the per cent of all children with that number of moves.

TABLE 3.2. Negative binomial regression on placement moves and Cox regression on time to first move (2000–2002 entry cohorts in 11 states)

Parameter	NEGATIVE BINOMIAL MODEL		COX REGRESSION MODEL	
	Placement rate ratio	Sig.	Hazard ratio	Sig.
Entry year (2000 as ref)				
2001	1.021	**	1.013	
2002	1.018	*	1.015	
Male vs. female	0.950	***	0.943	***
Start age (<1 as ref)				
1 to 5	1.375	***	1.224	***
6 to 12	1.687	***	1.223	***
13 to 17	2.127	***	1.034	*
Race (white as ref)				
Black	0.878	***	0.927	***
Hispanic	0.880	***	0.860	***
Other	0.772	***	0.720	***
First placement (foster care as ref)				
Congregate care	1.066	***	1.265	***
Kinship care	0.527	***	0.473	***
Other	1.512	***	3.882	***
Intercept	0.002	***		
Dispersion	1.759	***		
Number of cases	176,905		176,905	

*p<0.05; **p<0.01; ***p<0.001.

A comparison of the results of Cox regression model with those of the negative binomial model demonstrates that children with a higher rate of placement change, such as white children and children in congregate care, also tend to experience the first placement change more quickly. For children of different age groups, older children have a higher movement rate and quicker pace to first placement change. However, the results also show that teenagers have a slower pace to first placement change than children in the 1 to 5 and 6 to 12 year age groups. This is also contrary to the shorter median time to first placement move for teenage children compared to younger children, as shown in Table 3.1. This apparent discrepancy can largely be attributed to the fact that a much higher percentage of teenagers are initially placed in congregate

TABLE 3.3. Number of Children with Various Number of Moves during Each Six-month Interval and Summary Measure of Placement Stability for Each Interval (2000–2002 entry cohorts in 11 states)

Placement Interval (Duration in Months)	0 to 6	7 to 12	13 to 18	19 to 24	25 to 30	31 to 36	37 to 42	43 to 48
Total Children at interval start	176,905	114,695	85,485	64,962	50,408	39,123	30,162	19,663
Children who never move (stayers)	81,983	36,910	22,667	15,000	10,737	7,937	5,865	3,602
Children who move (movers)	94,922	77,785	62,818	49,962	39,671	31,186	24,297	16,061
Number of interval specific moves								
0	22,395	54,244	46,647	37,593	30,337	24,155	19,416	13,047
1	47,254	17,041	12,071	9,492	7,100	5,365	3,662	2,212
2 plus	25,273	6,500	4,100	2,877	2,234	1,666	1,219	802
Total Number of Moves	114,013	34,000	22,739	17,008	12,937	9,873	6,908	4,409
Total Number of Care Days	25,067,028	18,324,850	13,686,616	10,514,974	8,159,292	6,323,594	4,521,824	2,875,962
Moves per Child	0.64	0.3	0.27	0.26	0.26	0.25	0.23	0.22
Moves per 100 Days	0.45	0.19	0.17	0.16	0.16	0.16	0.15	0.15

Notes: The last four intervals are not shown in this table for space limitation.

care. Once the impact of the first placement setting is taken into account in the model, the hazard ratio of teenage children to first placement change is much reduced.

Movement trajectories

The number of movements by half-year placement intervals is given in Table 3.3 for all children placed in care during 2000 to 2002. The data in these tables can be interpreted as follows. For each time interval of six months, the total number of children starting the interval still in care is provided together with their total number of moves and care days used during the interval. The moves per child and moves per 100 days are calculated for each specific interval. Hence, the measures are based on the period-specific number of moves.

Both period-specific number of moves per child and number of moves per 100 days in care indicate a sharp decline in the rate of movement from the first to second six-month intervals: moves per child drop from 0.64 to 0.30 and moves per 100 days from 0.45 to 0.19. From the second to later intervals, the decline is more gradual for both moves per child and moves per 100 days. This demonstrates a trajectory with high rates of movement in the first six months and lower rates thereafter.

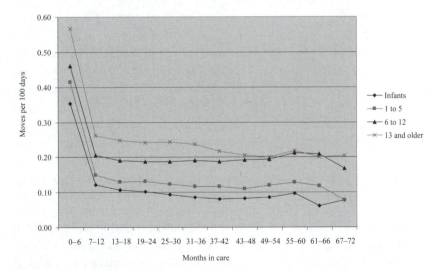

FIGURE 3.1 Period specific number of moves per 100 days by age at admission and time in care

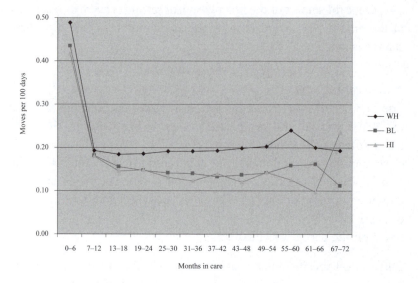

FIGURE 3.2 Period specific number of moves per 100 days by race/ethnicity and time in care

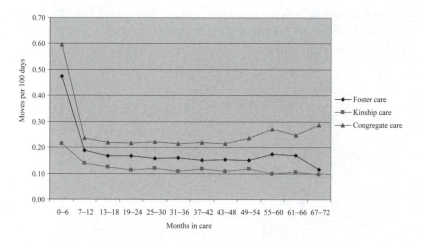

FIGURE 3.3 Period specific number of moves per 100 days by type of care and time in care

Figures 3.1, 3.2 and 3.3 show the movement trajectories for children of different age groups, races/ethnicities and first placement settings. They reveal nuances that are not captured by the summary measures of Table 3.1. The period-specific movement rate for the 13 years and older children drops in the latter placement intervals, whereas the rate for the

6 to 12 year olds remains stable. As a result, the rates for these two groups converge at the ninth interval (first six months of fifth year).

The movement trajectories for children of the three ethnic groups (white, black and Hispanic) converge in the second interval and then diverge with the movement rate for white children rising. The trajectories by first placement type indicate some increase in the later intervals in the movement rate for children in congregate care and foster care. For children in congregate care, the average moves per 100 days in the last few intervals is higher than the movement rate observed in the second interval.

Transitions between placement settings from first to second and second to third placement

Tables 3.4 and 3.5 demonstrate the patterns of transition between placement settings from the first to second placement and from the second to third placement. Four types of placements are differentiated: foster family homes, kinship homes, congregate care and other care types.[4]

TABLE 3.4. Transition from first placement to second placement setting during first foster care spell

First placement	TOTAL SPELLS	NO SECOND PLACE-MENT	SECOND PLACE-MENT	TYPE OF SECOND PLACEMENT			
				FOSTER	KIN-SHIP	CONGRE-GATE	OTH-ER
Foster care (PFC)	101,193 (100%)	43,712 (43%)	57,481 (57%)	39,777 (69%)	12,396 (22%)	4627 (8%)	681 (1%)
Kinship care (PKC)	33,061 (100%)	19,892 (60%)	13,169 (40%)	5765 (44%)	6082 (46%)	1083 (8%)	239 (2%)
Congregate care (PCC)	37,655 (100%)	17,663 (47%)	19,992 (53%)	7200 (36%)	2350 (12%)	9850 (49%)	592 (3%)
Other care types	4996 (100%)	716 (14%)	4280 (86%)	2766 (65%)	740 (17%)	617 (14%)	157 (4%)
Total	176,905 (100%)	81,983 (46%)	94,922 (54%)	55,508 (58%)	21,568 (23%)	16,177 (17%)	1669 (2%)

'Other care types' are mostly missing or unknown. The percentage data under 'type of second placement' refer to the percentage of the children with a second placement, excluding children without a second placement.

Altogether 94,922 children out of 176,905 have a second placement. While a majority of children in foster care (57%) and congregate care

---

4   Most children in the 'other' category have missing or unknown care type.

(53%) have a second placement, only 40 per cent of the children initially placed with relatives have a second placement. For most children with a second placement, their second placement setting is the same as their initial placement setting, be it conventional foster care, kinship care or congregate care. While 25 per cent of children initially placed in congregate care (48% of those with second placement) are transferred to more family-like settings (i.e. foster and kinship care), another 26 per cent (49% of those with second placement) move to another congregate care setting. There is also a small proportion of children in both foster care and kinship care who are transferred to the more restrictive congregate care.

TABLE 3.5. Transition from first–second placement combination to third placement setting during first foster care spell

FIRST–SECOND PLACEMENT	SPELLS WITH SECOND PLACEMENT	NO THIRD PLACEMENT	THIRD PLACEMENT	TYPE OF THIRD PLACEMENT			
				FOSTER	KINSHIP	CONGREGATE	OTHER
PFC-PFC	39,777 (100%)	18,249 (46%)	21,528 (54%)	16,926 (79%)	2562 (12%)	1726 (8%)	314 (1%)
PFC-PKC	12,396 (100%)	7702 (62%)	4694 (38%)	2625 (56%)	1834 (39%)	187 (4%)	48 (1%)
PFC-PCC	4627 (100%)	1583 (34%)	3044 (66%)	1538 (51%)	230 (8%)	1162 (38%)	114 (4%)
PKC-PFC	5765 (100%)	2468 (43%)	3297 (57%)	2038 (62%)	1007 (31%)	189 (6%)	63 (2%)
PKC-PKC	6082 (100%)	3686 (61%)	2396 (39%)	978 (41%)	1205 (50%)	157 (7%)	56 (2%)
PKC-PCC	1083 (100%)	278 (26%)	805 (74%)	247 (31%)	278 (35%)	258 (32%)	22 (3%)
PCC-PFC	7200 (100%)	2682 (37%)	4518 (63%)	2539 (56%)	717 (16%)	1132 (25%)	130 (3%)
PCC-PKC	2350 (100%)	1243 (53%)	1107 (47%)	360 (33%)	382 (35%)	346 (31%)	19 (2%)
PCC-PCC	9850 (100%)	4363 (44%)	5487 (56%)	1093 (20%)	462 (8%)	3630 (66%)	302 (6%)
OTHER	5792 (100%)	2336 (40%)	3456 (60%)	1920 (56%)	667 (19%)	553 (16%)	316 (9%)
Total	94,922 (100%)	44,590 (47%)	50,332 (53%)	30,264 (60%)	9344 (19%)	9340 (19%)	1384 (3%)

The 'OTHER' category includes any combination with the 'other care types'. The percentage data under 'type of third placement' refer to the percentage of the children with a third placement, excluding children without a third placement.

Table 3.5 shows that 53 per cent of the 94,922 children with a second placement also have a third placement, with 32 per cent in foster care, 10 per cent each for kinship and congregate care, similar to the per centage distribution for second placement. Regardless of the first placement type, children whose second placement is with kin are less likely to have a third placement. Although children placed in congregate care from an initial placement setting of foster and kinship care are only a small proportion of all children, they are the most likely to move again, with 66 and 74 per cent respectively placed for the third time. Over a third of the children with both first and second placements in congregate care are placed in congregate care again for the third time. About a quarter of the children who are transferred to congregate care from an initial placement of foster or kinship care move to another congregate care setting in the third placement.

In summary, while most children who have moved are likely to be placed in foster care or kinship care settings for their second or third placement, many of those who are placed in congregate care initially and/or in their second placement are likely to be placed again in congregate care. This is especially true for children whose first two placements are both in congregate care. These children also tend to have a higher movement rate, measured as either moves per child or per 100 days, during their stay in care.

Discussion

The current study addresses several questions regarding placement stability and change for children in foster care. First, the data from this analysis support previous findings that a substantial proportion of foster children experience no more than one placement. Additionally, movement activities are concentrated in the first few months of children's foster care stay.

Age proves to be a prominent variable in the current analyses. Adolescents tend to have a higher risk of placement change than younger children, especially infants. This is consistent with the literature suggesting that adolescents have more difficulty connecting to a family and remaining in substitute placement because of behaviour problems (e.g. Courtney *et al.* 2001). The finding that infants in either foster or kinship care generally have a lower average rate of movement is also consistent with most previous studies (James 2004; Wulczyn *et al.* 2003).

Although most previous local studies (e.g. James 2004; Wulczyn *et al.* 2003; Zinn *et al.* 2006) do not find significant variation in placement stability among children of different ethnic groups, our analysis of children in the 11 states shows white children to experience more frequent placement disruptions than black or Hispanic children. This is true even in the multiple regression results where child attributes and first placement type are taken into account. However, white children may not have a higher average number of moves per child. Actually, as shown in Table 3.1, since white children stay in care for a much shorter time than black children, their average number of placement moves is smaller.

There is some evidence in the literature regarding the qualitative differences between children who are chronic movers and their counterparts who move less frequently. These are often the children with extreme behaviour problems (James 2004). Indeed, the children with emotional and behavioural problems may have different movement dynamics from youth without (Barth *et al.* 2007). Our analysis found that children initially in congregate care have a much higher rate of disruption than children in foster care or kinship care settings and they tend to move from one congregate setting to another instead of foster homes or kinship care. However, despite the generally high placement disruption rate for children of all ages in congregate care, teenagers placed in foster homes have the highest level of placement disruption.

Practice implications

The findings from the current study are informative regarding child welfare practice with foster children. Clearly, placement stability is an essential goal. Children who remain in their first placement contend with less disruption in their lives. Based on the current data, different placement types may require different clinical emphases. Child welfare workers should provide substantial support to foster family homes in the first six months of placement, as this seems to be the most vulnerable period for children placed in these homes. Besides children in their first six months of placement, children in group care also have heightened movement rates later in the placement trajectory; services to stabilize the children in group care should be instituted during this period.

Second, the child welfare field must do a better job of tailoring services to the age of the child. General child welfare services (e.g. monthly foster care visits) may not be sufficient to prevent the higher rates of movement that characterize specific age groups. Work with infants may call for a more developmentally appropriate approach that limits the number of placement changes they experience given their need to attach to a primary caregiver (e.g. Clyman, Harden and Little 2002). Finally, while efforts should be made to place children in family like settings instead of institutions, we should also note the high level disruption for adolescents placed in foster homes mostly due to their behavioural problems and emotional disturbances. Some programmes based on methods used in treatment foster care, such as the KEEP foster-parent training interventions introduced in San Diego, California, are shown to have great potential in reducing placement instability for adolescents in foster family care and kinship care (Price *et al.* 2009; Smith *et al.* 2001).

References

Allison, P.D. (2005) *Fixed Effects Regression Methods for Longitudinal Data Using SAS.* Cary, NC: SAS Institute, Inc.

Barth, R. Lloyd, C. Green, R. James, S. Leslie, L. and Landsverk, J. (2007) 'Predictors of placement moves among children with and without emotional and behavioural disorders'. *Journal of Emotional and Behavioural Disorders 15,* 1, 46–55.

Chamberlain, P. Price, J. Reid, J. Landsverk, J. Fisher, P. and Stoolmiller, M. (2006) 'Who disrupts from placement in foster and kinship care?' *Child Abuse and Neglect 30,* 4, 409–424.

Clyman, R. Harden, B.J. and Little, C. (2002) 'Assessment, intervention and research with infants in out-of-home placement.' *Infant Mental Health Journal 23,* 5, 435–453.

Courtney, M. Piliavin, I. Grogan-Kaylor, A. and Nesmith, A. (2001) 'Foster youth transitions to adulthood: a longitudinal view of youth leaving care.' *Child Welfare 80,* 6, 685–717.

James, S. (2004) 'Why do foster care placements disrupt? An investigation of reasons for placement change in foster care.' *Social Service Review 78,* 4, 601–627.

Leathers, S.J. (2006) 'Placement disruption and negative placement outcomes among adolescents in long-term foster care: the role of behaviour problems.' *Child Abuse and Neglect 30,* 3, 307–324.

Newton, R.R. Litrownik, A.J. and Landsverk, J.A. (2000) 'Children and youth in foster care: disentangling the relationship between problem behaviours and number of placements.' *Child Abuse and Neglect 24,* 10, 1363–1374.

Price, J.M. Chamberlain, P. Landsverk, J. and Reid, J. (2009) 'KEEP foster-parent training intervention: model description and effectiveness.' *Child and Family Social Work 14,* 2, 233–242.

Rubin, D.M. O'Reilly, A. Luan, X. and Localio, R. (2007) 'The impact of placement stability on behavioural well-being for children in foster care.' *Paediatrics 119,* 2, 336–344.

Smith, D. Stormshak, E. Chamberlain, P. and Bridges-Whaley, R. (2001) 'Placement disruption in treatment foster care.' *Journal of Emotional and Behavioural Disorders 9,* 3, 200–205.

Stovall, C. and Dozier, M. (1998) 'Infants in foster care: an attachment theory perspective.' *Adoption Quarterly 2,* 1, 55–88.

U.S. Department of Health and Human Services (2002) *Child Welfare Outcomes 1999: Annual Report.* Washington, DC: USDHHS.

Wulczyn, F. Kogan, J. and Harden, B.J. (2003) 'Placement stability and movement trajectories.' *Social Service Review 77,* 2, 212–236.

Wulczyn, F. Hislop, K. and Chen, L. (2007) 'Foster Care Dynamics 2000–2005: A Report from the Multistate Foster Care Date Archive.' Working Paper, Chapin Hall Centre for Children, University of Chicago.

Zinn, A. DeCoursey, J. Goerge, R. and Courtney, M. (2006) 'A Study of Placement Instability in Illinois.' Working Paper, Chapin Hall Centre for Children, University of Chicago.

Commentary by Harriet Ward on:
Placement Stability and Movement Trajectories

Fred Wulczyn and Lijun Chen

This chapter contributes to the growing literature on the stability – or rather the instability – of care systems. It addresses an important issue, for the frequency with which children in care move from one placement to another is of grave concern in Australia, the USA, the UK, Canada and much of Europe (see Stein and Munro 2008). Frequent placement moves are likely to impact on children and young people's emotional and behavioural development, relationships with birth families, education and access to health care. Adverse consequences may be compounded by the context of constant change that characterizes so much of their life experience (Ward 2009). The questions we need to ask are:

- Who moves in care, when and why?

- What is it about care and care populations that engenders so much instability?

- How does placement instability impact on children and young people's long term life chances?

- Can we identify specific groups of children or specific time-points when changing placement can have a particularly adverse impact?

- How can the research evidence be utilized to improve policy and practice in this area?

Most research studies can only address some of these questions. However, taken together, their findings can provide the evidence base on which to develop policies and services that can provide greater stability for children in care. This chapter sheds further light on the characteristics of children who move, the placements they move from and the times at which moves are most likely to occur. The study is one of several that utilize administrative data, in this instance an extensive longitudinal dataset drawn from 11 US states over six years. While such databases have advantages, in that the samples are sufficiently large to allow for complex statistical analyses, there are also disadvantages. The main problem is that the researchers are restricted to data items collected by agencies for third parties, usually government bodies – they rarely have opportunities to insert new data items or access to additional data sources such as case-papers or interview material on a subset of children, that might help them explore how interesting findings might be interpreted.

For instance, this study found that many children experienced a high rate of movement in the first six months of the care episode, followed by lower rates thereafter. So the database can answer important questions such as *who* moved and *when*, but different data items are necessary to tell us *why* they moved. In the UK the majority of moves between placements are planned transitions, initiated by the agency as part of the case management process and these are often the reason for instability in the early months of the care episode (see Ward 2009). Administrative data do not distinguish between planned transitions and disruptions, caused by the breakdown of relationships between child and carer, yet the practice implications are very different.

Interview data from children and young people also give an added perspective. Moves to be placed with siblings may well be viewed positively, as may moves away from placements where the child is unhappy – and agencies sometimes refuse to allow such children to move because they need to meet their outcomes targets (see Sinclair *et al.* 2007; Ward 2009).

Placement stability is therefore a very complex issue. We need quantitative studies such as this one, but we also need additional data from a variety of sources in order to better understand the implications of their findings.

References

Sinclair, I. Baker, C. Lee, J. and Gibbs, I. (2007) *The Pursuit of Permanence: A Study of the English Care System.* London: Jessica Kingsley Publishers.

Stein, M. and Munro, E.R. (eds) (2008) *Young People's Transitions from Care to Adulthood: International Research and Practice.* London: Jessica Kingsley Publishers.

Ward, H. (2009) 'Patterns of instability: moves within the care system, their reasons, contexts and consequences.' *Children and Youth Services Review 31*, 1113–1118.

CHAPTER 4

Foster Care in the Netherlands: Correlates of Placement Breakdown and Successful Placement

Johan Strijker

This chapter opens with a description of foster care in the Netherlands. It then goes on to describe the results of a study into the characteristics of children in long-term foster care, the severity of the problems these children face during foster placement, the risk factors that may lead to placement breakdown and the association with the type of follow-up placement after breakdown.

National legislative and policy context for foster care

The Netherlands has 16.5 million inhabitants (in 395 km²), 3.8 million of whom are minors. In 2006 there were 20,951 children in foster care and 29,000 in residential care (Knorth 2005). As of 1 January 2007 there were 2,853 children in foster care – 35% of whom were younger than four years of age, while 28% belonged to an ethnic minority and 76% were there by court order. Fifty-three per cent of foster children stayed with their foster family for less than six months and 31% for more than a year. There were 12,808 foster families, one third of which were kinship families (*Factsheet Pleegzorg* 2007). Kinship care refers to a situation in which the child already had a genetic or psychological relationship with an adult in the foster family (e.g. a family member, teacher or neighbour) before the placement (Child Welfare League of America 1995). If the child had no such relationship before the placement, we refer in the Netherlands simply to foster care.

Until 1989 foster care was still available to children in need of temporary care, for example in order to attend a school or training institution far from home. The introduction of the Youth Care Act in 1989 removed this form of entitlement and made a formal referral a prerequisite for foster care. The Act stipulates that assistance should be carried out as quickly as possible, as briefly as possible, as 'lightly' as possible and as close as possible to home (known as the 'as-as-as-as' policy in the Netherlands). The Act distinguishes four kinds of youth care: in-home care (e.g. video-feedback intervention, families first), day care, foster care and residential care. The preferred sequence for care provision is as follows. Recourse should first be made to non-residential care in order to avoid an out-of-home placement for the child. Next comes daytime care if non-residential care is not appropriate. Here the child is placed at a day centre for treatment and the parent receives family assistance or therapy. If daytime care is not appropriate and the child has to be removed from home, foster care is preferred to residential care. The acceptance criterion for admission to foster care is 'Yes, provided that...' with the provision that there is nothing to suggest that the parent and/or child might constitute a danger to the foster family.

Foster care in the Netherlands comprises exclusively care within a kinship family or foster family and does not include, as in the USA, residential places, group homes or supervised independent living (Maluccio 2003). A referral for foster care is issued by the Office for Juvenile Care, the central access point for youth care. The case manager who issues the referral has final responsibility for the foster child and his or her original family during the period of care. One third of foster care placements are made on a voluntary basis and two thirds occur under a child protection order.

It is not possible to adopt a foster child in the Netherlands, even if parental rights have been revoked. Long-term foster care is the only option for an uninterrupted, stable place of residence. Because such care falls under the Youth Care Act, however, the judge needs to authorize continuation of the placement annually. This means that both foster child and foster parent live in a constant state of uncertainty about whether the case manager, perhaps under pressure from a parent, might terminate the placement. The legal situation that most closely approximates adoption is one in which parental rights have been revoked and the foster parent becomes the child's legal guardian.

It has been stated above that the 'long-term foster care' module can offer the child a long-term, stable upbringing setting. However, research findings from a small-scale study show that 44.9 per cent of placements broke down within 22 months (Strijker and Zandberg 2005). This highlighted the need for a larger-scale study to identify the antecedents of placement breakdown and to produce a comprehensive description of the characteristics of the foster care population. The following research questions were formulated for the implementation of the present study.

1. What are the characteristics of the children who enter care and of their parents?

2. What are the characteristics of the foster care system?

3. What are the care outcomes?

4. Where does the child go after leaving care?

Methodology

Design

A retrospective longitudinal research design was used to establish a correlation between the characteristics of the children and the care outcomes. Information about the foster children was collected from their files on three occasions. The first 'measurement moment' was the start of the foster care placement, when the prior history of the child and the parent was recorded from the files. The second was the situation surrounding the placement as described in the most recent evaluation plan. The period between the starting date for foster care placement and the date of the last evaluation plan averaged two years and four months. At the study's starting date, the cohort under investigation had been living with their foster families for at least six months. On average, the third 'measurement moment' was three years and four months after the first. Information about whether the foster child had changed residence was recorded from the files.

Research group

The research group comprised a cohort of 419 foster children aged 0–18 years ($M = 9.9$, $sd = 5.5$) who had been placed in long-term foster care by five care providers in the northern and eastern Netherlands between 1 September 2000 and 1 June 2004. The per centage of foster children aged 0–4 years was 21.2. Boys made up 49.9 per cent of the research group. The types of original family that the foster children came from were distributed as follows: both biological parents were present in 25.4 per cent of families, one biological parent was present in 72.9 per cent and both parents had died in 1.7 per cent. The status of the foster children was distributed as follows: 36.8 per cent resided in foster care on a voluntary basis, 46.6 per cent had a family guardianship arrangement and parental authority had been revoked in 16.6 per cent of cases. The majority of the children (52.9%) were living in non-relative foster homes, with a somewhat smaller percentage (47.1%) in kinship care. Three per cent of foster parents and 5 per cent of foster children belonged to an ethnic minority.

Procedure

All the information came from the foster children's files. In the event of missing data, the foster care worker was asked, often by phone, to supply the relevant information. Research data were collected on the spot by ten Master's students of special education at the University of Groningen as part of their practical training period with the foster care providers. The first author was present on the spot to assist each student with data gathering. He trained the students in records analysis and they had access to a protocol containing decision rules for processing the information. In the event of the slightest doubt about assigning scores to file information, they were instructed to use a consensus procedure, whereby the student and research leader decided in consultation how to score the information in question.

Instrument

The research instrument comprised a list of items devised for this study and grouped into three clusters, namely characteristics of the child, of the parents and of the foster care system.

The item variables in the 'child characteristics' cluster were attachment problems, physical abuse, emotional abuse, sexual abuse and neglect. Attachment problems meant that a diagnosis of attachment disorder had been made by a qualified professional or that a behavioural scientist suspected the presence of an attachment disorder based on reasonable indications. This cluster also contained the three scale variables from the abbreviated version of Barber and Delfabbro's Child Behaviour Checklist (2002), namely conduct (Cronbach's alpha=.74), hyperactivity (Cronbach's alpha=.68) and emotionality (Cronbach's alpha=.91). The item variable 're-placements' was recorded from the children's files with re-placement being defined as 'the transfer of a child between two places of residence which are not those of one or both of the parents'. Admission to a women's refuge centre was not considered a transfer under this definition because in such cases the child remained with the mother. However, in accordance with Farmer, Moyers and Lipscombe (2004), a return home was counted as a re-placement because the original family may have changed.

The item variables in the 'parent characteristics' cluster were drug problems (alcohol and/or drugs), sexual violence, physical violence and psychiatric problems (with referred treatment by a psychiatrist). The item variables in the 'care system characteristics' cluster were parent–child contact, visits home by the child, mother's attitude and whether or not the mother gave permission for her child to stay in the foster family. 'Parent–child contact' was operationalized in terms of the number of times per fortnight that the parent(s) visited the child, whether in the foster family's home, on neutral ground, or at the home of the parent(s). 'Visits home' is defined as the number of visits (a day, part of a day or a weekend) made by the child to the parental home over a two-month period. 'Mother's attitude' was operationalized in terms of the item variable 'what is the mother's attitude to the foster family placement?', with 'positive', 'ambivalent' and 'negative' as the response options. 'Mother's permission' was operationalized in terms of the item variable 'does the mother show that the child has her permission to be in the foster family?' with 'yes' and 'no' as the response options.

The psychosocial outcomes were measured using different variables. First, the severity of problem behaviour during the foster care placement was measured with the help of the abbreviated Child Behaviour Checklist referred to above. The scale variables were once again conduct (Cronbach's alpha=.90), hyperactivity (Cronbach's alpha=.76) and emotionality (Cronbach's alpha=.66). The second outcome was the result of the foster care placement, either continuing or prematurely ended. Placement breakdown meant that the foster child was removed from the foster family for reasons other than in keeping with the treatment plan or because the child had attained the age of 18. Information on this could be found in the child's file. Inter-rater reliability was calculated using 25 files. The average Pearson's *r* score for interval-level data was .87; the average Cohen's kappa score for nominal-level data was .51, a value that Landis and Koch (1977) regarded as moderate-to-high.

Summary of findings

Table 4.1 shows the characteristics of the children and their parents at the start of the long-term foster care placement. The events in the table were experienced 'at any time' by the foster child and the parent prior to the placement.

TABLE 4.1 Percentages and averages for child and parent variables at intake (N = 419)

PRIOR HISTORY OF THE CHILD (%)		PRIOR HISTORY OF THE CHILD *(M, SD)*		PARENTAL PROBLEMS	
Attachment problem	14.1%	Conduct disorder	1.4 (2.2)	Drugs/alcohol	33.5%
Physical abuse	24.4%	Hyperactivity	1.9 (2.1)	Physical violence	21.4%
Emotional abuse	31.1%	Emotionality	2.4 (1.9)	Psychiatric problems	30.4%
Sexual abuse	13.9%	Re-placement	1.0 (.4)		
Neglect	60.3%				

The number of foster children with an attachment problem was 14.1%. We could find no figures in the research literature for the prevalence of attachment problems in foster care. Dozier *et al.* (2001) give a figure of 48 per cent for the occurrence of insecure attachment. Approximately one quarter of foster children were physically abused. Six studies found abuse levels of between 20 and 25 per cent (Barber and Delfabbro 2002; Dubowitz *et al.* 1993; Garland *et al.* 1996; Iglehart 1993; James, Landsverk and Slymen 2004; Zinn *et al.* 2006). The percentage of emotionally abused foster children approximates the 26.8 per cent in the Barber and Delfabbro study (2002). One in seven foster children were sexually abused. Three studies found figures of between 11 and 15 per cent (Barber and Delfabbro 2002; Garland *et al.* 1996; James *et al.* 2004). The number of foster children who were neglected matches the per centages found in the studies by Courtney, Terao and Bost (2004) and Garland *et al.* (1996), which were 58.7 and 67.3 per cent respectively.

The averages for the variables of conduct, hyperactivity and emotionality are larger than those reported by Barber and Delfabbro (2002) for a research group of disruptive children – 0.94, 1.46 and 1.17 respectively at intake. The number of re-placements before the current long-term placement was 1.0, with an average length of stay of 1.5 years. This rate compares favourably with the reported average rates of 4.2 re-placements in 1.5 years (Leslie *et al.* 2000), 1.9 re-placements in 1.7 years (Pardeck 1984) and 1.8 re-placements in one year (Zinn *et al.* 2006).

One third of the parents in this study battled drug and alcohol problems. Shin and Poertner (2002) reported 38 per cent and Courtney *et al.* (2004) 42.6 per cent. The Courtney study also revealed that abuse of the partner occurred in 23.4 per cent of the original families. Almost one third of parents struggled with psychiatric problems; Shin and Poertner (2002) and Courtney *et al.* (2004) found per centages of 15.0 and 19.1, respectively.

What are the characteristics of the foster care system?

Table 4.2 combines two aspects of the foster care system – namely, the mother's attitude towards the placement and the characteristics of the care system.

TABLE 4.2 Percentages and averages for parent and care system characteristics (N = 419)

MOTHER'S ATTITUDE (%)		FOSTER CARE SYSTEM (*M, SD*)	
Negative attitude of mother	19.7	Parent–child contact frequency	2.2 (1.5)
No permission to live with foster family	46.1	Visits home	1.2 (1.8)
		Care worker–foster parent contact frequency	1.6 (1.0)
		Care worker–foster child contact frequency	1.4 (.9)

In one fifth of placements the mother had a negative attitude to the placement of her child in foster care and almost half of mothers made it clear that the child did not in fact have her permission to reside with the foster family. Recent research has shown that not obtaining psychological consent from the parent is associated with an increased likelihood of placement breakdown and an increased severity of conduct disorders and of hyperactive behaviour (Strijker and Knorth 2009).

Contact frequencies and visits by the child to the parent's home are presented over a two-month period. Parent–child contact is important for maintaining the bond between parent and child, working towards family reunification and preventing problem behaviour on the part of the child within the foster family (Proch and Howard 1986). In this study, the parent came almost twice as often to visit the foster child in the foster home. Recent research within foster care in the Netherlands has shown, however, that the frequency of visits by the parent to the child does not correlate with the occurrence of problem behaviour or with placement breakdown. In-home visits, on the other hand, are linked to the probability of placement breakdown (Strijker and Knorth in press).

Contact frequency between the foster care worker and the foster parent on the one hand and the foster child on the other differed only slightly. When visiting the foster family, the care worker also spoke to the child (provided he or she was old enough).

What are the outcomes?

Table 4.3 shows the outcomes for behaviour change and the status of the foster care placement on average three years and four months after its inception.

Statistically significant differences in the severity of problem behaviour were found between the start of the placement (see Table 4.1) and after a period of two years and four months in the foster family, with smaller averages on the second measure for conduct, $t(410) = 2.77$, $p < .01$, hyperactivity, $t(410) = 9.82$, $p < .0005$ and emotionality, $t(410) = 2.28$, $p < .05$. After an average of three years and four months, 46.8 per cent of foster children had another place of residence, although this home was intended as 'a family for life'. Of the 28 foster children who moved to another foster family, 65.2 per cent went to live with family or acquaintances. If we define placement breakdown as a premature termination of the placement for reasons such as conflict with the foster family (21.5%), problem behaviour of the foster child (21.3%), conflict with the foster family's own child (4.1%), conflicting allegiances (5.1%), the foster child's own decision (20.6%), psychiatric problems of the foster child (3.7%) and parental pressure (9.4%), then 31.7% of placements broke down.

TABLE 4.3 Percentages and averages for behaviour and outcome variables (N = 419)

BEHAVIOUR (M, SD)		OUTCOME (%)	
Conduct disorder	1.2 (1.7)	Continuation	38.8
Hyperactivity	1.7 (2.0)	Back home	18.5
Emotionality	1.6 (1.5)	Residential	11.5
		Supervised independent living	8.4
		Other foster family	6.7
		'Ageing out'	14.4
		Unknown	1.7

Destination following placement breakdown

In the published findings of another study by the present research team (Strijker, Knorth and Dickscheit 2008), a multivariate analysis shows that placement breakdown can be described in terms of the variables of age, conduct problems and re-placement. In other words, older children, children with serious conduct problems (at the start of the placement) and children with a greater number of re-placements are at greater risk of breakdown in long-term placements than young children, children with few serious problem behaviours and children who have experienced few or no re-placements. On the basis of this correlation, we investigated whether the type of destination following placement breakdown can be described in terms of these variables. In addition to averages and standard deviations for the destinations 'back home', 'residential', 'supervised independent living' and 'other foster family', Table 4.4 also shows the statistical results of the univariate analyses of variance (ANOVAs).

TABLE 4.4 Averages and standard deviations (n =158)

	BACK HOME (*n* = 76)	RESIDEN-TIAL (*n* = 47)	SUPERVISED INDEPEN-DENT LIVING (*n* = 35)	OTHER FOSTER FAMILY (*n* = 28)	*F*	
Age	10.2 (5.2)	10.5 (4.7)	15.5 (1.7)	10.9 (4.0)	12.65**	.17
Conduct	1.5 (2.1)	2.7 (3.0)	2.0 (2.7)	1.7 (2.0)	n.s.	
Re-placement	1.0 (1.4)	2.2 (2.1)	1.8 (2.7)	1.0 (1.3)	5.28*	.08

*$p < .01$; **$p < .001$; n.s. = not significant.

Statistically significant differences in group averages were found for the variables of age and re-placement. For 'age', the post hoc Bonferroni test gave statistically significant differences between the group 'supervised independent living' and the three groups 'residential', 'back home' and 'other foster family'. For 're-placement', the post hoc Bonferroni test gave statistically significant differences between the 'residential' and 'back home' groups and the 'residential' and 'other foster family' groups. In other words, following placement breakdown, older foster children were more likely to move to supervised independent living than younger children and children with a higher than average number of re-placements were more likely to move on to a residential care setting.

Discussion

It is not possible to adopt foster children in the Netherlands. For a long-term, stable upbringing setting a foster child has to rely on long-term foster care. Only children who are unable to return home are eligible for this type of care. The child and parent characteristics which this study identified as perhaps contributing to the need for care were consistent with those found in other studies. An exception was the average number of re-placements that the child had experienced, which was very small in comparison with the findings of other studies. This figure does not seem coincidental, as preliminary results from follow-up research show a similar average number of re-placements (1.2) in a research group of 252 long-term foster care placements (Dolfing, Sanderman and De Vries 2008). These figures show that in the Netherlands the number of movements across different placement settings is limited following an out-of-home placement.

Despite the expectation of a long-term placement, 31.7 per cent of placements ended prematurely within three years and four months. The risk factors identified in international research (Oosterman *et al.* 2007) – namely, age, conduct and re-placement – also apply to long-term foster care in the Netherlands. These factors have a prognostic correlation with the type of residence following placement breakdown. Younger foster children with few re-placements and few or no serious problem behaviour(s) go on to a family (either back home or to another foster family). Older children go on to supervised independent living, while foster children with relatively many re-placements and serious problem behaviour go to residential care (although this latter variable is not statistically significant). Long-term foster care therefore appears to be the preserve of young children with relatively few re-placements within the care system.

It was not only the factors of age, conduct and re-placement that showed a correlation with placement breakdown. The same was true of in-home visits and parental permission (Strijker and Knorth in press). Children who made a higher number of visits to the parental home and children whose parent did not give permission to live in the foster family were more likely to encounter placement breakdown. Children who go home often may experience difficulties bonding with the foster parent. And if the parent shows that her child does not have her permission to live with the foster family, the child may not be able to establish a bond with the foster parent. A child who feels drawn to the foster parent may experience conflicting allegiances. It should be noted that the frequency of visits between parent and child at another location (in the foster family's home or on neutral ground) was not associated with placement breakdown. Attachment problems (Strijker and Knorth in press) were associated with conduct but not with placement breakdown. Follow-up research should reveal how the factors of age, conduct, re-placement, in-home visits and attachment problems may be interlinked into a causal explanatory model of placement breakdown.

This study has two limitations which at the same time present a challenge for future research. The first is the lack of data about the foster families. Results from exploratory studies show that a more effective functioning of the foster family and access to more internal and external resources correlate with a reduced risk of placement breakdown. Follow-up research should include these variables and their correlation with placement outcomes.

The second challenge relates to the focus in this study of problem behaviour among foster children. The fact that the children experienced such events as abuse and witnessing domestic violence leads us to assume that a proportion of the foster children were traumatized and that the problem behaviour could arise out of this trauma. Until now there has been little or no systematic scientific research into standardized questionnaires about the type and severity of trauma among foster children.

Foster children bring their experiences with them into the foster family. The risk factors of age, severity of conduct disorders and replacements help determine not only the placement outcome but also the type of follow-up placement after breakdown. These factors can be identified before the foster placement in order to estimate the risk of breakdown. Close monitoring of placements involving these risk factors would be advisable.

References

Barber, J.G. and Delfabbro, P.H. (2002) 'The plight of disruptive children in out-of-home care.' *Children's Services: Social Policy, Research and Practice 5*, 201–221.

Child Welfare League of America (1995) *Standards of Excellence for Family Foster Care Services.* Washington, DC: Author.

Courtney, M.E. Terao, S. and Bost, N. (2004) *Midwest Evaluation of the Adult Functioning of Former Foster Youth: Conditions of Preparing to Leave State Care.* Chicago IL: Chapin Hall Centre for Children at the University of Chicago.

Dolfing, V. Sanderman, G.E. and De Vries, R.A. (2008) *(On)aangepast. Een empirisch onderzoek nar de aanpassing van pleegkinderen in pleeggezinnen.* Unpublished Master's thesis, University of Groningen, Groningen, the Netherlands.

Dozier, M. Stovall, K.C. Albus, K.E. and Bates, B. (2001) 'Attachment for infants in foster care: The roles of caregiver states of mind.' *Child Development 72*, 1467–1477.

Dubowitz, H. Feigelman, S. Harrington, D. Starr, R. Zuravin, S. and Sawyer, R. (1993) 'Children in kinship care. How do they fare?' *Children and Youth Services Review, 16*, 85–106.

Factsheet Pleegzorg 2007. Available from http://www.pleegzorg.nl/algemeen/Factsheet_Pleegzorg_2008.PDF, accessed on 20 February 2009.

Farmer, E. Moyers, S. and Lipscombe, J. (2004) *Fostering Adolescents.* London: Jessica Kingsley Publishers.

Garland, A.F. Landsverk, J.L. Hough, R.L. and Ellis-MacLeod, E. (1996) 'Type of maltreatment as a predictor of mental health service use for children in foster care.' *Child Abuse and Neglect 20*, 675–688.

Iglehart, A.P. (1993) 'Adolescents in foster care: predicting behavioural maladjustment.' *Child and Adolescent Social Work Journal 6*, 521–523.

James, S. Landsverk. J. and Slymen, D.J. (2004) 'Placement movement in out-of-home care: patterns and predictors.' *Children and Youth Services Review 26*, 185–206.

Knorth, E.J. (2005) 'Wat maakt het verschil? Over intensieve orthopedagogische zorg voor jeugdigen met probleemgedrag'. [What makes the difference? Intensive care and treatment for children and adolescents with problem behaviour.] In E.J. Knorth, A.E.M.G. Minnaert and A.J.J.M. Ruijssenaars (eds) *Verschillen onderscheiden.* Utrecht: Agiel Publishers, pp.11–41.

Landis, J.R. and Koch, G.G. (1977) 'The measurement of observer agreement for categorical data.' *Biometrics 33,* 159–174.

Leslie, L.K. Landsverk, J. Horton, M.B. Ganger, W. and Newton, R.R. (2000) 'The heterogeneity of children and their experiences in care.' *Child Welfare 79,* 315–334.

Maluccio, A.N. (2003) 'Processes and outcomes in family foster care: a selective North-American review.' *International Journal of Child and Family Welfare 4,* 133–140.

Oosterman, M. Schuengel, C. Slot, N.W. Bullen, R.A.R. and Dorelijers, T.A.H. (2007) 'Disruptions in foster care: a review and meta-analysis.' *Children and Youth Services Review, 29,* 53–76.

Pardeck, J.T. (1984) 'An exploration of factors associated with the stability and continuity of the foster care system in the United States.' *International Social Work 27,* 5–9.

Proch, K and Howard, J.A. (1986) 'Parental visiting of children in foster care.' *Social Work 31,* 178–181.

Shin, H.S. and Poertner, J. (2002) *The Well-Being of Older Youth in Out-of-Home Care Who Are Headed to Independence.* Urbana, IL: Children and Family Research Centre, University of Illinois.

Strijker, J. and Knorth, E.J. (2009) 'Factors associated with the adjustment of foster children in the Netherlands.' *American Journal of Orthopsychiatry.* Manuscript submitted for publication.

Strijker, J. Knorth, E.J. and Dickscheit, J. (2008) 'Placement history of foster children. A study of placement history and outcomes in long-term foster care.' *Child Welfare 78,* 107–125.

Strijker, J. and Zandberg, T. (2005) 'Breakdown in foster care.' *International Journal of Child and Family Welfare 2–3,* 76–87.

Zinn, A. DeCoursey, J. Goerge, R. and Courtney, M.E. (2006) *A Study of Placement Stability in Illinois.* Chicago, IL: Chapin Hall Centre for Children at the University of Chicago.

Commentary by Jorge F. del Valle on:
Foster Care in the Netherlands: Correlates of Placement Breakdown and Successful Placement

Johan Strijker

This chapter highlights the considerable discrepancies between legislative approaches to child welfare in different countries. The impossibility of adopting a foster child in the Netherlands, even in the case of the parents' rights having been revoked, obliges foster care to function as a definitive placement in such cases. However, in contrast to adoption, foster care requires constant supervision and as stressed in this chapter, foster children and foster parents are dependent on the foster care being approved by the authorities each year, which results in feelings of uncertainty. On making international comparisons in foster care research it is very important to take into account such legislative aspects, which condition the type of intervention carried out and the role played by foster care in each country.

Through a retrospective longitudinal study with a sample of 419 children in long-term foster care, the characteristics of children, parents and the foster care system were studied and analysed in relation to fostering outcomes, with a particular focus on cases of breakdown. A very important finding is that nearly a third of cases (31.7%) end in breakdown, in spite of being defined as long-term fostering cases requiring great stability (by virtue of the above-mentioned impossibility of adoption). These breakdowns are associated with variables such as higher age of the children, behaviour problems and re-placement experiences, confirming the results of other studies in a range of countries. In this research, moreover, children who more frequently visit their birth parents' home and those cases in which there is no parental permission for the fostering also present higher probability of breakdown. Interference from the birth family is also confirmed as a highly relevant factor in the development of the foster care.

Finally, the study shows that residential context after breakdown is related to the child's profile, so that younger children and with fewer behaviour problems tend to move to another family (family reunification or new fostering), whilst the older ones with fewer behaviour problems go on to supervised independent living programmes and the older ones with more behaviour problems appear to end up in residential care.

This study highlights once more the importance of behaviour problems in foster children and how they strongly influence issues of permanence and stability, as well as the need in some cases to return to residential care at the end of the process. Early and preventive attention to such problems, with appropriate diagnoses and therapeutic interventions, is still a challenge to be met in many countries. Coordination of the mental health and child welfare systems is a need that should not be further postponed in the political agenda.

CHAPTER 5

Profile and Scope of Foster Care in Spain

Jorge F. del Valle and Mónica López

National legislative and policy context of foster care

The current child welfare system in Spain was set up by the legislation of 1987 that reformed the Civil Code in matters relating to foster care and adoption (*Ley 21/1987*). This law radically changed the child welfare system, introducing principles such as support for families to avoid separation from the child, return to the family as a priority option in cases where separation had become necessary, the definition of residential care as a last resort and the use of foster care as the most beneficial alternative, as well as facilitating the adoption process.

It is important to stress that foster care has existed as a child protection measure in Spain only since 1987, so that programmes in this area date back scarcely more than 20 years. In these two decades, the development of child protection services has revolved basically around the attempt to reform a system based almost exclusively on residential care, creating and maintaining foster care programmes, providing intervention services in support of families and streamlining and facilitating adoption processes.

The development of foster care in Spain is difficult to quantify in view of the lack of a national statistical database, since, despite the annual publication of child protection data, these figures refer to quite general aspects and are of doubtful reliability. Only through a relatively recent and specific study was it possible to collect information on all the Autonomous Regions and present national data (del Valle and Bravo 2003). That research concluded that of a total of 31,368 children in out-of-home care at the end of 2002, 45.3% were in residential care, 46.8% in kinship care and just 7.9% in non-relative foster care. Thus, Spain has two characteristics in this context that distinguish it from other European countries: on the one hand, the high use of residential care, which accounts for nearly half of out-of-home placements and, on the other, an enormous predominance of kinship care (85.5%) compared to foster care provided by unrelated families (14.5%).

As far as research is concerned, no empirical studies had been published until quite recently. One of the first was carried out in the Autonomous Community of the Principality of Asturias and involved the assessment of needs in kinship care (del Valle, Alvarez-Baz and Bravo 2002) with a sample of 568 children. This research, which revealed a precarious situation of these foster families, primarily grandparents, and the lack of support they received, would open up a line of work on extended families in other regions (Lumbreras, Fuentes and Bernedo 2005; Molero *et al.* 2007; Montserrat 2007; Palacios and Jiménez 2009). The year 2003 saw the publication of the first study assessing a foster care programme (Amorós *et al.* 2003); subsequently, these same authors would publish a review of foster care and adoption in Spain (Palacios and Amorós 2006). The group led by Professor Amorós was pioneering in the development of instruments and resources for supporting foster care processes, especially training materials for foster parents. The work of this research team – together with that of Professor Palacios's group – has contributed enormously to the development of foster care in our country (Amorós, Fuertes and Roca 1994; Amorós *et al.* 2002; Amorós *et al.* 2005). An overview of the foster care situation highlights the fact there is a clear legal initiative in favour of foster care as the preferred option in cases of out-of-home placements and that all the national and regional legislation define it as such, especially for children under the age of six. However, only kinship care has developed in a way comparable to the case of residential care and programmes with non-relative caregivers account for less than a tenth of such placements. Some of the reasons for this will become clear from what follows here.

On the other hand, while the 1987 legislation established the concept of foster care as a temporary measure with a view to eventual family reunification, the Constitutional Child Protection Law (1996) opened up the possibility of long-term and permanent foster care, without limit of time to remain in foster care, probably with the aim of providing guarantees for kinship caregivers.

Overview of methodology

In order to describe the main characteristics of foster care in Spain we shall analyze a recent study funded by the Ministry of Work and Social Affairs, which is the only research dealing with this type of data (del Valle *et al.* 2008a). It is a descriptive study of those involved in foster care, including children, birth families and foster parents, which also examines fostering processes. This is complemented by a study on closed cases revealing how the placements turned out and permitting a tentative assessment of results.

The sample was made up of 649 fostered children in six different Autonomous Communities (Madrid, Catalonia, Andalusia, Galicia, Castilla-León and Valencia) which cover both rural and urban regions and some with a well-developed foster care system and others in which this resource is less widespread. The sample included kinship care cases (292) and others where the foster families were unrelated to the child (357) and was composed in a stratified way in proportion to the number of foster care cases in each Community. With this total sample we carried out an analysis of foster care profiles and processes. Moreover, in order to analyze the results of the foster care, approximately half were closed cases, so that these analyses can be applied to a subset of 321 cases (142 kinship care and 179 non-kinship care). Samples were randomly selected from open cases at the moment of collecting data and from closed cases in the last ten years. Although we tried to get two samples of 350 children (for foster and kinship care), some problems collecting kinship care cases made necessary to reduce that subsample to 292 children.

The instrument employed was a data-collection form for the profiles of the children and families, as well for providing information on the process and the reason it finished (in the closed cases). The design of the instrument took into account the relevant variables usually considered in the literature in this field: (a) Children: gender, age at fostering, age at opening the protective care case, diagnosed disability, serious illness, legal status; (b) Birth families: marital status, psychosocial problems in father and mother; (c) Foster caregivers: age, single/couple, educational level, income, own children, previous fostering, multiple fostering; (d) Fostering process: previous situation, short- or long-term, judicial intervention, visits, place of visits; (e) Outcomes (for closed cases): duration, reason for closure, final situation.

The procedure consisted of sending a researcher to each Autonomous Community, where with the help of social workers and analysing the foster programme files, they compiled the data on the profiles and processes.

The data presented here were analysed by means of descriptive statistical techniques and difference analyses (basically between kinship and non-kinship care), chi-squared for the qualitative data and Student *t* for the quantitative data. Statistical significance is set at $p \leq .05$.

Summary of findings

Children profiles

The sample included similar proportions of boys (49%) and girls. Mean age of the children on being fostered was almost seven years, with no differences between kinship and non-kinship care. In contrast, there was a significant difference as regards the age of the children when the protection file was opened, which was 4.6 in non-kinship care and 6.3 in kinship care. This indicates that in kinship care cases the beginning of the fostering coincided with the opening of the case, whilst in non-kinship cases there is a mean delay of more than two years between the opening of the case and the fostering decision, which – as will be seen later – is a period children spend in residential care. On the other hand, we know that in 52 per cent of kinship care cases there was already informal fostering by these families, which had sometimes lasted for years and only later became formalized.

[1]TABLE 5.1 Children's and birth families characteristics in kinship and non-kinship care (N = 649)

CHILDREN'S CHARACTERISTICS	KINSHIP CARE (n = 292)	FOSTER CARE (n = 357)
Gender		
Female	53.1%	49.9%
Age at placement		
M	6.94 (sd = 5.18)	6.95 (sd = 4.56)
Age at opening of case		
M*	6.29 (sd = 5.04)	4.57 (sd = 3.97)
Disability*	3.1%	8.1%
Serious illnesses	5.5%	9.2%
Legal status		
Care order	68.6%	87.1%
Voluntary placement	31.4%	12.9%
BIRTH FAMILIES' CHARACTERISTICS	**KINSHIP CARE (n = 280)**	**FOSTER CARE (n = 344)**
Marital status*		
Married	19.2%	28.2%
Divorced	48.4%	38.8%
Widowed	16.8%	10.7%
Single mother	15.2%	22%
Father		
Substance abuse*	33.2%	18%
Alcoholism	13.9%	11.6%
Prison*	20.7%	14%
Poverty	8.9%	13.7%
Mother		
Substance abuse*	40%	25.6%
Alcoholism	12.9%	9.6%
Prison	13.9%	14.1%
Poverty	22.5%	27.6%
Mental disorder	17.9%	20.1%
Prostitution	7.9%	9.6%

*$p \leq .05$ (t/χ^2).

The legal status of foster children can be *care order* (rights of the parents are suspended and custody of the child is assumed by the regional authorities) or *parental request* (because of a risk situation; in these cases parents conserve their rights). As the data show, care order cases are more numerous.

---

1   Tables 5.1 to 5.3 are reprinted from del Valle *et al.* (2009) with permission from Elsevier.

Other relevant data include those on the incidence of some special characteristics, which show that there are more than double the number of children with disabilities in non-kinship care compared to kinship care and also that there are more cases with serious health problems.

Birth family profiles

The profiles of biological families differ significantly between kinship care and foster care (we shall use the latter term to refer to foster care by unrelated families) in various respects. As regards marital status, there are more cases of divorce and widowhood/widowerhood in kinship care, whilst single mothers are more common in foster care. A study of psychosocial problems in biological parents revealed that drug-dependence is the most common characteristic, accounting for 40 per cent of mothers and 33.2 per cent of fathers in kinship care, whilst in foster care this proportion is lower. Following this problem in order of frequency, for fathers, are prison and alcoholism, both again more common in kinship care. In mothers, drug-dependence is followed in order of frequency by mental health disorders (more common in foster care) and also prison and alcoholism. It can be concluded that in Spain drug-dependence in parents is a highly important factor influencing the fact that relatives take over the care of children in the form of kinship care.

Foster caregivers

As would be expected, foster caregiver profiles differ considerably from kinship to foster care. In kinship care, 60 per cent are grandparents and 32 per cent are uncles/aunts, with greater frequency of maternal than paternal family. Mean age is over 50. On the other hand, in foster care the mean age is lower and it is important to note that the standard deviation, that is, the variability of the data, is much smaller than in kinship care. This is the case not only because there are grandparents who are quite elderly (up to 85 years old), but also because in almost 6 per cent of cases kinship caregivers are under 30 (older siblings of the child or young uncles/aunts).

TABLE 5.2 Characteristics of kinship and non-kinship caregivers ($n = 623$)

CHARACTERISTICS	KINSHIP CARE ($n = 281$)	FOSTER CARE ($n = 343$)
Age*		
Men*	54.3 (SD = 14.1)	47.7 (SD = 8.4)
Women*	52.2 (SD = 13.5)	46.2 (SD = 8.6)
Foster carer(s)*		
Couple	63.3%	82.9%
Woman alone	35.6%	14.1%
Man alone	1.1%	3%
Educational level*		
Higher	5.6%	40.3%
Intermediate	10.4%	32.2%
Primary	58.9%	26%
No formal education	25.1%	0.6%
Annual income*		
24,001€ +	5.6%	40.1%
12,001–24,000€	26.2%	39.4%
6001–12,000€	48.5%	17.3%
6000€ or less	19.7%	3.3%

* $p \leq .05$ (t/χ^2).

The sociodemographic and economic indicators reveal the great precariousness of resources of kinship caregivers. Whilst 40.3 per cent of foster caregivers have higher education (university level), this is the case in only 5.6 per cent of kinship caregivers; indeed, a third of the latter have no formal education at all, but this situation is found in less than 1 per cent of foster caregivers. Consequently, 40.1 per cent of foster caregivers earn over 24,000€ a year, but only 5.6 per cent of kinship caregivers earn such salaries and a fifth of them earn less than 6000€ a year, a situation found in only 3.3 per cent of non-kinship caregivers.

Among these foster caregivers it is important to stress that 82.9 per cent are married couples and 59 per cent have their own children, who in 77 per cent of cases are older than the children fostered and in 4 per cent are adopted. In kinship care we find, on the other hand, that in 35.6 per cent of cases the caregiver is a single woman, nearly always a grandmother, which implies added difficulty due to lack of social support.

A particularly relevant finding and common to the two types of foster care, is that the vast majority of caregivers were fostering for the first time and around 20–30 per cent were fostering more than one child. It appears it is not easy to find families who repeat the fostering experience in our country.

The fostering process

The situation of children prior to the foster placement varies considerably between the two types of care. In the case of foster care, the majority of the children were in residential care before being fostered (69.5%); in contrast, just 22.6 per cent of those fostered by relatives had previously been in residential care. An important finding and one which indicates a considerable difference with respect to other countries, is that just 15.1 per cent of children in foster care and 8.2 per cent in kinship care had been fostered previously and although some had been with two families previously, there was only one case in the whole sample where the child had been with three foster families.

Approximately 60 per cent of cases had visits from their parents, with no differences between types of foster care. What did differ greatly was the type of location in which these visits occurred, since in the case of kinship caregivers 38.8 per cent of parents visited their children in the (kinship) foster home itself, whilst this occurred in only 6.8 per cent of non-kinship care cases. In this latter type of care the most common situation was to use neutral points (38.5%), which were used in just 9.1 per cent of kinship care cases. Neutral points are services developed by social agencies to facilitate a place where children can meet their parents in case of need for supervised visits and also in situations of conflictive divorces.

On the other hand, there is also a difference as regards the need for judicial intervention (which occurs when the parents are in disagreement with the fostering decision), given that this occurred in 46.5 per cent of foster care cases and only 22.9 per cent of kinship care cases, suggesting parents are more favourable to fostering by their own relatives than by unrelated families.

Assessment of closed cases

A subset of 321 cases were already closed, which meant that their results could be assessed, at least in a broad sense. Duration of the fostering differed, with means of 4.8 years in kinship care and 3.4 years in foster care. Also, apart from tending to be longer-lasting, kinship care showed greater variability.

TABLE 5.3 Analysis of closed cases in kinship and non-kinship care (n = 321)

VARIABLES	KINSHIP CARE (*n* = 142)	FOSTER CARE (*n* = 179)
Duration		
M (years)*	4.82 (sd = 4.18)	3.41 (sd = 2.86)
Distribution		
– 1 year	15.7%	26%
1.1 – 3 years	27.1%	28.3%
3.1 – 5 years	16.4%	19.1%
5.1 – 7 years	19.3%	14.5%
+7 years	21.5%	12.1%
Reasons for termination*		
Technical decision	36.4%	46.8%
Reached adulthood	44.3%	24.3%
Disruption	15.7%	25.4%
Other	3.6%	3.5%
Final situation after **technical decision***	(*n* = 51)	(*n* = 81)
Return to family	64.7%	27.2%
Adoption by fosterers	3.9%	42%
Adoption by others	0	9.9%
New placement	21.6%	6.2%
Residential care	9.8%	11.1%
Other	0	3.7%
Final situation after **reaching adulthood***	(*n* = 48)	(*n* = 37)
Return to family	2.6%	8.1%
Adoption by fosterers	0	13.5%
Remaining with fosterers	92.7%	64.9%
Independence	4.7%	13.5%
Final situation after **disruption**	(*n* = 21)	(*n* = 42)
Return to family	14.3%	9.5%
New placement	9.5%	9.5%
Residential care	61.9%	71.4%
Other	14.3%	8.8%

*p ≤ .05 (t/χ^2).

Reasons for closing the case were divided into three types: disruptions, due to problems arising in the process; coming of age of the foster children; and technical decisions for change or cessation of the measure (for example due to family reunification or an adoption). Significant differences were found between these reasons, since in kinship care the most common was reaching adulthood (44.3%, compared to 24.3% in foster care). On the other hand, in foster care the main reason for cessation was technical decision (46.8%, compared to 36.4% in kinship care). Disruption was the reason in 15.7 per cent of kinship care cases and 25.4 per cent of foster care cases.

Subsequently, we analysed the situation of the child when the foster care had ceased, which obviously greatly depends on the reason for closing the case. Cases ended because of disruption showed no differences by type of foster care and the vast majority of children went into residential care. Average age of these children was around 12 years (with no differences according to type of fostering) at the time of the disruption, but it is important to point out that their mean age on being fostered was around nine years.

As regards those cases that are closed due to the child reaching adulthood, there are significant differences, since in kinship care practically all of them remain living with the foster parents, whilst this occurs in 64.9 per cent of (non-kinship) foster care cases which end this way. This latter figure, considering that these are unrelated families, is quite striking; indeed, if in addition we take into account that in another 13.5 per cent of cases the children are adopted on coming of age, a total of 78.4 per cent of those in non-kinship care whose case ends for this reason continue living with their foster parents afterwards.

Finally, when the reason for cessation is a technical decision, the most common outcome in kinship care is reunification with the biological family, occurring in 64.7 per cent of such cases, followed by 21.1 per cent in which the child goes to new foster parents. On the other hand, in non-kinship care, the most common decision is adoption, accounting for more than half of the cases, the majority having been adopted by the foster caregivers themselves. This is a highly controversial practice in our country, with the majority of Regions preventing kinship caregivers from adopting so as to avoid generating confusion with adoption programmes. Even so, some Regions are not opposed to this practice and even encourage it and this results in a substantial percentage of such cases in our sample, but which actually come from just a single Region among the six studied. A further important finding is that in foster care, reunification with the biological family occurs less frequently than in kinship care, being found in only 25 per cent of cases.

Reasons for closure of a case and the child's subsequent situation indicate that foster care in Spain shows great stability, since many children remain for a long time with their foster caregivers and even beyond reaching adulthood, with very few passing from one foster family to another. This, which is logical and more common in kinship care, is also occurring in foster care, so that it is unsurprising if these foster families have no previous experience of fostering. It would seem that in our country foster placements are experiences with a tendency to be long-term and even to result in definitive cohabitation or adoption. Thus, it is to be expected that these families do not repeat the fostering process, resulting in a constant need to seek new foster families. It can be concluded that what has failed to emerge in Spain is the figure of the volunteer family that consecutively fosters different children, as is commonly found in other countries.

Limitations of the study and future research lines

There is a genuine problem in Spain with regard to data monitoring in the social services in general and in child welfare in particular. Each of the 17 Autonomous Regions has its own criteria for registration and for the definition of indicators, which makes comparisons quite difficult. Therefore, in research covering several Regions, the type of information in the files and the recording methods differ from one to another, leading to considerable problems of data-collection.

The present study cannot claim to be anything more than descriptive and although its importance is considerable given that it is the first time this type of data has been obtained in our country, there is still a great deal to be done. One of the major and most urgent objectives is the outcomes assessment by means of medium- and long-term follow-up studies, assessing psychosocial aspects of young people who were fostered at some time. This type of research, which in Spain has already been done in the case of residential care (del Valle *et al.* 2008b), has yet to be applied to foster care.

Another priority goal would be to carry out studies on factors that correlate with disruptions, or with the achievement of objectives such as family reunification, on which there is also an absence of research in Spain.

Implications for policy and practice

Foster care has been a legal alternative in this country for little over 20 years, so that it is still only gradually taking hold and is far from problem-free. The main forms of intervention continue to be residential care and kinship care, since there has always been a cultural tradition of informal 'fostering' by members of the extended family in cases of need. In the wake of the 1987 legislation introducing foster care, such informal foster care situations became formal, with the concomitant advantage for the foster parents of receiving various types of benefit (though generally insufficient).

However, foster care programmes designed to recruit families that volunteer to foster children with whom they have no family relationship are having very little success. They account for 8 per cent of out-of-home placements in our country and many Regions are having considerable problems in recruiting families and maintaining them. Spain has had no culture of foster care and no such culture is being successfully introduced, since few families are opting to embark on this experience. Moreover, the results of our research reveal that when such families are recruited for foster care, the children tend to stay long-term and even continue living with the family after reaching adulthood and/or are adopted by the family. Thus, it is not surprising that these families tend not to foster again and processes tend to resemble adoptions more than temporary foster care (which was the concept set out in principle by the legislation).

On the positive side, for the children, in contrast to what occurs in other countries, foster care is characterized by great stability and in many cases even provides a definitive solution that goes beyond adulthood. This stability is also reflected in the fact that it is not common to find frequent changes from one foster family to another, even though when there are disruptions the tendency is for the child to return to residential care.

One of the challenges for the future in child welfare policy in Spain is adequate attention and support for kinship care, since there are many cases in which relatives take care of abused or neglected children, often elderly grandparents in precarious social and economic circumstances and to whom the authorities are only just beginning to pay due attention. As regards non-relative foster care, its application should be increased through investment in recruitment campaigns and, above all, by means of programmes equipped to provide support and supervision so that the fostering experiences of these families are good ones and a culture is created around foster care as a positive concept. But with this in mind, the authorities will have to set up programmes that increase family reunification rates through family support services, so that cases of foster care do not become prolonged indefinitely. One of the priorities identified in a recent review (del Valle, Bravo and López 2009) is that of making foster care placements for the youngest children and ceasing the use of residential care for those aged under six and this policy has indeed been introduced in the agenda of some Regions. What is important above all else is to break the pattern whereby authorities take the easy option of residential care, which for so long had been the only alternative.

References

Amorós, P. Fuertes, J. and Roca, M.J. (1994) *Programa para la formación de familias acogedoras.* Valladolid: Junta de Castilla y León y Ministerio de Asuntos Sociales.

Amorós, P. Jiménez, J. Molina, C. Pastor, C. Cirera, L. and Martín, D. (2005) *Programa de formación para el acogimiento en familia extensa.* Barcelona: Obra Social. Fundación La Caixa.

Amorós, P. Palacios, J. Fuentes, N. León, E. and Mesas, A. (eds) (2002) *Programa para la formación de familias acogedoras de urgencia y diagnóstico.* Barcelona: Fundación La Caixa.

Amorós, P. Palacios, J. Fuentes, N. León, E. and Mesas, A. (eds) (2003) *Familias Canguro: Una experiencia de protección a la infancia.* Barcelona: Fundación La Caixa.

del Valle, J.F. Alvarez-Baz, E. and Bravo, A. (2002) 'Acogimiento en familia extensa. Perfil descriptivo y evaluación de necesidades en una muestra del Principado de Asturias.' *Bienestar y Protección Infantil 1,* 1, 34–56.

del Valle, J.F. and Bravo, A. (2003) *La situación del acogimiento familiar en España.* Madrid: Ministerio de Trabajo y Asuntos sociales. Available from www.gifi.es/admin/publications/archives/77025_Acogimiento_2003.pdf, accessed October 2009.

del Valle, J.F. Bravo, A. Alvarez, E. and Fernanz, A. (2008b) 'Adult self-sufficiency and social adjustment in care leavers from children's homes: a long-term assessment.' *Child and Family Social Work 13,* 1, 12–22.

del Valle, J.F. Bravo, A. and López, M. (2009) 'Foster care in Spain: implementation and current challenges.' *Papeles del Psicólogo 30,* 1, 33–41.

del Valle, J.F. López, M. Montserrat, C. and Bravo, A. (2008a) *'El Acogimiento Familiar en España. Una evaluación de resultados.'* Madrid: Ministerio de Trabajo y Asuntos Sociales.

del Valle, J.F. López, M. Montserrat, C. and Bravo, A. (2009) 'Twenty years of foster care in Spain: profiles, patterns and outcomes.' *Children and Youth Services Review 31,* 8, 847–853.

Lumbreras, H. Fuentes, M.J. and Bernedo, I.M. (2005) 'Perfil descriptivo de los acogimientos con familia extensa de la provincia de Málaga.' *Revista de Psicología Social Aplicada 15,* 1–2, 93–117.

Molero, R. Moral, M. J. Albiñana, P. Sabater, Y. and Sospedra, R. (2007) 'Situación de los acogimientos en familia extensa en la ciudad de Valencia.' *Anales de Psicología 23,* 2, 193–200.

Montserrat, C. (2007) 'Kinship foster care: a study from the perspective of the caregivers, the children and the child welfare workers.' *Psychology in Spain 11,* 1, 42–52.

Palacios, J. and Amorós, P. (2006) 'Recent changes in adoption and fostering in Spain.' *British Journal of Social Work 36,* 6, 921–935.

Palacios, J. and Jiménez, J.M. (2009) 'Kinship foster care: protection or risk?' *Adoption and Fostering, 33,* 3, 67–75.

Commentary by Anne Dorthe Hestbæck on:
Profile and Scope of Foster Care in Spain

Jorge F. del Valle and Mónica López

First of all, it is worth noticing that before 1987 Spain did not have any legal system for placing children in foster care. Not until two decades ago, foster care was included in the Civil Code as the most beneficial out-of-home care intervention, trying to state residential care as a last resort for 24-hour care. On the one hand, thus, professional foster care is a relatively new phenomenon in Spain. On the other hand, though, there has been a cultural tradition for using foster care informally through generations, but without public support or control.

With 45 per cent of all children being cared for in residential care, Spain resembles Denmark, but, in turn differs much from the other Scandinavian countries, Norway and Sweden, in this respect. A special characteristic of the Spanish out-of-home care landscape is that by far the largest proportion of children in foster care is placed in kinship care (85 per cent). In Denmark, for example, we find less than 15 per cent of the children in foster care placed in kinship care and network care altogether.

Another special characteristic of a foster care system with most children in kinship care is that – contrary to most other foster care systems – being in foster care in Spain has been a very stable experience for the children. The number of foster care break downs has been extremely low: very few children have exited care and later on re-entered care; and very few children have been passed on from one foster family to another. Thus, a positive secondary effect is the high degree of stability in foster care, giving the child a realistic possibility of relating and attaching to a (new) family. Most other countries are struggling with the unplanned breakdowns that from an overall perspective seem to be detrimental to the child's development. The negative secondary effect of the Spanish system is that the regions are missing a stable group of foster carers that stay in the system as professionals who on and on are available for new children.

The Spanish chapter describes a child welfare system in the process of reorganizing itself. A challenge for the Spanish system in the years coming is to develop foster care as a professional intervention programme. This requires, among other things, the recruitment of an increased number of professional foster carers who are available for the child welfare agencies for taking new children into foster care for a longer time span. Also, it requires new types of training of, support for and remuneration of foster care. These criteria need to be met if Spain shall succeed in breaking *'the pattern whereby authorities take the easy option of residential care, which for so long had been the only alternative'*.

CHAPTER 6

Reunification in Australia: Insights from South Australia and New South Wales

Elizabeth Fernandez and Paul Delfabbro

Introduction

With the continuing application of mandatory child abuse reporting and growing economic uncertainty in already disadvantaged areas an increasing number of children are the subject of child abuse reports and removal to care decisions. At the same time, the complexity of the psychological and social problems prevalent in out-of-home care populations has grown steadily, very likely because placements are increasingly used as a last resort for only the more serious cases (Australian Senate 2005; Wood Report 2008). In this chapter, a brief review of these trends is provided along with an analysis of the legislative and policy context that governs Australian out-of-home care. To achieve this end, two Australian states, New South Wales (NSW), the largest in population and South Australia (SA), one of the smallest are discussed as examples to highlight the current status of Australian out-of-home care. It will be argued that ongoing research about the causes of the current growth in out-of-home care numbers needs to be complemented by greater attention to the other side of the system: reunification or restoration, or how children go home.

A system that is able to return children home will be better able to maintain an adequate supply of placements for new children entering care and assist in maintaining the attachments between children and their biological parents. More broadly, better understanding reunification may also have important policy implications. Reunification research may offer insights into whether certain vulnerable population groups (e.g. Aboriginal children) are perhaps unfairly represented in the care system. Knowing why different children enter, how long they stay in care and what helps them go home is therefore central to this area of research. Accordingly, this chapter will provide evidence from two significant research projects that examined the issue of family reunification. Included in this analysis will be a discussion of the methodologies employed, principal findings, how stable the care experience is and the implications of this work for policy and practice in Australia.

Legislative and policy context

Trends in the changing nature of foster care are provided in Table 6.1 which summarizes the nature of out-of-home care in the two relevant states in 1997 and 2007 (Australian Institute of Health and Welfare 2009). As indicated in Table 6.1, there has been a dramatic increase in the number of children coming into care (a 60% increase in South Australia and 85% in New South Wales). Other distinctive features include the relatively low proportion of children in residential care compared with other countries such as the United States, the high rates of kinship care (a third to almost a half) and the significant over-representation (according to their representation in the population) of Aboriginal children in the care system.[1] Around a quarter of children coming into care are aged under four years and just over half are 10 years or older. NSW has a higher proportion of children in kinship care, but a smaller proportion in residential care.

In South Australia and New South Wales, children can be placed into care for short-term orders of less than a year either through parental authority and custody agreements, or be placed into longer-term guardianship via a court order. In custody arrangements, the day-to-day care of the child passes to the care system, whereas a guardianship transfers full parental responsibility and decision-making to the State.

---

1   Aboriginal people represent only 2–3 per cent of the total Australian population in SA and NSW.

TABLE 6.1 Profile of out-of-home care in South Australia and New South Wales

	SOUTH AUSTRALIA	NEW SOUTH WALES
Total population	1.5 million	6.5 million
0–17 year olds with a care and protection order (rate per 1000 children)	1997: 3.3 2007: 5.4	1997: 3.7 2007: 6.6
Population in care	1997: 1172 2007: 1881	1997: 5764 2007: 10,639
New orders (2007)	888	3495
Placement types (2007) Parents + order Foster care Residential care Kinship care Other	41 (2.2) 874 (46.5) 120 (6.4) 647 (34.4) 199 (10.6)	594 (5.6) 4645 (43.7) 359 (3.4) 4918 (46.2) 123 (1.2)
Age profile (years) 0–4 5–9 10–14 15–17	476 (21.7) 504 (26.8) 570 (30.3) 331 (17.6)	2472 (23.2) 3329 (31.3) 3411 (32.1) 1421 (13.4)
% Aboriginal	440 (23.4)	2880 (27.1)

Source: Australian Institute for Health and Welfare (2008). Audit of children in care, 20 June 2007.

In both States, the relevant legislation requires priority to be given to the child's right to be raised in the biological family to prevent placement. If a separation becomes necessary, the child should be returned to his or her family as soon as possible. In New South Wales, the legislation limits the length of the duration of episodes in out-of-home care and requires periodic court reviews to monitor progress against a predetermined care plan for each child. To ensure permanency, the system should attempt to achieve the following outcomes in order of priority: family reunification, guardianship, long term foster care and adoption. For reunification to occur, parents are expected to demonstrate progress in meeting goals and conditions and there should be evidence that the system has made reasonable efforts to provide supportive services.

Reunification research in South Australia

Methods and analytical strategies

The principal source of findings relevant to reunification in South Australia is derived from a longitudinal study conducted by Barber and Delfabbro (2004) and described in various papers (e.g. Barber and Delfabbro, 2005; Delfabbro, Barber and Cooper 2000). In this study, 235 children (121 boys, 114 girls, 17% Aboriginal) referred for new placements (other than respite or remand) of two or more weeks' duration in 1999–2000 were selected and tracked for up to three years thereafter. Detailed information concerning the child's demographics, previous placement history and social background was collected via case-file reviews and interviews with case-workers. Information concerning the child's psychosocial wellbeing, placement movements and living arrangements were obtained at 4, 8, 12, 18 and 24 months.

Reunification was analysed both descriptively using flow-charts, but also using proportional hazard models or Cox regression, a method which has now become commonly used by child welfare researchers. Proportional hazard modelling is a multivariate technique that enables researchers to determine the probability of a given child remaining in care based on specified predictor variables.

South Australian findings

Rate of reunification and significant predictors

A first stage of the South Australian analysis examined the rate of reunification across each of the follow-up points (Figure 6.1). As indicated in Figure 6.1, around 40 per cent of children who entered care in 1999–2000 had returned to their birth families two years later. Re-entry rates were generally low (only ten cases came back into care). The most striking feature of Figure 6.1 is that that around 90 per cent of children who were reunified returned home within the first eight months. Thereafter, reunification was very unlikely. Only 10 per cent of reunifications occurred from the eight-month to the two-year point, whereas just over 60 per cent of reunifications occurred in the first four months.

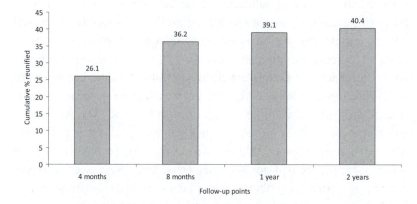

FIGURE 6.1 Cumulative percentage of children reunified in South Australia over time

Several consistent factors explained why children went home early. For around 40 per cent of cases, the mother's health or wellbeing had improved. In another quarter of cases, reunification had involved going to the home of the other birth parent, whereas another one in five went home because the order had expired.

Why children entered care and reunification

The South Australian study showed that the most common factor seen to be contributing to the child's entry into care was child abuse. Within the sample, 12 per cent had been sexually abused, 25 per cent physically abused, 37 per cent subjected to emotional abuse and 28 per cent had been subject to neglect. Around one third of parents had ongoing substance abuse problems, mental illness or disabilities. These factors, as well as demographic factors and placement history, contact with birth families (telephone or direct visits), were analysed in relation to the child's status (still in care vs. reunified) at each of the different follow-up points. Significant predictors were only found for the four-month and two-year points.

The proportional hazards models undertaken at the four-month follow-up point showed that aboriginality, neglect and parental problems were most strongly associated with the probability of reunification. In particular, it was found that Aboriginal children were five times less likely to be reunified in the short-term. Children subject to neglect were 2.8 times less likely to be reunified, whereas children whose parents had illnesses or substance abuse problems were over twice as likely to go home. When these three significant factors were entered into the regression equation, it was possible to determine the probability of children being reunified after exactly 120 days (four months) based on a combination of factors. As shown in Table 6.2, the likelihood of reunification was influenced by the combination of variables considered. A child was very unlikely to go home if he or she was Aboriginal unless the cause of the problem was a parental problem (e.g. illness), whereas non-Aboriginal children had up to a 58 per cent chance of going home if they had not been neglected and been placed into care because of a parental problem. Other factors such as the frequency of family contact with birth families were significant at a univariate level, but did not appear in the final multivariate model.

TABLE 6.2 Probability of reunification after 120 days

	PARENTAL PROBLEMS NOT REASON FOR PLACEMENT	PARENTAL PROBLEMS REASON FOR PLACEMENT
Neglect		
Aboriginal	.02	.42
Non-Aboriginal	.09	.21
No neglect		
Aboriginal	.05	.12
Non-Aboriginal	.27	.58

Source: Delfabbro *et al.* (2003).

Similar analyses were conducted to examine the factors that contributed to subsequent reunifications (i.e. at four months and two years). These results showed that Aboriginal children were 2.5 times more likely to be reunified, particularly after one year, whereas the number of previous placements prior to the entry into care decreased the likelihood of reunification. In other words, even though Aboriginal children were less likely to be reunified in the short-term, they were more likely to fall into the 'late' reunification group. From inspection of cases, it was found that the factors contributing to reunification were much more variable (e.g. parents returning after an absence, sudden departure of abusive partner, new housing obtained, return from prison).

Reunification research in NSW

The New South Wales Reunification Study followed the care careers of 294 children over four years focusing on factors associated with entry to care, the post placement experience and reunification or restoration outcomes. Findings from the overall study are described in Fernandez (1996) and Fernandez (1999). The sample, drawn from the NSW Department of Community Services, included children aged 0–15 who were new entries to care and who had spent a minimum of two weeks in care. Data were collected through personal interviews with caseworkers and study of case files that included information concerning relevant child and family characteristics. The profile of children in terms of age was: 40 per cent under five; 24.5 per cent 6–10 years and 35.5 per cent 11 years and over (21 per cent Aboriginal).

The analyses examined the children's substitute care careers to indicate the changing likelihood that a child would be (1) reunified with biological parents, (2) experience a change of placement within given intervals of time over the four year period and how these outcomes were influenced by child-, parent- and placement-related variables. The first analysis examined the length of time in care until reunification, whereas the second analysed the pattern of movement into another placement (up to three placements were considered).

The study drew on event history analysis (Allison 1984) using 'time till event' as the dependent variable and used a number of predictors, including: age, sex, ethnicity, family structure, income status, type of placement, number of placements and reasons for entry to care. The analysis was undertaken in stages. The first analysis used the whole spell of care for each child from entry to care to the end of the study period to identify patterns of restoration. The next analysis focused on the spell of each of the first three placements. Typically, from each placement a child can be either restored, continue in the same placement or transfer to another placement as a result of breakdown or planned move. The second analysis is concerned with length of time in each placement until transfer to another placement.

Results of the NSW study

Figures 6.2 and 6.3 show that most children return home after the first five months in care, with 50 per cent going home after their first placement, 26 per cent from the second placement and 24 per cent

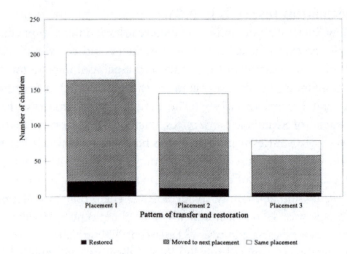

FIGURE 6.2 Individual placement careers

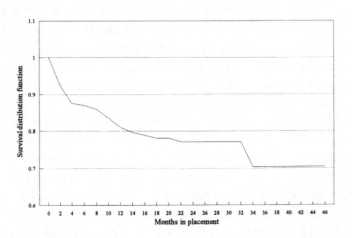

FIGURE 6.3 Restoration as event: all placements

from subsequent placements. The findings suggest a declining rate of restoration with each subsequent placement. All restorations from first placement occur in the first four month interval (Figure 6.4). In contrast, while there are some restorations in second placement in the first two month interval, children were restored as late as the twelfth month (Figure 6.5).

Examining each placement to identify patterns of experiencing both events restoration and replacement the patterns that emerge are: restorations which take place from the first placement occur in the first

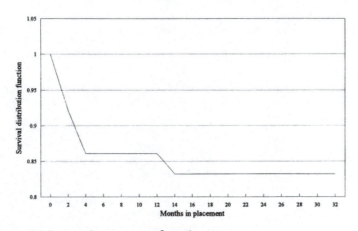

FIGURE 6.4 Restoration as event: first placement

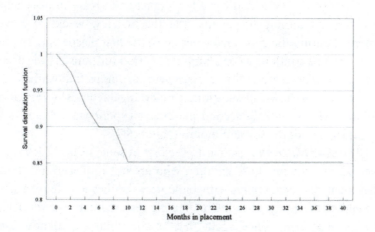

FIGURE 6.5 Restoration as event: second placement

four months. Of those who transfer to a second placement 50 per cent are replaced in the first two months, a further 25 per cent move in the next two months and 16 per cent experience a change of placement in the next interval of four months. The first six months of the placement appear to be a time when several important decisions relating to both restoration and change of placement are concentrated. A small per centage (7%) of children who have not moved in the first six months experience changes in placement in the subsequent 12 months. After this period, however, the children who survive in their first placement have a stable experience, the maximum duration being 32 months (Figure 6.6).

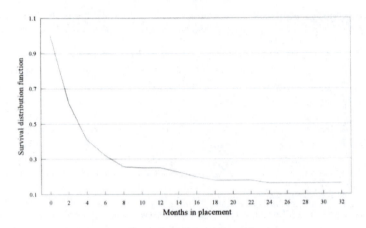

FIGURE 6.6 Subsequent placement as event: first placement

The *second placement* shows a less dramatic decrease in per centage of children returning to parents after the first few weeks than were observed during the comparable period of the first placement. The first seven months continue to be a high risk period for transfers to another placement. The reasons for re-placement are more frequently (72%) related to breakdown in substitute care arrangements. The rest of the children who survive in second placement experience stable care arrangements until the fortieth month (Figure 6.7).

The *third placement* is similar to the first in some respects. It extends over 32 months for those children who are not re-placed in a fourth placement or not reunited with biological families and have reached the end of the study period. Children are restored until the fourteenth month, suggesting once again that as the child experiences more placements the likelihood of rapid restoration declines. The majority of placements transfers (91%) occur in the first seven months. By the twelfth month, however, a stable pattern of care is evident for those children who continue in care in their third placement (Figures 6.8 and 6.9).

Additional analyses of reunification

Additional analyses undertaken to understand how restoration or reunification is influenced by explanatory variables and whether this varies by placement, are reported in Table 6.3.

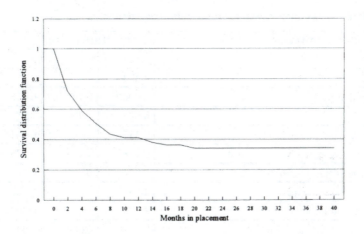

FIGURE 6.7 Subsequent placement as event: second placement

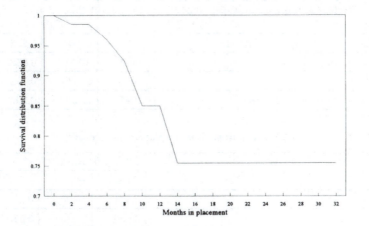

FIGURE 6.8 Restoration as event: third placement

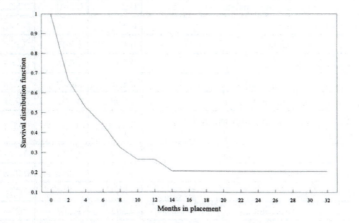

FIGURE 6.9 Subsequent placement as event: third placement

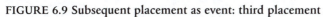

TABLE 6.3 All placements with restoration as event

EXPLANATORY VARIABLES	EVENT: RESTORATION		
	Estimate	x^2	*p*
Intercept	4.874	–	–
Age in days	0.00005	0.196	0.658
Sex (female)	0.885	4.799	0.2*
Background (Aboriginality)	1.337	13.426	0.001*
Family composition (two parents)	0.578	1.142	0.285
Income status (wages)	0.234	0.122	0.727
Accommodation (public)	1.837	13.592	0.0002*
Legal status (court ordered)	1.999	15.149	0.0001*
Type of I placement (family)	-0.031	0.004	0.949
Three or more placements	1.762	12.051	0.0005
Reasons for placement as compared to child's behaviour			
Environmental/situational factors	0.192	0.046	0.828
Parent illness/disability	-0.155	0.020	0.888
Child abuse/neglect	-0.690	0.716	0.398
Parent behaviour/functioning	-1.047	1.705	0.192

TABLE 6.4. Second placement with third placement as event

EXPLANATORY VARIABLES	EVENT: RESTORATION		
	Estimate	x^2	*p*
Intercept	0.674	1.300	0.254
Age in days	0.0002	0.000	0.856
Sex (female)	0.118	0.160	0.689
Family composition (single parent)	0.231	0.340	0.560
Income status (benefits)	0.599	2.153	0.142
Accommodation (public)	0.441	1.725	0.189
Legal status (court ordered)	0.723	1.956	0.162
Type of I placement (residential)	0.706	3.010	0.052*
Type of II placement (residential)	0.008	0.001	0.981
Reasons for placement as compared to child's behaviour			
Environmental/situational factors	0.967	3.225	0.0725
Parent illness/disability	0.557	3.888	0.048*
Child abuse/neglect	0.834	4.388	0.036*
Parent behaviour/functioning	0.604	1.417	0.233

* $P<.05$

Restoration : significant variables (Table 6.3)

- *Sex* – Girls can expect to remain in care 2.4 times as long before restoration as boys. (Figure 6.10)

- *Accommodation* – Children whose parents were living in public or transitory accommodation at the time of their entry to care expect to remain in care 6.28 times as long before restoration as children who have been in ownership or private accommodation.

- *Legal status* – Children who enter care under court orders wait 7.38 times as long before restoration as children who enter care under voluntary, non court ordered arrangements. (Figure 6.11)

- *Aboriginality* – Children from Aboriginal backgrounds remain in care 5.26 times as long before restoration as children from non-Aboriginal backgrounds.

- *Number of placements* – Children who have experienced three or more placement changes wait 5.8 times as long before restoration in comparison with children who had one or two placements. (Figure 6.12)

The findings on reasons for entry to care and restoration patterns follow.

Restoration and reasons for entry to care

The reasons for placement describe the routes through which children enter the system and may well influence their careers in care and options for leaving care. The relationship between each of the reasons for entry to care and time before restoration is depicted in Table 6.4.*

TABLE 6.5 Arbitrary days comparison of time in care before restoration according to reason for placement

REASONS	RESTORATION FROM ALL PLACEMENTS	
	EXPONENTIAL	INDICATIVE DAYS
Child behaviour (set at 365 days)		365
Environmental and situational factors	1.213	441
Parent illness/disability	0.856	313
Child abuse/neglect	0.501	183
Parent behaviour/functioning	0.351	127

Children who entered care for reasons of their behavioural or emotional problems have a tendency to experience longer careers in care before restoration than those in other categories of reasons (Table 6.5).

For the purpose of comparison with other reasons the author set 365 days as an arbitrary representation of the time spent in care before restoration by the group of children whose behavioural problems were the reason for entry to care. By comparison it would appear that children in care because of their parents' alleged behaviour or functioning in the parental role spend the shortest time in care before restoration (127 days). Where the reasons for admission to care were neglect and abuse or parent's illness or disability, the period in care before restoration is comparatively 183 days and 313 days, respectively. In comparison with other reasons, the children whose families were confronted with environmental and situational factors spend 441 days in care before being restored. Their long stay in care suggests that the problems of their families arising from poverty, disadvantage, housing and lack of formal and informal supports are not easily addressed by services available in the community. A number of factors may explain the early return of those children in the abuse and neglect category. It may be they were in care under short term orders during court proceedings and the case was either not established due to lack of evidence, or that the neglect or abuse was less severe, or that parents were receiving help and consequently the level of risk was reduced.

Restoration and type of placement
In the analysis of restoration from first placement the trend reflects earlier restoration from foster family placements. It is two or three times as likely that family placement leads to restoration in the first five months for foster family placements compared to residential placement. When further time intervals in first placement are taken into account the family placements are still more likely to lead to restoration. Thus if a child spends 365 days in a residential placement before restoration the same child in a family placement would spend 252 days in care before restoration.

Experience of placement movement: significant variables
In the analysis of the children's likelihood of experiencing a re-placement or movement to a subsequent placement if not restored, a

lower survival rate for family placement is noted. For instance in focusing on third placement as the hazard event for children in their second placement, children experience more stability in residential placements than family placement. It takes twice as long to experience a change of placement from a residential setting than a family placement. Thus if a child spends 365 days in a residential placement before being transferred to a third placement, by contrast, the model predicts this child would experience a transfer from family placement in 180 days.

While this analysis contributes insights into the relative contributions of child, family and placement related factors to reunification and other placement trajectories the analysis overlooks the impact of other system variables such as caseload size, frequency of worker contact, worker training and experience that may contribute to reunification outcomes.

Conclusions and policy and practice implications

Both studies yielded findings that appear consistent with many similar studies conducted internationally on reunification and placement trajectories. Both studies showed that the probability of going home decreases the longer children are in care, although it is acknowledged that these results may not necessarily generalize to longer durations in care (Bullock, Little and Milham 1993; Fanshel and Shinn 1978; Fanshel, Finch and Grundy 1989; Goerge 1990). The vast majority of children who return home do so within the first year and this is usually because the problems that contributed to their entry into care are potentially resolvable (e.g. parental illnesses). As the NSW research showed, reunification also occurs when children have not been placed on court orders. Decisions to restore children placed in care on a voluntary basis are less constrained by legislative requirements and agreements about reunifying are more easily negotiated by parents.

Both of these findings highlight the critical role of early intervention and service supports for families when their children become involved in the care system. In Australia, the decision options and decision-time for placements are often very restricted when children come into care. While on one hand, statutory departments are often unable to continue to place children on short-term orders and are left with having to apply for long-term orders, families are provided with relatively little time to challenge this application once it has been filed. The most common result will, therefore, be that the child will remain in care on a long-term order. Even when this occurs, it may still be the case that an intention to reunify is built into case plans, but this can prove to be difficult to realize in practice because of the lack of sufficient resources and services to assist families as well as the lack of time for case-planning and reviews. The trends highlighted in the NSW study on placement instability imply that child welfare services should provide extensive support to carers and children in the early months of placement when care arrangements are vulnerable to breakdown.

These results also show how broader family, child and environmental factors are related to the likelihood of reunification. Previous studies have emphasized the importance of factors such as: substance abuse (Marsh *et al.* 2006; Miller *et al.* 2006; Terling 1999), social support for families (Festinger, 1996; Terling, 1999), offending in families (Frame, Berrick and Brodowski 2000), mental health issues in parents (Festinger 1996), whereas others have focused on the ongoing prevalence of risk factors in the household that preclude successful reunification or which contribute to re-entry (Appleyard *et al.* 2005; Fraser *et al.* 1996). Many studies have shown how the complexity of the child's behavioural and emotional problems can influence outcomes (Barth *et al.* 2008; Goerge 1990; Lau *et al.* 2003). Farmer (1992) has drawn attention to the importance of changes in the composition of households (e.g. the departure of abusive partners) as critical factors in reunification. The NSW research confirmed a number of these findings. In terms of family composition, the odds of reunification were greater for children from single parent households than two parent households including step parents. In considering reasons for placement as predictor of children's placement status the NSW analysis indicated that children who enter care for emotional and behavioural problems experience poorer chances of restoration and a greater likelihood of placement instability. It would appear that as they are the source of the need for care, the investment of resources in therapeutic services to ameliorate their problems and facilitate restoration should be a priority.

The fact that Aboriginal children are likely to spend longer in care in both studies is also consistent with international research that has revealed similar difficulties in achieving reunification for minority groups (Fein, Maluccio and Kluger 1990; Hubbell *et al.* 1986; Wulczyn and Goerge 1992). Aboriginal families generally experience significantly higher rates of social disadvantage, higher rates of domestic violence and substance abuse than non-Aboriginal families (Delfabbro *et al.* 2009). They are also

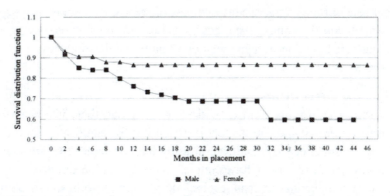

FIGURE 6.10 Restoration as event: all placements (by gender)

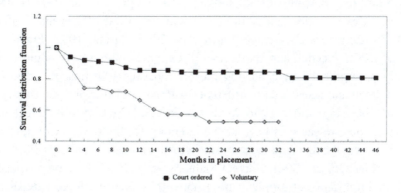

FIGURE 6.11 Restoration as event: all placements (by legal status)

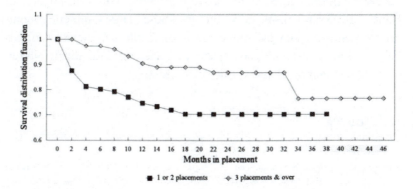

FIGURE 6.12 Restoration as event: all placements (by number of placements)

likely to face greater difficulties in being able to challenge court orders because of the geographical remoteness of some communities, language barriers and the complex and adversarial nature of court processes that require dedicated legal representation to understand and contest.

Future Directions

Despite the insights yielded by these two studies, there is a need for further research into the factors contributing to reunification and the longer term effects of reunification using larger samples that are stratified by age. It is known, for example, that reunification can give rise to ongoing challenges in families, including an increase in internalizing and externalizing behaviours and greater family stress once children return (e.g. Bellamy 2008; Landsverk *et al.* 1996; Lau *et al.* 2003; Taussig, Clyman and Landsverk 2001) and that these effects may differ according to a child's age (Barth *et al.* 2008; Farmer 1992; Frame *et al.* 2000; Needell and Barth, 1998). Reunification research could also be strengthened by achieving greater consistency in how the term is defined and researched in different Australian jurisdictions (see Barth *et al.* 2008; Fernandez 1996; Maluccio, Fein and Davis 1994). For example, some researchers have drawn attention to the need to distinguish between short, medium and long-term reunification patterns (Barber and Delfabbro 2004), whereas Maluccio *et al.* (1994) have emphasized the importance of supplementing statistical models with more detailed qualitative analyses of individual placement histories. Some guidance in these matters is likely to follow from large studies currently being conducted in the United States (Barth *et al.* 2008; Wulczyn, Kogan and Harden 2003) and in Australia. In these studies, large samples of young people being tracked over time can address the complexities in this field of inquiry and track the trajectory of classes of individual children who share common characteristics or profiles.

References

Allison, P.D. (1984) *Event History Analysis: Regression for Longitudinal Event Data*. USA: Sage Publications.

Appleyard, K. Egeland, B. van Dulmen, M.H.M. and Sroufe, L.A. (2005) 'When more is not better: the role of cumulative risk in child behaviour outcomes.' *Journal of Abnormal Psychology and Psychiatry 46*, 235–245.

Australian Institute of Health and Welfare (2009) 'Child protection Australia 2007–08.' *Child Welfare Series* no. 45, Cat. no. CWS 33. Canberra: AIHW.

Australian Senate (2005) *Protecting Vulnerable Children: A National Challenge.* Canberra: Community Affairs References Committee.

Barber, J.G. and Delfabbro, P.H. (2004) *Children in Foster Care.* London: Taylor and Francis.

Barber, J.G. and Delfabbro, P.H. (2005) 'The long-term psychological consequences of placement disruption in foster care.' *Children and Youth Services Review 27,* 329–340.

Barth, R. Weigensberg, E. Fisher, P. Fetrow, B. and Green, R. (2008) 'Reentry of elementary aged children following reunification from foster care.' *Children and Youth Services Review 30,* 353–364.

Bellamy, J.L. (2008) 'Behavioural problems following reunification of children in long-term foster care.' *Children and Youth Services Review 30,* 216–228.

Bullock, R. Little, M. and Milham, S. (1993) *Going Home: The Return of Separated Children from Their Families.* Aldershot: Dartmouth Publishing Company.

Courtney, M.E. (1994) 'Factors associated with the reunification of foster children with their families.' *Social Service Review 68,* 81–108.

Delfabbro, P.H. Barber, J.G. and Cooper, L. (2000) 'Placement disruption and dislocation in South Australian substitute care.' *Children Australia 25,* 16–20.

Delfabbro, P.H. Barber, J.G. and Cooper, L.L. (2003) 'Predictors of short-term reunification in South Australia subsitute care.' *Child Welfare, 82,* 27–51.

Delfabbro, P.H. Borgas, M. Rogers, N. Jeffreys, H. and Wilson, R. (2009) 'The social and family backgrounds of infants in care and their capacity to predict subsequent abuse notifications: a study of South Australian out-of-home care 2000–2005.' *Children and Youth Services Review 31,* 219–226.

Fanshel, D. and Shinn, E.B. (1978) *Children in Foster Care: A Longitudinal Study.* New York: Columbia University Press.

Fanshel, D. Finch, S.J. and Grundy, J.F. (1989) 'Modes of exit from foster family care and adjustment at time of departure of children with unstable life histories.' *Child Welfare 68,* 391–402.

Farmer, E. (1992) 'Restoring children on court orders to their families: lessons for practitioners.' *Adoption and Fostering 17,* 7–15.

Fein, E. Maluccio, A.N. and Kluger, M.P (1990) *No More Partings: An Examination of Long-Term Family Foster Care.* Washington DC: Child Welfare League of America.

Fernandez, E. (1996) *Significant Harm: Unravelling Child Protection Decisions and Substitute Care Careers of Children.* Avebury: Ashgate Publishing.

Fernandez, E. (1999) 'Pathways in substitute care: representation of placement careers of children using event history analysis.' *Children and Youth Services Review 21,* 377–416.

Festinger, T. (1996) 'Going home and returning to foster care.' *Children and Youth Services Review 18,* 383–402.

Frame, L. Berrick, J.D. and Brodowski, M.L. (2000) 'Understanding re-entry to out-of-home care for reunified infants.' *Child Welfare 79,* 339–369.

Fraser, M.W. Walton, E. Lewis, R.E. Pecora, P.J. and Walton, W.K. (1996) 'An experiment in family reunification: correlates of outcomes at one-year follow-up.' *Children and Youth Services Review 18,* 335–361.

Goerge, R.M. (1990) 'The reunification process in substitute care.' *Social Service Review 64,* 422–457.

Hubbell, R. Hirsch, G, Barrett, B. Condelli, L. and Plantz, M. (1986) *Evaluation of Reunification for Minority Children.* Washington, DC: CSR Inc.

Landsverk, J. Davis, I. Ganger, W. Newton, R. and Johnson, I. (1996) 'Impact of child psychological functioning on reunification from out-of-home care.' *Children and Youth Services Review 18,* 447–462.

Lau, A.S. Litrownik, A.J. Newton, R.R. and Landsverk, J. (2003) 'Going home: the complex effects of reunification on internalizing problems among children in foster care.' *Journal of Abnormal Child Psychology 31*, 345–358.

Maluccio, A.N. Fein, E. and Davis, I.P. (1994) 'Family reunification research: research findings, issues and directions.' *Child Welfare 53*, 489–504.

Marsh, J.C. Ryan, J.P. Choi, S. and Testa, M.F. (2006) 'Integrated services for families with multiple problems: obstacles to family reunification.' *Children and Youth Services Review 28*, 1074–1087.

Miller, K.A. Fisher, P.A. Fetrow, B. and Jordan, K. (2006) 'Trouble on the journey home: reunification failures in foster care.' *Children and Youth Services Review 28*, 260–274.

Needell, B. and Barth, R.P. (1998) 'Infants entering foster care compared to other infants using birth status indicators.' *Child Abuse and Neglect 22*, 1179–1187.

Taussig, H.N. Clyman, R.B. and Landsverk, J. (2001) 'Children who return home from foster care: a 6-year prospective study of behavioural health outcomes in adolescence.' *Paediatrics 108*, e10.

Terling, T. (1999) 'The efficacy of family reunification practice: re-entry rates and correlates of re-entry for abused and neglected children reunified with their foster families.' *Child Abuse and Neglect 23*, 1359–1370.

Wood Report (2008) *Special Commission of Inquiry into Child Protection Services in New South Wales.* Sydney: NSW Government.

Wulczyn, F. and Goerge, R.M. (1992) 'Foster care in New York and Illinois: the challenge of rapid change.' *Social Service Review 66*, 278–294.

Wulczyn, F. Kogan, J. and Harden, B.J. (2003) 'Placement stability and movement trajectories.' *Social Service Review 76*, 212–236.

Commentary by Elaine Farmer on:
Reunification in Australia: Insights from South Australia and New South Wales

Elizabeth Fernandez and Paul Delfabbro

Reunification as a topic is under-researched not only in Australia but also in the UK and to a lesser extent in the US. These two Australian studies remind us that even when the court process is well structured to provide oversight of children in care, the intentions of policy makers may be frustrated by lack of services to families to avoid out-of-home care or promote reunification.

Both studies are of particular interest in their use of proportional hazard modelling to determine the probability of children remaining in care or going home. They found, as has other research, that voluntarily accommodated children returned home more quickly than those on court orders, that most children were reunified within the first five to eight months of being in care and that neglected children and those with multiple placements in care are not returned quickly. In addition, they found that Aboriginal children were much less likely to be reunified quickly (within four months), although they were often reunified at a later stage, in common with other international research which shows similar difficulties in reunification for black and minority ethnic groups. They argue that Aboriginal families experience extremely high levels of disadvantage and poverty and may find it difficult to challenge court orders, all of which would delay return. In common with the US and other research it was also found that children with behavioural and emotional problems (who are usually older) and those from the poorest and most disadvantaged backgrounds spent a long time in care before return. The Australian studies also found that the odds of reunification were greater for children from single parent than two parent households, whereas (a slightly different point) some US studies have shown that children from single parent families return home more slowly than those with two parents.

As the authors argue it will be useful in the future to analyze reunification data in relation to age, since research has shown that different factors relate to reunification for different age groups, to consider different sub-groups and the different factors that lead to return, including push factors from children, parents and the child welfare system. In addition, it is important to consider the outcomes of return, since between 15 per cent and half of returns disrupt (depending on whether it is a first return and on the length of the follow-up) and repeated returns are common. The quality of the returns for children also need to be considered since research has shown that between a quarter and half of returned children are maltreated and that the psychosocial outcomes of many reunified children are poor (Biehal 2006). It will also be useful to continue to investigate the reasons for the differential rates of reunification for Aboriginal children and to consider which other factors, such as family structure, might account for this (Harris and Courtney 2003) as well as to investigate whether there are higher rates of return breakdown for this group (see e.g. Shaw 2006).

References

Biehal, N. (2006) *Reuniting Looked After Children with Their Families: A Review of the Research.* London: National Children's Bureau.

Harris, M.S. and Courtney M.E. (2003) 'The interaction of race, ethnicity and family structure with respect to the timing of family reunification.' *Children and Youth Services Review,* Special Issue on the Over representation of Children of Colour in the Child Welfare System, M.E. Courtney and A. Skyles (eds), 5–6, 409–429.

Shaw, T.V. (2006) 'Re-entry into the foster care system after reunification.' *Children and Youth Services Review 28,* 1375–1390.

Part Three:
The Foster Care Experience:
<u>A Life Course Perspective</u>

CHAPTER 7

Very Young Children in Care in England: Issues for Foster Care

Harriet Ward and Emily R. Munro

Introduction

Social workers have to make impossibly difficult decisions that can have major consequences for the life chances of very vulnerable children and families, often on the basis of incomplete evidence. If they separate children unnecessarily from parents who may be able to provide a 'good enough' standard of care, they stand accused of failing to support vulnerable families, a criticism that gains added weight when supported by evidence that the care system can often fail to meet children's needs (House of Commons Children, Schools and Families Committee 2009; Social Exclusion Unit 2003). Yet those who allow children to remain in abusive families, in the hope or expectation that the support provided will enable struggling parents to provide adequate, non-abusive care, may find they have seriously compromised a child's life chances if their decisions have been over optimistic. If a child dies, they may find themselves pilloried by the media. Following a recent highly publicized case, social workers in the London borough concerned faced what amounted to a witch hunt from members of the general population, urged on by a popular press, intent on avenging the unnecessary death of a child (McCulloch 2008). The complexity of such decisions is particularly evident when children are very young, for abused and neglected infants are more likely to die than older children, yet the decision to separate a baby from its mother is a particularly emotive one and the European courts have upheld that 'there must be extraordinary and compelling reasons before a baby can be removed from its mother, against her will, immediately after birth' (*K and T. v. Finland* 2001). This chapter explores the issues raised by placing young children from very difficult home circumstances in foster care in England.

National legislative and policy context of foster care

The Children Act 1989 provides the legislative framework that underpins the provision of child welfare in England and Wales. The most recent national statistics show that of the 59,500 children and young people looked after by local authorities (i.e. in public care) in England on 31 March 2008, 42,300 (71%) were placed in foster care. Following a number of fluctuations, the numbers of children in care are currently about the same as when the Children Act 1989 was implemented in 1991 (59,834). However while the size of the care population is relatively similar, the numbers of children placed in foster care have increased substantially and the per centage has risen by 13 per cent (see Department for Children, Schools and Families 2008; Rowlands and Statham 2009). Only 14 per cent of children in the care population are now placed in institutional settings (including residential special schools), a proportion that has been decreasing over several years; many of these children will have run the gamut of a series of failed foster placements before entering residential care (see Ward, Holmes and Soper 2008). A small number of children (4500; 8%) are subject to care orders but placed with their own parents, often as a preliminary to complete reunification and case closure; another relatively small group (2600 children; 4%) are in adoptive placements awaiting a final order. Increased interest in adoption in the last decade is partly a response to findings from studies such as the one reported in this chapter (see Department of Health 2000).

While the child's welfare is the paramount consideration for the courts in making decisions, resources are inevitably an issue for local authorities which are chronically short of cash: foster care, particularly with family and friends, is a popular option not only because children are thought to benefit from these placements, but also because they are relatively cheap. A recent study found that maintaining a child for a week in residential care costs on average eight times as much as foster care with strangers, 9.5 times as much as foster care with relatives and 12.5 times as much as a placement with their own parents (Ward *et al.* 2008). Following a recent legal judgment (*R v. Manchester City Council* 2001) local authorities have been required to increase the allowances they pay to family and friends carers. In response to evidence that a shortage of foster carers has resulted in large numbers of children being placed far from their homes, the new Children and Young Persons Act 2008 has also introduced requirements for local authorities to ensure that there are sufficient numbers of foster carers available within their areas.

The Children Act 1989 is based on the belief, also enshrined in the United Nations Convention on the Rights of the Child, that 'children are generally best looked after within the family, with parents playing a full part in their lives'. The responsibilities of the state, in the form of the local authorities and their partner agencies that deliver child welfare services, reflect this principle: local authorities have a duty to provide services to support children and their families in their own homes; to return children looked after by them to their families unless this is against their interests; and to endeavour to provide contact between looked after children and their parents unless this is not reasonably practicable or consistent with their welfare (Department of Health 1989, para 1.8). Care placements are therefore expected to be short and followed by swift reunification. Parents have enduring responsibility for their children and although a local authority acquires parental responsibility for children who are committed to care through the courts (placed on a care order), 'any person who is a parent or guardian of the child [also] retains parental responsibility for him and may exercise this responsibility independently of the authority, provided that he does not act incompatibly with the care order' (Department of Health 1989, para 5.4). The legislation also reflects a number of other key principles: of particular relevance to this chapter are the primary principle that, when a court determines any question with regard to their upbringing, the welfare of the child shall be the paramount consideration (Section 1(1)); and the principle that practitioners and carers should work in partnership with parents (see Department of Health 2001).

Local authorities also have a duty to place children with parents, relatives or friends wherever such arrangements are consistent with their welfare (Section 23(6)). Where suitable kinship placements are not available, local authority foster care is the preferred option, largely because it replicates the family setting that is thought to be conducive to children's wellbeing. However the increase in the proportion of children placed in foster care and the changes in culture wrought by the Children Act 1989 have had a profound impact on the nature of foster care and the manner in which it is delivered.

Changes in foster care

First, the principle that practitioners and carers should work in partnership with parents has radically altered the nature of the fostering task. The Children Act 1989 accelerated an emerging trend away from the perception of foster care as an exclusive, quasi-adoptive arrangement in which birth parents played only a minimal role, towards more inclusive work with birth families, the objective of which is reunification. Foster parents are no longer expected to replace children's parents but to work in partnership with them, facilitating contact and eventual return – a point emphasized by the change in nomenclature to foster carer. Those prospective foster carers who are unable to accommodate what is a radical change of position are not considered appropriate applicants, for the regulations on recruitment state that:

> The applicant's attitudes and expectations in relation to contact between parents and children, visits by parents and relatives to the foster parents' home and working with parents in pursuance of the aims of the placement and the plan for the child will be particularly important. The social worker should seek to clarify whether attitudes and opinions are dogmatic or amenable to training and change. It is essential that the applicant is aware of the day to day implications of working with parents and is prepared to accept training and support to achieve the required partnership with parents. (Department of Health 2001, para 3.26)

While traditionally foster carers were seen as volunteers who offered a home to a child in return for an allowance to cover their expenses, they are increasingly expected to play a more professional role and to participate in the management of the case, working in partnership with social workers and family placement workers as well as with parents (see Poirier, Chamberland and Ward 2006). This change in the nature of the fostering task has been one of the key factors that have led to increased calls for professionalization of foster carers; they spend far more time with children who are placed in care or accommodation than do the practitioners involved and once their unique role and expertise are acknowledged it is difficult to argue that they should be anything other than full members of the 'team around the child'.

Second, the increase in the proportion of children and young people placed in foster care reflects both the principle that children are best brought up in families (and a foster family is the best substitute for a birth family if no kinship placement is available) and a widening understanding of the diverse needs of children who can be successfully placed in these settings. Whereas 20 years ago young offenders and young people with extensive behavioural problems or profound disabilities were not generally considered suitable for foster care, a number of specialist foster programmes have been shown to be relatively effective in meeting their needs (Chamberlain and Reid 1998).

Extending the population for whom foster care is considered a viable option, together with the concomitant increase in the number of specialist fostering schemes, has had a major impact on the emerging debate concerning the professionalization of the fostering service as a whole (Kirton 2007). Foster carers recruited to work on specialist schemes are trained to offer a highly skilled service; a number of them have formal qualifications in teaching or psychology. They have spearheaded initiatives to develop foster care into a professional service with appropriate working conditions, holiday entitlement and adequate levels of remuneration.

The study discussed in this chapter illustrates how some of the issues raised by the implementation of the legislation and the policies and practice which grew up around it has impacted on the lives of very young children in care and accommodation. In particular it demonstrates some of the unforeseen consequences of policies designed to promote the wellbeing of children in care or accommodation and shows how changes in the nature and expectations of foster care, although undoubtedly beneficial for the majority, can have their downside, particularly in relation to infants who cannot swiftly return home to their birth families.

The study

The study derived from a wider longitudinal research project concerning 242 children who entered the care of six English local authorities between 1 April 1996 and 31 March 1997 and were still looked after on 1 April 1998. The needs, experiences and outcomes of children in this wider study were tracked for at least 3.5 years after entry to care (see Darker, Ward and Caulfield 2008; Sempik, Ward and Darker 2008; Skuse and Ward 2003; Ward 2009). Initial analysis of this dataset showed that by far the largest age group of this long stay sample were infants who had entered care before their first birthday; there was also evidence that these babies had experienced substantial instability while looked after; indeed no significant differences were found in the numbers of placements experienced by the 0–4 and 5–9 age groups (see Ward 2009). Concerns about the care experiences of these very young children led to a further in-depth study of the decision-making process that had influenced their life pathways.

The subset consists of a sample of 42 babies who were all looked after for at least a year. A comprehensive case file search was conducted to trace chronologically all changes of primary carer, household composition and domicile experienced by each child from birth until they ceased to be looked after (or until 1 April 2002, when they were aged 5–6, if they were still in care). Changes experienced before, during and after care were all included in the chronology. Changes of care plan and legal status were also recorded, as were reasons for key decisions and causes of delay. Case file data were supplemented by semi-structured interviews held with social workers, team leaders, family placement workers, children's guardians and, where possible, parents and carers. Further interviews focusing on wider resource, practice and policy issues were conducted with a local authority solicitor, the chief clerk of the family proceedings court and the assistant director of children and families services in each authority. In total 122 interviews were conducted; however, because of the difficulties in gaining access, only 12 of these were with parents or current carers.

Findings[1]

The sample was composed of an equal proportion of boys (21) and girls (21); the majority (31; 74%) were white British or Irish; there was

---

1   Comprehensive findings from this study can be found in Ward, Munro and Dearden, 2006

one black Caribbean child and ten were of mixed heritage. As we know, all were placed in care or accommodation before their first birthdays; in fact 34 (81%) had been admitted before they were six months old. Five years after they had been admitted, when the study ended, just over half of the sample (23; 55%) had been adopted; a third (14; 33%) had returned to their birth parents, two had been placed with other relatives on permanent orders (residence orders) and three were still looked after by the local authorities. The average time from separation to permanence was 29 months for those children who were placed for adoption and 34 months for those who were reunited with their birth families.

Given the underlying principle that children are best looked after by their own families, we would expect that such very young children would be unlikely to be admitted or stay long in care unless they came from families with extensive needs and this proved to be the case. They came from families with a high incidence of alcohol and drug related problems, mental ill health, domestic violence and homelessness; at least 17 mothers and three fathers had had some involvement with children's social care during their own childhoods and 14 had themselves had experience of care. Almost all these very young children (37; 88%) had been placed on the child protection register, either at birth because they were deemed to be at risk, or before their first birthday because they had been abused or neglected. Abuse or neglect was the primary reason for entry to care for three quarters of the sample (31; 74%); while parental illness or addiction was the second most frequent reason.

A high proportion of the children (15; 36%) had health problems. In at least eight cases these were attributable to abuse: four babies suffered from drug withdrawal symptoms at birth, two had foetal alcohol syndrome and two had complex needs following non-accidental head injuries. Such problems are likely to have meant that many of these young children were difficult to care for in infancy – thereby placing additional demands on those who looked after them.

There is a tendency to associate frequent and unsettling changes of domicile and primary carer with local authority care, yet many of these very young children had had very similar experiences in the few months before they became looked after. Before they entered care nearly half (18; 46%) of the sample had had at least two primary carers and five (12%) had had four or more. While 12 (31%) had had one domicile,

11 (28%) had had four or more. Changes of domicile and carer had often been accompanied by changes of household as new partners and children joined or left the family unit. It was evident that many of the children had had few opportunities to develop those attachments that are known to be a prerequisite to the formation of secure and lasting relationships in later life (see for instance Bowlby 1979; Zeanah and Emde 1994).

Their experience of abuse, their health problems and the instability of their first few months are likely to have meant that these very young children required a high standard of stable, compensatory care. Above all they needed opportunities to develop a sense of security and attachment to a primary care giver who could offer them stability. However the data suggest that, while they were looked after by local authorities, the life pathways of a substantial proportion of the sample served to compound rather than to mitigate their earlier experiences of unpredictability and transience.

TABLE 7.1 Placement types (N=141)

	FREQUENCY	%	CUMULATIVE %
Placement with parent(s)	17	12.1	12.1
Relatives as foster carers	13	9.2	21.3
Foster care with others	77	54.6	75.9
Prospective adoptive placement	20	14.2	90.1
Mother and baby unit/family assessment centre	9	6.4	96.5
Hospital admission	5	3.5	100.0
Total	141	100.0	

During the course of their care episodes the sample experienced 141 placements. As Table 7.1 shows, the vast majority (90%) were in family settings, mostly with unrelated foster carers (55%); a smaller proportion were with kinship carers (9%), own parents (12%) and prospective adopters (14%). The few placements in institutional settings were either admissions to hospital (4%) or placements in mother and baby homes or assessment centres (6%). The latter were intended to assess parenting capacity and the child was accompanied by one or both parents.

There were variations in the length of different placement types. Many were very short: the mean length of placements with unrelated foster carers was seven months; however 30 (39%) of these lasted for one month or less.[2] In comparison, the mean length of placements with parents (14 months)[3] and relatives and friends (16 months)[4] was significantly longer.

The short length of placement reflected the frequency with which children moved around the care system. Table 7.2 shows the number of placements the children experienced during the period that they were looked after. Only five (12%) of these babies stayed in the same placement throughout their care episode; 18 (43%) had two or three and 19 (45%) had four or more.

The definition of a placement is that used at the time in the government guidance: a period of seven days or more. Very temporary placements of less than seven days are not included in this table; however data collected from the children's case files showed that many of them experienced additional short term moves in and out of hospital or to stay for a few nights with respite carers while foster carers were temporarily unavailable; for such very young children these would have added to their experience and understanding of impermanence (see Ward, Munro and Dearden 2006, pp.46–47).

TABLE 7.2 Total number of placements per child

NUMBER OF PLACEMENTS	NUMBER OF CHILDREN	%	CUMULATIVE %
1	5	11.9	11.9
2	10	23.8	35.7
3	8	19.0	54.8
4	9	21.4	76.2
5	3	7.1	83.3
6	6	14.3	97.6
Total	42	100.0	

It is important to ask why such very young children who clearly needed to become attached to parents or parent substitutes who were able to provide them with a safe, stable and loving environment throughout their childhood had so few opportunities to do so while they were

2   Median: 4 months; standard deviation: 9.03.

3   Median: 10 months; standard deviation: 13.95.

4   Median:13 months; standard deviation: 13.28.

looked after by local authorities. It was possible to establish both from the case files and through interviews with social workers the reasons for 100 of the 101 changes of placement they experienced (see Table 7.3).

TABLE 7.3 Reasons for placement changes for 42 children while looked after[5]

REASON FOR CHANGE	PERCENTAGE OF MOVES (N=100)
Planned transitions	
Planned move to new placement	59
Foster carers need relief	8
Child ceased to be looked after	8
Unplanned transitions	
Placement no longer available	4
Residential assessment broke down	5
Placement with parent broke down	7
Placement with relatives/friends broke down	5
Placement with local authority foster carers broke down	4
Not know	1
Total	**100**

As Table 7.3 shows, the vast majority of moves were planned transitions, undertaken as an integral part of the case management process. A number of these were very positive *purposive* moves, undertaken to progress a child towards permanence; moves into prospective adoptive placements or placements with birth parents under the protection of a care order, with the aim of permanent reunification, come into this category. However many of these planned transitions were resource or practice led moves from short term to long term placements, or from ill-matched foster carers to those who shared the children's race, religion and culture, or who could offer accommodation to a whole sibling group and therefore reunite a family that had initially been split (see also Munro and Hardy 2006). While many of these moves were in a positive direction, a number might have been avoided with better resources or more realistic forward planning. If, as appears evident, stability is of fundamental importance to such very young children, then any move has its negative side. Very small children who have had

---

5   Reprinted from Ward, H., Munro, E. and Dearden, C. (2006)

excessive experience of instability and transience may reach a point where it is more important to promote their chances of developing stable attachments than to ensure that they are placed with well matched carers who can meet their other needs.

Twenty-one (21%) placements disrupted; this is the same per centage of disruptions at the carer's request for looked after children of all ages noted in the wider study from which this sample was drawn (see Ward 2009),[6] and it is surprising that the rate was so high. Placements with parents, either in their own homes or in a residential assessment setting, broke down if it became evident that the baby's needs were not being met, or that the parent could not cope. A number of these placements had been ordered by the courts because evidence of neglect or abuse had not been considered sufficient; social workers had often anticipated a negative outcome and the breakdown provided the necessary proof to free the child for adoption. These experiences are undoubtedly damaging for both parent and child and demonstrate the need for the collection of sound evidence at an early stage of case management when abuse or neglect are suspected. Nine placements with relatives, friends and local authority foster carers disrupted and four more were withdrawn when the carer decided they could no longer continue to foster. Some of these placements ended when it became apparent that the child would need a long-term placement; others ended because of tensions between carers and birth families. Both the excessive number of planned moves and the high rate of disruptions were indicative of some of the unintended consequences for foster care of implementing the Children Act 1989.

Implications for policy and practice

Although over half the children were eventually adopted, the initial care plans demonstrated an expectation that the majority would be swiftly reunited with their birth families. This is in line with the Children Act 1989 principles and indeed 25 per cent of children who enter the English care system return home within eight weeks. However the infants in this study were not part of that group. They came from families with high levels of need to whom they could not swiftly return. Because this was not understood at the point of entry to care, they tended to be

---

6   The datasets are not strictly comparable as the babies were followed for 24 months longer than the wider sample.

found short term temporary placements. When it later became apparent that they could not return home, a subsequent, longer term placement had to be found. For some children this happened more than once as attempts were made to unite them with siblings who were also looked after or to match them with carers better suited to their needs than those who had originally been found. Both the wider study from which the sub-sample of babies was drawn and another major study of the English care system have found that children tend to move from one placement to another for at least the first two years of a care episode (see Sinclair *et al.* 2007; Ward 2009). The frequent moves from one placement to another had a particularly adverse impact on these young children's chances of developing secure attachments to adults capable of responding to their needs, especially in light of their early adverse experiences. In the words of one adoptive parent:

> I would like to say that…children do not bounce. Yes, they are resilient, but if you move a child several times before its adoption then the adoptive parents are going to have a very long struggle to get them to realise that this is where they are for good, this is where you're going to stay. (Munro and Ward 2008, p.230)

Although three foster carers succeeded in adopting babies who had been placed with them, others were discouraged from doing so. These carers were not thought to be suitable as adoptive parents, although by the time the question arose they had looked after the babies for at least a year and attachments had been formed. The expectation, however, that the placement would not be for long had meant that children had been placed with carers who were considered too old to look after them permanently; there were also indications that some foster carers did not meet a more rigorous standard of care expected of adoptive parents, even though by then they had had long term care of the children.

Other cases demonstrated some of the difficulties inherent in the expectation that carers would work in partnership with birth parents. Parents were encouraged to spend substantial amounts of time with these very young children in order to facilitate opportunities for bonding with them in a safe setting. However extensive contact within the foster carer's home placed a considerable burden on their own family and could become intolerable, particularly if more than one young child were placed with the same carer. Where contact took place outside the carer's home other problems arose as carers were expected to spend considerable time transporting children to and from the venue. The tensions that arose over contact could lead to the disruption of a placement. Other placements disrupted when foster carers found they had inadequate support in dealing with very demanding or aggressive parents.

Foster carers had an exceptionally difficult role to perform: on the one hand they had to nurture the children and help them to form attachments, while on the other hand they had to distance themselves in order to accept that their own relationship with the child would probably be short term and that one of their key tasks was to promote the child's bond with the birth parent. Attempts to acknowledge their more professional role were not necessarily beneficial for the children concerned. For instance, some foster carers did not expect to take these children on their family holidays and so respite placements had to be found. These entailed yet another move for children whose lives had been characterized by transience. Increased professionalization of foster carers, with better regulated working conditions, including formal holiday entitlement, is likely to reinforce this trend. And yet in many respects, professionalization should benefit the children concerned as it should lead to higher standards of foster care and reduce the temptation to exploit their good will. This is one of the 'wicked issues' to which Kirton (2007) refers in an important paper which explores some of the 'vital elements to fostering that may be lost if professionalization is implemented in a way that encourages calculative approaches to care' (p.12).

Conclusion

The study discussed above is one of several funded by the UK government in order to gather evidence to underpin future policy development. Policy is often constructed with little regard to research evidence, but in this area findings from a number of studies have informed developments, particularly in the area of adoption (see for instance Parker 1999; Selwyn and Sturgess 2001; Selwyn *et al.* 2006; Ward 2009).

Since this study was completed, the Adoption and Children Act 2002 has been introduced, with the intention of facilitating adoption, improving the position of foster carers and speeding up the process. The Children and Yong Person's Act 2008 is designed to improve placement stability and strengthen the planning and review process when children become looked after; revised regulations and guidance are currently being developed. There are also initiatives to improve social work training and the quality of care offered to looked after children. Two major research initiatives into issues concerning adoption (Thomas, forthcoming) and safeguarding children (Davies and Ward forthcoming) should extend the evidence base further. However many of the findings from this study raise ethical issues that need to be more openly debated. These include questions about our societal expectations of foster carers and their appropriate relationship with birth parents, children and professionals; our expectations of parents and their relationships with children whom they have abused; and finally the most fundamental question, what we really mean when we claim that the welfare of the child should be our paramount consideration.

References

Bowlby, J. (1979) *The Making and Breaking of Affectional Bonds.* New York NY: Routledge.

Chamberlain, P. and Reid, J. (1998) 'Comparison of two community alternatives to incarceration for chronic juvenile offenders.' *Journal of Consulting and Clinical Psychology 66*, 4, 624–633.

Darker, I. Ward, H. and Caulfield, L. (2008) 'An analysis of offending by young people looked after by local authorities.' *Youth Justice 8,* 2, 138–148.

Davies, C. and Ward, H. (forthcoming) *Overview of Research Initiative on Safeguarding Children.* London: Jessica Kingsley Publishers.

Department for Children, Schools and Families (2008) *Children Looked After in England Including Adoption and Care Leaving, Year Ending 31 March 2008.* London: DCSF.

Department of Health (1989) *An Introduction to the Children Act 1989.* London: HMSO

Department of Health (2000) *Prime Minister's Review of Adoption; Report from the Performance and Innovation Unit.* London: Department of Health.

House of Commons Children, Schools and Families Committee (2009) *Looked After Children: Third Report of Session 2008–9,* HC111-1. London: The Stationery Office.

K. and T. v. Finland (Appn no 25702/94) ECHR 16 July 2001; [2001] 2FLR 673.

Kirton, D. (2007) 'Step forward? Step back? The professionalization of fostering.' *Social Work and Social Sciences Review 13,* 1, 6–24.

McCulloch, A. (2008) 'Baby P. Campaign: The Sun at its Worst.' Available from www.communitycare.co.uk/blogs/social-care-experts-blog/2008/11, accessed on 7 August 2009.

Munro, E.R. and Hardy, A. (2006) *Placement Stability: A Review of the Literature. Report to the Department for Education and Skills.* Loughborough: CCFR.

Munro, E.R. and Ward, H. (2008) Balancing parents and very young children's rights in care proceeding: decision-making in the context of the Human Rights Act 1998. *Child and Family Social Work, 13,* 2, 227–234.

Parker, R. (1999) *Adoption Now: Messages from Research.* London: The Stationery Office.

Poirier, M.-A. Chamberland, C. and Ward, H. (2006) 'Les interactions entre les adultes qui prennent soin d'un enfant placé en famille d'acceuil: Une étude sur les pratiques quotidiennes de collaboration.' *La revue Internationale de l'éducation Familiale: Recherches et Interventions 20,* 51–86.

Rowlands, J. and Statham, J. (2009) 'Numbers of children looked after in England: a historical analysis.' *Child and Family Social Work 14,* 79–89.

R (on the application of L. and others) v. Manchester City Council; R (on the application of R. and another v. Same [2001] EWHC Admin 707, CO/965/2001.

Selwyn, J. and Sturgess, W. (2001) *International Overview of Adoption: Policy and Practice.* Bristol: School for Policy Studies.

Selwyn, J. Sturgess, W. Quinton, D. and Baxter, C. (2006) *Costs and Outcomes of Non-Infant Adoptions.* London: BAAF.

Sempik, J. Ward, H. and Darker, I. (2008) 'Emotional and behavioural difficulties of children and young people at entry to care.' *Clinical Child Psychology and Psychiatry 13*, 2, 221–233.

Sinclair, I. Baker, C. Lee, J. and Gibbs, I. (2007) *The Pursuit of Permanence: A Study of the English Care System.* London: Jessica Kingsley Publishers.

Skuse, T. and Ward, H. (2003) *Outcomes for Looked After Children: Children's Views of Care and Accommodation. Interim Report to the Department of Health.* Loughborough: Centre for Child and Family Research.

Social Exclusion Unit (2003) *A Better Education for Children in Care.* London: HMSO.

Thomas, C. (forthcoming) *Overview of Studies in the Adoption Research Initiative.*

Ward, H. (2009) 'Patterns of instability: moves within the care system, their reasons, contexts and consequences.' *Children and Youth Services Review.*

Ward, H. Holmes, L. and Soper, J. (2008) *Costs and Consequences of Placing Children in Care.* London: Jessica Kingsley Publishers.

Ward, H. Munro, E.R. and Dearden, C. (2006) *Babies and Young Children in Care: Life Pathways, Decision-making and Practice.* London: Jessica Kingsley Publishers.

Zeanah, C. and Emde, R. (1994) 'Attachment Disorders in Infancy and Childhood.' In M. Rutter, E. Taylor and L. Hersov (eds) *Child and Adolescent Psychiatry: Modern Approaches.* Oxford: Blackwell Scientific Publishers

Commentary by Peter Pecora on:
Very Young Children in Care in England: Issues for Foster Care

Harriet Ward and Emily R. Munro

This chapter illustrates how no multi-faceted policy that is as far-reaching as the Children Act of 1989 governing child welfare practice in England and Wales can be universally positive for all children in all kinds of circumstances. Informed and experienced practitioners, policymakers and researchers will find themselves in agreement with many of the practice principles outlined in the Act – no matter what country one dwells on. The Act correctly emphasizes key principles such as family preservation whenever possible, child placement in the least restrictive setting and foster parent collaboration with birth parents and workers. And yet there are issues that have yet to be resolved.

One of the major contributions of the chapter is the focus on a group of children who make up a sizeable proportion of those placed in many countries – infants. This is an especially vulnerable population who, according to the study data, are experiencing living situation instability at a crucial growth period in their lives (Centre on the Developing Child at Harvard University 2007; Shonkoff and Phillips 2000). Depending upon what country frames your experience, several findings from this study may surprise you, such as:

- Five years after placement and when the study had ended, over half the sample (23 or 55%) had been adopted.

- Only a tiny proportion of the remaining children who had not been reunified had been placed with other relatives in permanent orders (two children).

- Living situation instability preceded placement of these children. Nearly half (18 or 46%) of the children had had two or more primary carers and 12% (five) had had four or more!

- Living situation instability was also present for many infants – even after they entered care, with 43 per cent with 2–3 and 45 per cent with four or more placements – excluding moves of less than seven days.

While many of these moves were in a positive direction, some negative moves might have been avoided with better resources, better matching of child and foster parent, or more realistic planning that would take into account the fact that many of the parents were so troubled that reunification was unlikely. Some placements disrupted when foster carers found they had inadequate support in dealing with very demanding or aggressive parents. These facts and dynamics underscore the need to consider carefully how some aspects of the Children Act of 1989 need to be re-considered and the needs of certain children planned for differently. The authors raise concerns that all child welfare systems today should be carefully examining and discussing.

References

Centre on the Developing Child at Harvard University (2007) *A Science-Based Framework for Early Childhood Policy: Using Evidence to Improve Outcomes in Learning, Behaviour and Health for Vulnerable Children.* Boston, MA: Author. Available from www.developingchild.harvard.edu, accessed on 26 September 2007

Shonkoff, J. and Phillips, D. (2000) *From Neurons to Neighbourhoods: The Science of Early Childhood Development.* Washington, DC: National Research Council and Institute of Medicine.

CHAPTER 8

Fostering Adolescents in England: What Contributes to Success?

Elaine Farmer

Introduction

Foster care is the preferred option in the UK for looking after children who cannot live with their parents. In 2007, for example, 71 per cent of children in the care system in England were living in foster families rather than in residential care (DCSF 2008). In Sinclair and colleagues' study (2007) a third of children first entered foster care aged 10 or over, whilst a quarter had entered care under the age of 11 and remained there into adolescence (Biehal 2009). Two thirds of looked after children are under a care (court) order and the majority (62%) enter care because of abuse or neglect, although problems in getting on with their families are common in adolescent admissions.

There has for some time been concern about the ability of foster care to deliver stability for children (see Berridge and Cleaver 1987; Sinclair *et al.* 2007; review of American studies by Wulczyn and Chen, Chapter 3 of this volume) or to give adequate attention to the health care and educational needs of looked after children (Berridge *et al.* 2008; Blyth and Milner 1993; review of these studies in Flynn, Paquet and Marquis, Chapter 14 of this volume.)

There has also been increasing concern about the insufficient supply of foster carers and such shortages apply in particular to placements for adolescents, minority ethnic children and sibling groups (e.g. ADSS 1997; Triseliotis *et al.* 1995; Waterhouse 1997). The independent foster care sector has developed in response to this gap by offering enhanced remuneration and support to carers (Sellick 2007). Moreover, in the US, Canada and now the UK, pressures on child care agencies and a growing commitment to family-based care, have led to increasing numbers of children being placed with the extended family (see Mc-Fadden, 1998). Recent legislation (Adoption and Children Act 2002 and Children and Young Persons Act 2008) and policy changes in England have been introduced to promote the use of kinship care, so the number of kin placements is expected to rise sharply (Farmer and Moyers 2008).

Foster care for adolescents is widely used, yet surprisingly little is known about what makes it work well (Berridge 1997). Given the consistent evidence that it is more problematic to provide foster care for adolescents than for younger children and that the disruption rate for the placements of fostered adolescents is high (e.g. Sinclair, Gibbs and Wilson 2004), the study described here was undertaken to provide information about what helps to make adolescent foster placements succeed.

This chapter considers the factors that our study found were significantly related on statistical tests to our two outcome measures: placement disruption and placement quality (see below). The use of the words *statistically significant* have been used sparingly, but should be assumed unless stated otherwise.

Methods

Our study of foster care for adolescents was funded by the Department of Health in England (Farmer, Moyers and Lipscombe 2004). The objective was to discover how far foster carers' parenting strategies and the supports they receive relate to the outcomes of placements for adolescents and what other factors relate to the stability and effectiveness of placements. Two outcomes were considered. One was whether the placement broke down within one year and 44 per cent did. The other was placement quality. Placements were considered to be of good quality or 'successful' when they were continuing well or had had a planned positive ending by the one year follow-up (47%). They were rated as poor quality when they had disrupted or were continuing but showed evidence of severe difficulty (53%).

The study utilized a one year prospective, repeated measures design and was based on a consecutive sample of young people aged 11–17 who had recently moved to a new placement. The young people were drawn from specialist and mainstream fostering schemes in 14 local authorities and two independent fostering agencies. These agencies were asked to refer young people aged 11–17 who had recently been placed in family foster care, regardless of where they previously lived, about whom reasons for admission included professional or family concern about their current behaviour and/or emotional well-being. Respite, mother and baby and kin placements, , young people with severe learning difficulties and asylum seekers were not included in the sample.

This yielded a sample of 68 young people. Seven parents (3% of referrals), nine young people (4%), 16 foster carers (8%) and two social workers refused consent. We do not know how many new placements that met our criteria were not referred but those referred who did not participate were not statistically different from those who did, in terms of age, gender or ethnicity. There did not therefore appear to be any major response bias.

Data for this study were collected through a review of the young people's case files, semi-structured interviews with the young people, their foster carers and social workers and using standardized measures. Interviews were conducted three months after the start of placement and again after nine months, or at the point of disruption if this occurred earlier. After appropriate permissions had been obtained, initial contact with the foster carers and young people was made by a letter from the researchers, requesting their participation.

Foster carers were asked at both interviews to complete the 28-item version of the General Health Questionnaire (GHQ) (Goldberg and Hillier 1979) as a measure of their psychosocial functioning and the strain in their lives. Both the foster carers and the young people also filled in the Strengths and Difficulties Questionnaire at both time points (Goodman 1994, 1997) which measured the young people's behaviour and adjustment. Significance was assessed using Chi-square or Fisher's exact test (two-tailed) and relationships were considered to be statistically significant where $p<0.05$.

The strength of this research methodology was in being able to follow a sample of fostered young people prospectively over time and in depth. The principal limitation was in the sample size and the study could not assess whether services helped reduce replacement.

The sample

The young people

Of the 68 young people, 51 per cent were girls and 49 per cent boys, the majority were aged 13–15 years old and 18 per cent were from minority ethnic backgrounds. Most (71%) were accommodated voluntarily and the remainder were on care or supervision (court) orders.

The foster carers

The majority (69%) of foster carers in the sample were couples. Over half (53%) of the primary carers were 41–50 years old and most (93%) were white British. Nearly a quarter (24%) had been fostering for 5–10 years, 21 per cent for 10–15 years and 18 per cent for 15 years or more, so they were an experienced group. Sixty-two per cent of the carers were part of specialist teenage fostering schemes, which were managed separately from mainstream fostering and provided somewhat better support but did not provide treatment foster care.

An analysis of the factors which were significantly related to the two outcome measures follows.

Formal support services

Pre-placement

Placements disrupted more often when social workers had not been open with carers about the extent of the young people's difficulties and had provided inadequate information about school attendance and plans for their education and long-term care. Foster carers were able to deal with some very difficult behaviour when the young people had been no more difficult than they had expected, that is they knew what they were taking on, the child's problems had not been downplayed and, in addition, social workers responded to their requests for assistance.

The young people too wanted more information about the foster families before they moved in with them. Most had not felt sufficiently involved in pre-placement decisions and if an introductory visit was not possible telephone contact with the carers and/or information in booklet form about the foster family might have been helpful.

Placements were also more likely to disrupt if the carers' gender preference had been overridden. These preferences were generally based on well-founded concerns about the effect, for example, of placing a teenage girl in a household of boys. An unexpected finding was that placing young people of a similar age to those in the foster family did not produce particular difficulties and could sometimes be helpful. However, when the foster carers had a birth child between two and five years younger than the fostered young person, placements were at increased risk of disruption, probably because these younger children were more vulnerable to being affected by high risk or violent behaviour by the fostered adolescents.

During the placement

Four elements of the formal support system which were available to all the foster carers were investigated in depth. These were the family placement worker, foster carer groups which met regularly usually facilitated by a social worker, the child's social worker and the out of hours service, which was generally emergency duty team cover for all comers but was more rarely provided by family placement workers. The first two specialist services were broadly effective, the other two generic ones much less so. Family placement workers provided consistent high quality support. The foster carer groups were important for half the carers and might have had higher attendance if child-sitting had been provided and the carers allowed 'to have a moan'. However, foster care was rarely prioritized by busy children's social workers or general out of hours services and the deficits in these parts of the formal support system often led to carers feeling poorly supported *overall*.

We mapped in detail each carer's satisfaction with each type of service against their ratings of overall support from the local authority. It emerged that foster carers experienced local authority support rather like a net: it was only as strong as its weakest point. All the four formal support services noted above needed to be in place if foster carers were to feel adequately supported. If one part was weak, their overall ratings were low, even when other supports were in place. For example, a carer who was very satisfied with her family placement worker, group and the child's social worker was very dissatisfied with the out of hours service and rated herself as overall 'not well supported'.

The weakest point in the local authority support 'net' was the service offered by the young people's social workers. The considerable difficulties in contacting them (experienced by 70% of carers) and low levels of visiting by some (21% saw the child and 37% the carers less often than monthly) were significantly related to carers feeling under strain and poorly supported. Inability to contact social workers left a range of pressing issues related to the young people and their families unresolved. Foster carers were particularly upset when they thought that the child needed specialist help and it was not forthcoming. A number of findings in the study showed that lack of support from the young people's social workers was related to poorer placement outcomes, whilst there were significantly more successful placements when social work support was good.

Over a third of the young people were seeing a specialist for counselling and carers felt better supported when this was the case. Over and above this, there were more successful placements when young people reported that they were receiving such assistance. Foster carers' requests for such help should always be taken seriously.

Young people's social workers visited the foster carers with good social and local professional support more often than those with poorer support networks (see also Quinton 2004). If services are to match individual needs better, family placement workers and social workers need to find out more about the support foster carers receive from friends, relatives and local professionals to identify those who lack adequate support and consider how to reach those who do not readily request or use help.

Real partnership with foster carers had often not been achieved. Just under half (44%) of the foster carers felt that their views were seldom or never taken seriously within Children's Services and fewer than half (46%) felt that they were an important member of the team which had responsibility for the young person.

The foster carers' informal supports
Carers who received a lot of support from their own children (including adult children in the family or nearby) had fewer disruptions. Carers' younger children who lived in the family wanted their views to be listened to and their difficulties acknowledged, including the stresses of bedroom sharing, feelings of jealousy and lack of attention. More recognition is needed of the important role played by the carers' children in supporting placements. In addition, there were significantly more

successful placements when the carers were receiving substantial support from family members, their social networks or local professionals.

Education

Low confidence in schoolwork was significantly related to disruption and low confidence in social relationships at school were linked to low success rates in placements. In addition, young people with particular skills and interests, such as sporting ability or involvement in a drama group (developed at school or at home), had an increased chance of having a successful placement.

Young people's behaviour and characteristics

Young people with histories of aggressive behaviour or with no attachment to an adult before the placement (for example because of failed adoption or long-term care) experienced increased levels of disruption. Hyperactivity (Quinton *et al.* 1998) and conduct problems in the placement also predicted poor outcomes. Local authorities need to consider organising more extensive packages of support for such placements if they are to survive. Such approaches might include for example, shared care between two foster families (where children regularly receive assistance or time out in the other family), dedicated respite care or purchasing therapeutic counselling.

The young people's relationships with other children

Young people who by follow-up had had a negative impact on the other children in the placement had poorer outcomes on both of our outcome measures (see also for example Quinton *et al.* 1998; Triseliotis 1989). Carers were willing to deal with much difficult behaviour unless it had a detrimental effect on the other (including fostered) children in the family, at which point they would seek to end the placement. These effects were not apparent at the start of the placement but emerged as the placements went on. It is therefore very important for professionals to monitor the impact of fostered adolescents on other children in the family over the course of the placement, so that assistance can be provided when problems arise, either by modifying or neutralizing the behaviour of the fostered young person or by supporting or protecting the child of the family.

Parenting skills

Strain and parenting skills

Many of the foster carers faced the arrival of a newly placed young person when they were already under significant pressure from stressful life events such as bereavements, accidents, illness or recent fostering breakdowns. Two fifths (41%) had experienced four or more of these stresses in the six months before the adolescent's placement. The presence of the fostered adolescent was often itself stressful. The more strain on carers, during and *before* the placement began, the more often placements disrupted. Strain had an impact on carers' capacity to parent well: strained carers (in particular those who reported that stress had had an intense impact on them) responded less sensitively to the young people, disliked them more often and showed them less warmth (Farmer, Lipscombe and Moyers 2005).

These findings suggest that family placement workers should review the stresses on carers *before* each placement is made, as well as during its course, in order to match those who are under a great deal of strain (and who have reported that it is having a strong impact on them) with less demanding adolescents and/or to offer them enhanced levels of support or a paid break.

The contribution of parenting skills to outcomes

At the time of the first interviews three parenting approaches were significantly related to later placement outcomes (Lipscombe, Farmer and Moyers 2003; Lipscombe, Moyes and Farmer 2004). There were fewer disruptions when the foster carers had been able to respond to the young person's 'emotional age' when it was younger than their chronological age (see also Farmer and Pollock 1998). Such responsiveness indicates understanding that many looked after young people function emotionally at a level well below their chronological age and need regular opportunities for play and nurture appropriate to a much younger child to meet these unmet needs.

There were also fewer disruptions when the young people had been able to talk about their past histories with their carers, implying time made to share difficult issues and carer capacity to hear painful past events. There were also significantly more successful placements when the carers monitored the activities of the young people outside the house (see also Lowe, Hellett and Stace 2007). This required skill and an extended view of the foster carer role and was important for those young people who were unable to keep themselves safe or out of trouble when away from the foster family (Farmer and Pollock 1998).

The particular difficulties of single carers

One third of the foster carers were looking after the adolescents alone and they were more disadvantaged than couple carers: they received less training, lower levels of local authority services and less support from local professionals even though they had weaker social support networks. For single carers support from their friends was therefore particularly important. In addition, significantly fewer of the single carers took active steps to facilitate the young people's education or attended the foster carer groups, principally because of the lack of childminding, pressure on their time if they worked and a feeling that the groups were not serving their needs. Increased understanding of the needs of single carers and some supplementary services might well benefit lone foster carers and the young people they look after.

Contact

Almost two thirds of the young people had contact with someone which the researchers judged was detrimental to them (Sinclair 2005) and difficulties with contact were significantly related to higher disruption rates (Moyers, Farmer and Lipscombe 2006). The main problems were repeated rejection from parents (e.g. not speaking to young people for whole weekends), unreliability in visiting and exposure to risk (including physical and sexual abuse by family members). As a result, the young people often returned from contact visits extremely upset and acted out their distress in disturbed behaviour. Over the one year follow-up poor quality contact remained poor for many young people (57%).

The young people who had contact with their maternal grandparents had more successful placements because grandparents often ensured that contact with other relatives occurred and provided enriching relationships themselves. Overall, the widespread idea that adolescents can manage their own contact was not borne out in the study. More work with parents might be useful to help them to negotiate meaningful contact with their children, whilst the involvement of other family members such as grandparents, who can offer a positive relationship, is to be encouraged. There is also a real need for work with young people to help them to integrate the reality of their parents' actions in ways which allow them to move on and make use of other more sustaining relationships. There is a need for further research on contact for adolescents and to test out findings about the impact of placing adolescents close in age to other children in the foster family.

Foster carers' previous work experience and training

The length of time carers had previously spent fostering did not affect outcomes but those who had other relevant work experience such as nursing, teaching or social work had significantly more successful placements. This is likely to be because they were able to transfer their skills, knowledge and training from work to the foster carer role. Two types of training also related to greater success with placements: training in dealing with birth parents and in 'letting children go'. These may have been chance findings or having attended such training might relate to a greater depth of fostering experience. Two fifths of the foster carers said that the young person's contact with birth family members had had a negative effect on them and together these findings suggest that dealing with birth parents and understanding transitions for children are important areas for training. In addition, the findings mentioned earlier suggest that placement outcomes are likely to be improved if training includes helping foster carers to respond to young people's emotional and developmental age, talking to young people about the past and about difficulties in their relationships with their families and monitoring adolescents' activities outside the home.

Clarification of responsibility for key tasks

There were gaps in the practice of this sample of experienced foster carers that were likely to have an impact on the young people's future life chances. Training and greater clarification of who is responsible for these tasks is important. Two fifths of the carers did not discuss sexual health or sexuality with the young people even though many looked after young people are poorly informed about normal sexual development, sexual health and contraception. Half of the foster carers had little involvement with schools, including 20 who reported having no contact with the young people's school teachers. Two fifths of the carers showed little encouragement for the young people to develop age-appropriate life skills that would prepare them for leaving care and later life, such as budgeting, helping with cooking meals and completing forms. Moreover, foster carers were significantly less sensitive to the needs and anxieties of girls than boys. The interviews revealed some girls whose real unhappiness about their placements were not apparent to their foster carers.

Implications for policy and practice

In conclusion, much greater emphasis is needed on giving foster carers full and honest information about young people before placement and training for foster carers should include a focus on the key parenting skills from the study and on managing contact. Clarification of responsibility for key tasks such as sex education, educational involvement and life skills is also needed. More proactive work is required in relation to contact with family members, especially in helping young people cope with continuing parental rejection and in encouraging the involvement of relatives who can offer them more positive relationships.

The impact of a fostered young person on the other children in the family needs careful monitoring so that intervention can be provided when necessary. Counselling and other specialist help for fostered teenagers is important in its own right and in the maintenance of placements. Foster carers' requests for such help should always be taken seriously.

Substantial packages of support are needed for carers who take young people who are hyperactive or have serious conduct problems. Moreover, foster carers who are already under a great deal of strain before placement require less challenging adolescents, much increased support or a break between placements. Foster carer strain is reduced by regular and reliable availability of the young person's social worker, continuity of social work help and taking carers' views seriously.

The study suggests that improved support is related to less foster carer strain and that the foster carers with substantial social networks and local professional support at follow-up offered more warmth to young people, met their needs more fully, were more satisfied with the placements and the young people they fostered showed improved well-being. It is clearly important to maintain and improve the support given to foster carers to limit their feelings of strain, thereby enhancing their ability to parent the young people in their care and helping to maintain placements.

References

Association of Directors of Social Services (ADSS) (1997) *The Foster Care Market: A National Perspective.* Ipswich: Suffolk Social Services.

Berridge, D. (1997) *Foster Care: A Research Review.* London: The Stationery Office.

Berridge, D. and Cleaver, H. (1987) *Foster Home Breakdown.* Oxford: Basil Blackwell.

Berridge, D. Dance, C. Beecham, J. and Field, S. (2008) *Educating Difficult Adolescents: Effective Education for Children in Public Care or with Emotional and Behavioural Difficulties.* London: Jessica Kingsley Publishers.

Biehal, N. (2009) 'Foster Care for Adolescents.' In G. Schofield and J. Simmonds (eds) *The Child Placement Handbook.* London: British Association for Adoption and Fostering.

Blyth, E. and Milner, J. (1993) 'Exclusion from school: a first step in exclusion from society?' *Children and Society 7,* 3, 255–268.

Department for Children, Schools and Families (DCSF) (2008) *Statistics for Education: First Release, Children looked after by Local Authorities in England, Year Ending 31 March 2008.* London, DCSF.

Farmer, E. and Pollock, S. (1998) *Sexually Abused and Abusing Children in Substitute Care.* Chichester: Wiley.

Farmer, E. and Moyers, S. (2008) *Kinship Care: Fostering Effective Family and Friends Placements,* London: Jessica Kingsley Publishers.

Farmer, E. Lipscombe, J. and Moyers, S. (2005) 'Foster carer strain and its impact on parenting and placement outcomes for adolescents.' *British Journal of Social Work 35,* 2, 237–253.

Farmer, E. Moyers, S. and Lipscombe, J. (2004) *Fostering Adolescents.* London: Jessica Kingsley Publishers.

Goldberg, D.P. and Hillier, V.F. (1979) 'A scaled version of the General Health Questionnaire.' *Psychological Medicine 9,* 139–145.

Goodman, R. (1994) 'A modified version of the Rutter Parent Questionnaire including extra items on children's strengths – a research note.' *Journal of Child Psychology and Psychiatry 35,* 8, 1483–1494.

Goodman, R. (1997) 'The Strength and Difficulties Questionnaire: a research note.' *Journal of Child Psychology and Psychiatry 38,* 581–586.

Lipscombe, J. Farmer, E. and Moyers, S. (2003) 'Parenting fostered adolescents: skills and strategies' *Child and Family Social Work 8,* 4, 243–255.

Lipscombe, J, Moyers, S and Farmer, E. (2004) 'What changes in "parenting" approaches occur over the course of adolescent foster care placements.' *Child and Family Social Work 9,* 347–357.

Lowe, K. Hellett, J. and Stace, S. (2007) *Teenagers in Foster Care: Promoting Positive Relationships, A Training Course.* Brighton: Trust for the Study of Adolescents.

McFadden, E.J. (1998) 'Kinship care in the United States.' *Adoption and Fostering 22,* 3, 7–15.

Moyers, S. Farmer, E. and Lipscombe, J. (2006) 'Contact with family members and its impact on adolescents and their foster placements.' *British Journal of Social Work 36,* 4, 541–559.

Quinton, D. (2004) *Supporting Parents: Messages from Research.* London: Jessica Kingsley Publishers.

Quinton, D. Rushton, A. Dance, C. and Mayes, D. (1998) *Joining New Families: A Study of Adoption and Fostering in Middle Childhood.* Chichester: Wiley.

Sellick, C. (2007) 'Towards a mixed economy of foster care provision.' *Social Work and Social Sciences Review 13*, 1, 25–40.

Sinclair, I. (2005) *Fostering Now: Messages from Research.* London: Jessica Kingsley Publishers.

Sinclair, I. Gibbs, I. and Wilson, K. (2004) *Foster Placements. Why They Succeed and Why They Fail.* London: Jessica Kingsley Publishers.

Sinclair, I. Baker, C. Lee, J. and Gibbs, I. (2007) *The Pursuit of Permanence: A Study of the English Care System.* London: Jessica Kingsley Publishers.

Triseliotis, J. (1989) 'Foster care outcomes: a review of key research findings.' *Adoption and Fostering 13*, 3, 5–17.

Triseliotis, J. Borland, M. Hill M. and Lambert, L. (1995) *Teenagers and the Social Work Services.* London: HMSO.

Waterhouse, S. (1997) *The Organisation of Fostering Services: A Study of the Arrangements for Delivery of Fostering Services in England.* London: National Foster Care Association.

Commentary by Robbie Gilligan on:
Fostering Adolescents in England:
What Contributes to Success?

Elaine Farmer

As Kelly (2000) has observed, foster care is still the 'workhorse' of the care system serving large numbers of children, whatever the debates about its merits. This paper by Farmer flags yet again important concerns about the level of (in) stability experienced by many children and young people. Yet it is worth remembering that the difficulties that may exist seem most pronounced in the Anglo American or English language countries. There is at least some evidence of more stability in foster care in at least some continental European countries (e.g. Sweden and France), thus suggesting that issues with how foster care plays out in practice may be to do as much with cultural, organizational or other factors, as with the nature of the form of care itself.

Farmer rightly gives much attention to 'support', although it is important to acknowledge that this term hides a great deal of variation in how it is defined or manifested in reality.

The paper correctly distinguishes between formal and informal support. It pays more attention than is often the case to the nature of informal support that carers may access. In the case of formal support it highlights the role of social workers. But while there are not a lot of data presented on the precise nature of what social workers offered to carers in these cases, it is very likely that there is a lot of variation. Mainstream social workers are not delivering on some highly manualized programme. They each interpret their role in foster care according to some mix of factors related to local agency custom and practice, professional experience and training and biographical influences. Farmer's work here reminds us that foster care practice and training (for carers and social workers) needs to become much more alert and sophisticated in relation to theory and practice of formal and informal support in foster care.

The findings in relation to strain on foster carers help point up for social workers that problems do not have a hermetically sealed existence. The fact that a professional has a pre-occupation with an issue such as the needs of a young person in care and the capacity of a foster carer to respond does not mean that all other realities of the human condition have been screened out, or are somehow put on hold or frozen by special dispensation of the social worker. There is no quota of bad things happening in people's lives, however unfair that may seem. Other things, good and bad, impinge on the carer's reality, day in day out, again highlighting the importance of close connection to the carer's evolving daily reality and their need for attuned support. The study provides a valuable reminder that single carers may have additional and specific needs for support, given the findings in this study that they have weaker networks and a tendency to be given less support.

From this reader's perspective, the study highlights, in its necessarily brief coverage, negative aspects of family contact and the harm that may flow from detrimental contact. However, it does offer two important insights. First, that contact with grandparents may be especially valuable, given their potential 'hub' role in relation to supporting wider contact within the extended family, as well as their being supportive in their own right. The implication would seem to be that decisions about contact with parents should be clearly separate from decisions about contact with grandparents – and siblings. Second, the study cautions against professionals or adults off-loading onto adolescents responsibility for decisions about contact. We should certainly listen to the views of young people, but adults must take final responsibility. The paper identifies family contact as one of the key areas for attention in the training of foster carers and also notes that those carers in the study with some form of relevant professional training had significantly more successful placements. This finding may also speak to the importance of the carers' overall level of education and the related issue of the young person's educational progress which gets surprisingly little attention in this study as reported here.

References

Kelly, G. (2000) 'Outcome Studies of Foster Care.' In G. Kelly and R. Gilligan (eds) *Issues in Foster Care: Policy, Practice and Research.* London: Jessica Kingsley Publishers, pp.59–84.

CHAPTER 9

Rates of Mental, Emotional and Behavioural Disorders among Alumni of Family Foster Care in the United States: The Casey National Alumni Study

Peter J. Pecora, Catherine Roller White, Lee Ann Murdock, Kirk O'Brien, Ronald C. Kessler, Nancy Sampson and Irving Hwang

Mental health among children in the foster care system

While the rate of foster care placements in the United States has been slowly decreasing, 496,000 children were in foster care as of 30 September 2007, with about 783,000 children served during the 2007 federal fiscal year (US Department of Health and Human Services 2009). Most children are placed in foster care because of child abuse or neglect, but a sizable number are placed due to challenges created by mental, emotional or behavioural problems (Barth, Wildfire and Green 2006; James Bell Associates 2004).

The effects of child abuse and neglect on childhood, adolescent and adult outcomes are numerous and diverse. Research has shown that while many maltreated youth show resilience in the face of such adversity, others struggle with mental, emotional and behavioural disorders; risk taking behaviour; social disadvantage; and physical health problems. Child maltreatment not only has a direct impact, but an indirect one as these impacts compound each other (Kendall-Tackett and Giacomoni 2003; National Research Council and the Institute of Medicine 2009).

As a result, a substantial proportion of children placed in foster care need mental health services. A recent study of the National Survey of Child and Adolescent Well-Being (NSCAW) by Stahmer and colleagues (2005) involved a large sample of children being served by public and voluntary child welfare agencies who were under the age of six (mean age of 2.6 years). They found that scores for cognitive, behavioural and social skills for 45.7 per cent of these children would likely qualify them for early intervention services. More specifically, based on the Vineland Adaptive Behaviour Scale screener (Sparrow *et al.* 1984), 14.9% of preschoolers were significantly more likely to have adaptive behaviour risk than infants and toddlers (6.2%). Additionally, in terms of behavioural functioning, approximately 25–30% of the children in both age groups scored in the at-risk range, making this the most prevalent area of difficulty. The NSCAW study also found that 47.9% of the children aged 2 to 14 years with completed child welfare investigations had clinically significant emotional or behavioural problems, measured using the Child Behaviour Checklist (Achenbach 1991).

Older youth are susceptible to these issues as well. A study of 19–20 year olds conducted by Brandford and English (2004) found that 42% had indicators for depression. Meanwhile, self-reports of mental health functioning made by older adolescents in foster care have indicated rates of approximately 25% for borderline clinically significant internalizing behavioural problems and 28% for externalizing behavioural problems (Auslander *et al.* 2002).[1] This is significantly higher than children in the general population. Another study, however, compared a sample of pre-emancipation youth in foster care with a matched sample of other youth and found that youth in care did not differ from the comparison sample on measures of well-being, including depressed mood, problem behaviour and self-esteem (Farruggia *et al.* 2006).

---

1   See Pecora *et al.* (2009) for more information about this and other studies.

Selected international research

Other countries have been focusing on these areas for many years and in some cases have extensive data bases. For example, in Denmark 20 per cent of children in out-of-home care have at least one psychiatric diagnosis compared to 3 per cent of children in the country as a whole. Further, 48 per cent of the children in care scored within the abnormal range of the Strengths and Difficulties Questionnaire, compared to 5 per cent of children of the same age (Egelund and Lausten 2009).

In England, the Office of National Statistics recently completed separate surveys of the mental health needs of children in out-of-home care ('looked after children') in England, Scotland and Wales. The first national survey of the mental health of young people looked after in England has also recently been completed by the same team (Meltzer *et al.* 2003). The International Classification of Diseases and Related Health Problems 10th Edition (ICD-10) classification was used to gather data from a wider range of care providers (foster care staff, parents, residential care workers) as well as young people aged 11–17 years and teachers. The sample was comprised of 1039 looked after children drawn from 134 local authorities across England. With regard to prevalence, 45 per cent of looked after young people aged 5–17 years were assessed as having a mental disorder – including 37 per cent with clinically significant conduct disorders, 12 per cent with emotional disorders, anxiety or depression and 7 per cent were rated as hyperactive. This is in contrast to one in ten in the general population (McAuley 2009; Meltzer *et al.* 2003).

Study purpose

The purpose of the current study was to examine prevalence rates of mental, emotional, behavioural and substance abuse disorders of adult alumni of foster care. Questions addressed in this special set of analyses include:

1. What are the prevalence and recovery rates of mental, emotional, behavioural and substance abuse disorders of alumni of foster care?

2. How do those rates compare to young adults in the general population?

3. For alumni of foster care, do the rates differ by race/ethnicity?

The sample included young adults who were placed in foster family care between 1966 and 1998 in 23 field offices of a private foster care agency in the United States. The current set of analyses focused on detecting similarities or differences among mental health functioning between alumni of different racial/ethnic groups.

Method

Agency background

Casey Family Programs (Casey) is a national operating foundation that supports youth in care and foster families through direct services and system improvement efforts in child welfare. Alumni in the current study were served in long-term family foster care provided by Casey from 1966 to 1998. Casey focused on serving children referred by public child welfare agencies who were less likely to be returned home or adopted than children in public agencies. A variety of services were provided to children, including permanency planning (planned long-term foster care, guardianship, adoption, kinship care) and transition services for youth emancipating (ageing out) from foster care (Pecora *et al.* 2010).

Participants

Inclusion criteria for alumni in the study were: (a) placement in Casey foster care between 1966 and 1998; (b) placement with a Casey foster family for at least 12 consecutive months; and (c) exit from Casey foster care for at least 12 months prior to being interviewed. All alumni were served by one of 23 Casey field offices in operation in 1998 in 13 states: Arizona (Phoenix and Tucson); California (Walnut Creek/Bay Area and San Diego); Hawaii (Hilo and Honolulu); Idaho (Boise); Louisiana (Baton Rouge); Montana (Helena and Missoula); North Dakota (Bismarck and Fort Berthold); Oklahoma (Oklahoma City); Oregon (Portland); South Dakota (Pine Ridge, Rapid City and Rosebud); Texas (Austin and San Antonio); Washington (Seattle, Tacoma and Yakima); and Wyoming (Cheyenne).

The sample included 1068 adult foster care alumni served by foster families and caseworkers of Casey. Demographic characteristics by race/ethnicity for each group are shown in Table 9.1. White alumni comprised the largest racial/ethnic group (52.1%), followed by American Indian and Alaska Native alumni (18.3%). The sample was fairly evenly split by gender (52.2% male; 47.8% female). Participants' average age was 30.6 years and ranged in age from 20 to 49, with 54.8% of alumni having entered Casey foster care in the 1980s. Most participants were served in the Western United States (California, Oregon and Washington; 48.4%), though a sizeable proportion were served in the Great Plains (Montana, Wyoming, North Dakota and South Dakota; 34.9%).

TABLE 9.1 Demographic characteristics by race/ethnicity

	HISPANIC/LATINO (%)	BLACK (%)	AMERICAN INDIAN OR ALASKA NATIVE (%)	WHITE (%)	OTHER (%)	TOTAL (%)
% of study sample	11.9	13.1	18.3	52.1	4.7	100.0
Gender						
Male	50.8	48.5	56.7	52.6	45.2	52.2
Female	49.2	51.5	43.3	47.4	54.8	47.8
Age at time of interview*						
20–25	31.4	35.9	25.1	20.2	27.2	24.8
26–29	28.7	33.2	23.9	20.4	23.1	23.8
30–34	20.2	19.0	22.2	26.4	23.0	23.7
35–49	19.7	11.9	29.0	32.9	26.7	27.6
Decade entered Casey foster care*						
1966–1979	17.6	19.8	34.0	34.8	28.5	30.3
1980–1989	58.6	54.3	56.3	53.0	60.5	54.8
1990–1998	23.8	26.0	9.7	12.2	11.0	14.9
Region served in care*						
Southwest	27.7	25.8	4.4	7.9	7.2	11.9
Great Plains	21.7	8.8	49.1	41.6	11.7	34.9
Hawaii	10.9	5.0	1.5	1.2	39.6	4.7
California	8.6	18.4	6.4	6.6	0	8.0
Northwest	31.1	42.1	38.6	42.6	41.4	40.4
Sample size	127	140	195	556	50	1068

*Indicates a significant difference between racial/ethnic groups as tested by chi-square, $p < .05$.

Materials
CASE RECORDS
Case record reviews included demographics (e.g. decade entered foster care and region served in care); risk factors (e.g. reasons for foster care placement, child maltreatment); and foster care experiences (e.g. type of placement, length of time in care).

INTERVIEWS
Interview data included birth parent information (e.g. health and mental health status, substance use, employment and parenting style) and some foster family and foster care experience information (e.g. relationships with other caring adults; child maltreatment; and access to educational and mental health services).

ASSESSMENT
Mental health diagnoses for alumni of foster care were assessed during the interview using the Composite International Diagnostic Interview (CIDI). The CIDI is a non-clinician administered standardized interview developed by the National Institutes of Health Alcohol, Drug Abuse and Mental Health Administration and the World Health Organization for use in epidemiological studies and is often used for research and clinical assessment (Haro *et al.* 2006; Kessler and Üstün 2004; Wittchen, Üstün and Kessler 1999). The CIDI was used to assess lifetime and 12-month psychological disturbances and substance dependencies among alumni.

BASELINE
Comparison data for the general population were provided by the National Co-morbidity Study – Replication (Kessler *et al.* 2005; Kessler and Merikangas 2004). Data were restricted to participants ages 20 to 49 and were post-stratified on age, gender and race/ethnicity to match the National Study sample.

Procedure
The study data collection phase began in 1999 with case record reviews conducted by teams of research staff (reviews were completed for

1582 Casey alumni).[2] Interviews for the Casey National Alumni Study (Casey National Study) were conducted between 2000 and 2002. Professionally trained interviewers from the University of Michigan Survey Research Centre (SRC), unfamiliar with study hypotheses, conducted one-on-one interviews with 1068 alumni. The adjusted response rate was 73.4 per cent (adjusted for members of the sample who were inaccessible due to incarceration (3.4%), psychiatric institutionalization (0.7%), or death (3.9%)).

Weighting and analysis

Case records were available for the entire population from the Casey study. However, because some alumni were unavailable for interviews, a weight was created to account for non-responses. Variables used to create the statistical weight included age, gender, race/ethnicity, region and background variables such as reason for placement. The weighting improved the ability to generalize to the population of adults from which the sample was drawn by estimating data as if the entire sample of 1582 alumni had been interviewed.[3]

Descriptive statistics (i.e. frequencies) are presented for the past 12 months and lifetime mental health prevalence. In addition, recovery rates, which are defined as having a lifetime diagnosis of a mental health disorder, but not experiencing it in the previous 12 months, are also presented. Last, bivariate and multivariate examinations of differences in outcomes by race/ethnicity are presented. For the multivariate analyses, logistic regressions were conducted to examine differences

---

2   A random sample of 40 case records was selected for an inter-rater reliability check. Each record was reviewed by a trained staff member and a 'gold standard' reviewer, who had the most extensive case record review training and the most consistent performance. These four raters reviewed a group of case records randomly selected for verification purposes. Only variables that had acceptable inter-rater reliability (Cohen's Kappa greater than or equal to .70) were retained.

3   Specifically, propensity score matching was used to weight the data by estimating a logistic regression equation (Hosmer and Lemseshow 1989) separately that distinguished survey respondents from non-respondents (treated as a dichotomous dependent variable) based on pre-placement characteristics. The predicted probabilities generated from these equations were used to weight the data without case-level matching so that survey respondents had distributions on pre-placement characteristics comparable to the original total agency sample. This matching improved the ability to generalize to the population from which the sample was drawn by weighting the data so that differences between the samples did not bias the results (Braitman and Rosenbaum 2002) This matching procedure was completed after the first technical report was issued (Pecora *et al.* 2003) so sample size and some findings vary slightly.

in outcomes by race/ethnicity after controlling for demographics, risk factors and foster care experiences.[4]

Results

Current (past year) mental health diagnoses

Almost half (45.5%) of alumni had at least one current (past year) mental health diagnosis and 12.6 per cent had three or more current diagnoses. The most common diagnosis was Post-Traumatic Stress Disorder (PTSD) with 20.2 per cent alumni experiencing PTSD in the past year; in comparison, 4.3 per cent of the general population experienced past year PTSD. Other common past year diagnoses included Major Depressive Episode (14.6%), Modified Social Phobia (11.6%) and Panic Disorder (11.1%).

As a group, alumni of foster care experienced significantly higher rates of current (past year) mental, emotional and behavioural disorder than adults in the general population for all disorders assessed except Anorexia. Within each ethnic group, however, comparisons between the general population and alumni were mixed. White alumni had higher rates than the white general population for six of the nine disorders assessed, but there were no differences for three disorders. Alumni of other racial/ethnic backgrounds had fewer differences compared to their peers in the general population: rates of current disorders were higher among black alumni compared to blacks in the general population for four of nine disorders; among alumni of other racial/ethnic backgrounds, rates were higher for four disorders; among Hispanic/Latino alumni, rates were higher for three disorders; and among American Indian and Alaska Native alumni, rates were higher for two disorders. Relatively small sample sizes may explain some of the lack of differences in rates between alumni and the general population. There were no disorders for which the general population had higher lifetime or past year rates.

Among alumni, there was a significant difference in prevalence rates by race/ethnicity for Alcohol Dependence, controlling for demographics, risk factors and foster care experiences. American Indian and Alaska Native alumni had 3.58 times higher odds of having past year Alcohol Dependence compared to white alumni ($p<.01$).

---

4   The full list of control variables is available from the study authors.

TABLE 9.2 Current (past year) mental health diagnoses by race/ethnicity

MENTAL HEALTH DIAGNOSIS	CASEY NATIONAL STUDY						GENERAL POPULATION (NCS-R)					
	Hispanic/ Latino % (SE)	Black % (SE)	American Indian or Alaska Native % (SE)	White % (SE)	Other % (SE)	Total % (SE)	Hispanic/ Latino % (SE)	Black % (SE)	American Indian or Alaska Native % (SE)	White % (SE)	Other % (SE)	Total % (SE)
At least one diagnosis	52.0* (4.8)	39.9* (4.5)	51.0* (3.7)	44.2* (2.1)	38.2* (7.2)	45.5* (1.6)	20.8 (4.5)	20.6 (3.4)	25.1 (6.9)	26.0 (1.5)	10.3 (3.9)	23.0 (1.3)
Three or more diagnoses	12.4* (3.1)	10.4* (2.7)	15.8* (2.6)	12.4* (1.4)	9.0* (4.5)	12.6* (1.0)	2.1 (0.8)	2.8 (1.1)	5.3 (2.8)	3.4 (0.8)	0.0 (0.0)	2.9 (0.5)
Major Depressive Episode	16.3* (3.5)	11.9 (2.9)	15.3 (2.6)	14.8 (1.5)	13.7 (4.9)	14.6* (1.1)	9.6 (1.9)	11.9 (2.0)	11.3 (3.8)	11.7 (0.9)	6.0 (3.0)	11.0 (0.7)
Panic Disorder	7.4 (2.4)	13.3* (3.0)	13.2* (2.5)	10.6* (1.3)	12.7* (4.6)	11.1* (1.0)	4.5 (1.5)	5.3 (1.3)	4.7 (2.2)	3.6 (0.6)	0.0 (0.0)	4.0 (0.6)
Modified Social Phobia	11.5 (3.1)	6.9 (2.2)	11.3 (2.3)	13.3* (1.4)	5.6 (3.2)	11.6* (1.0)	10.2 (2.9)	8.2 (1.8)	10.5 (2.5)	9.6 (1.1)	4.2 (2.7)	9.2 (0.7)
Generalized Anxiety Disorder	8.1* (2.7)	7.4 (2.3)	11.4 (2.2)	8.8* (1.2)	5.6 (3.2)	8.8* (0.9)	1.3 (0.6)	5.3 (1.8)	6.9 (3.4)	4.6 (0.6)	1.3 (1.4)	3.9 (0.5)
Alcohol Dependence[†§]	3.4 (1.9)	3.5* (1.6)	8.1 (2.1)	2.2 (0.6)	7.6 (4.3)	3.8* (0.6)	2.7 (1.8)	0.3 (0.3)	4.0 (3.2)	2.9 (0.8)	1.3 (1.4)	2.3 (0.5)
Drug Dependence	2.2 (1.3)	4.6* (1.9)	5.9 (1.7)	3.3* (0.8)	0.0 (0.0)	3.6* (0.6)	0.7 (0.4)	0.2 (0.2)	3.6 (3.2)	1.0 (0.3)	0.0 (0.0)	0.8 (0.3)
Post-Traumatic Stress Disorder	17.4* (3.5)	18.7* (3.4)	23.7* (3.1)	20.6* (1.7)	15.0* (5.4)	20.2* (1.2)	2.7 (0.9)	6.6 (2.1)	7.6 (3.4)	4.2 (0.6)	0.0 (0.0)	4.3 (0.6)
Anorexia	0.0 (0.0)	0.0 (0.0)	0.0 (0.0)	0.0 (0.0)	0.0 (0.0)	0.0 (0.0)	0.0 (0.0)	0.0 (0.0)	0.0 (0.0)	0.0 (0.0)	0.0 (0.0)	0.0 (0.0)
Bulimia	0.8 (0.8)	0.7 (0.7)	3.3 (1.3)	2.9* (0.7)	4.1 (2.9)	2.5* (0.5)	0.4 (0.3)	0.5 (0.4)	0.0 (0.0)	0.4 (0.4)	0.0 (0.0)	0.4 (0.2)
Sample size	127	140	195	556	50	1068	349	353	83	1632	76	2493

* indicates a significant difference between alumni and the general population as tested by two-proportion z-test, P<.05 at the bivariate level.
§ Indicates a significant difference between racial/ethical groups as tested by overall chi-square x p<.05 at the bivariate level.
† Indicates a significant difference between racial/ethical groups as tested by overall chi-square p<.05, controlling for demographics, risk factors and foster care experiences.

Lifetime mental health diagnoses

Lifetime prevalence rates for mental, emotional or behavioural disorders were fairly high. For example, 32.4 per cent of alumni had experienced a Major Depressive Episode at some point in their lives, with a slightly lower per centage having experienced PTSD (28.2%). One in five (19.1%) alumni had experienced Modified Social Phobia, Alcohol Dependence (18.3%), Panic Disorder (18.2%) or Generalized Anxiety Disorder (17.8%).

As a group, alumni of foster care experienced significantly higher rates of lifetime disorders than the general population for all disorders assessed. For example, 18.2% of alumni had lifetime Panic Disorder, compared to 5.4% of the general population. Within each ethnic group, alumni of foster care generally had higher rates of lifetime disorders than the general population. White alumni had higher rates than the general population on all nine disorders assessed and alumni of other backgrounds had higher rates on all but two disorders (Modified Social Phobia and Anorexia) when compared to their general population counterparts. Rates of lifetime mental, emotional or behavioural disorders were higher among black alumni compared to blacks in the general population for five of nine disorders; among Hispanic/Latino alumni, rates were higher for five disorders; and among American Indian and Alaska Native alumni, rates were higher for four disorders. There were no disorders for which the general population had higher lifetime rates.

Among alumni, there were significant differences in rates by racial/ethnic group at the bivariate level for Major Depressive Episode, Panic Disorder, Alcohol Dependence and Drug Dependence. Controlling for demographics, risk factors and foster care experiences, the only disorder with significantly different rates by racial/ethnic group was Alcohol Dependence. American Indian and Alaska Native alumni had 2.23 times higher odds of having lifetime Alcohol Dependence compared to white alumni ($p<.01$).

Recovery rates for mental health diagnoses

Recovery rates, the per cent of alumni who experienced a particular disorder in their lifetime but not in the past year, varied widely by diagnosis, from only 28.2 per cent of alumni recovering from PTSD to 100 per cent of alumni recovering from Anorexia. Recovery rates among

TABLE 9.3 Lifetime mental health diagnoses by race/ethnicity

MENTAL HEALTH DIAGNOSIS	CASEY NATIONAL STUDY						GENERAL POPULATION (NCS-R)					
	Hispanic/ Latino % (SE)	Black % (SE)	American Indian or Alaska Native % (SE)	White % (SE)	Other % (SE)	Total % (SE)	Hispanic/ Latino % (SE)	Black % (SE)	American Indian or Alaska Native % (SE)	White % (SE)	Other % (SE)	Total % (SE)
Major Depressive Episode§	28.9* (4.3)	21.7 (3.6)	33.0 (3.4)	35.5* (2.0)	35.2* (7.1)	32.4* (1.4)	16.9 (2.2)	18.2 (2.2)	26.1 (5.1)	22.0 (1.0)	17.1 (6.3)	20.1 (0.9)
Panic Disorder§	11.0 (2.9)	19.6* (3.5)	23.9* (3.1)	17.2* (1.6)	21.2* (5.8)	18.2* (1.2)	6.8 (1.9)	5.6 (1.4)	6.1 (2.5)	5.2 (0.7)	0.0 (0.0)	5.4 (0.6)
Modified Social Phobia	20.4 (4.0)	11.4 (2.8)	18.4 (2.8)	21.3* (1.7)	15.7 (5.6)	19.1* (1.2)	13.3 (2.9)	12.6 (2.5)	17.6 (4.1)	14.3 (1.4)	8.4 (3.8)	13.6 (0.8)
Generalized Anxiety Disorder	12.9* (3.2)	17.3* (3.3)	19.8 (2.8)	19.0* (1.6)	11.6* (4.6)	17.8* (1.2)	3.1 (1.2)	6.9 (1.8)	11.0 (3.9)	8.7 (0.8)	2.8 (2.2)	6.9 (0.7)
Alcohol Dependence†,§	12.6* (3.3)	14.7* (3.1)	29.2* (3.4)	16.4* (1.6)	22.1* (6.3)	18.3* (1.2)	5.1 (2.1)	1.1 (0.6)	13.5 (3.7)	7.7 (0.9)	2.5 (2.0)	5.8 (0.6)
Drug Dependence§	14.3* (3.4)	12.5* (3.0)	24.2* (3.2)	16.3* (1.6)	13.8* (5.4)	16.9* (1.2)	3.6 (1.1)	1.2 (0.4)	9.5 (3.1)	5.0 (0.8)	1.3 (1.4)	3.9 (0.5)
Post-Traumatic Stress Disorder	26.5* (4.1)	24.4* (3.8)	35.2* (3.5)	27.5* (1.8)	23.0* (6.3)	28.2* (1.4)	5.0 (1.3)	8.6 (2.2)	9.8 (3.4)	8.0 (1.0)	0.0 (0.0)	7.2 (0.8)
Anorexia	0.0 (0.0)	0.0 (0.0)	1.9 (1.0)	2.4* (0.6)	3.7 (2.6)	1.8* (0.4)	0.5 (0.5)	0.0 (0.0)	0.0 (0.0)	1.0 (0.5)	0.0 (0.0)	0.6 (0.3)
Bulimia	1.9 (1.3)	1.5 (1.0)	5.2 (1.6)	5.1* (0.9)	8.0 (3.9)	4.4* (0.6)	0.7 (0.6)	1.4 (0.9)	6.7 (5.1)	1.9 (0.7)	0.0 (0.0)	1.6 (0.3)
Sample size	127	140	195	556	50	1068	349	353	83	1632	76	2493

Comparing alumni to the general population: *Indicates a significant difference between alumni and the general population as tested by two-proportion z-test, $p < .05$ at the bivariate level.

Comparing racial/ethnic groups for alumni only: †Indicates a significant difference between racial/ethnic groups as tested by overall chi-square, $p < .05$, controlling for demographics, risk factors and foster care experiences. §Indicates a significant difference between racial/ethnic groups as tested by overall chi-square, $p < .05$ at the bivariate level.

alumni (as a group) were higher than those in the general population for five of nine disorders: Major Depressive Episode, Panic Disorder, Modified Social Phobia, Generalized Anxiety Disorder and Alcohol Dependence. Recovery rates were higher for the general population than for alumni for PTSD and Bulimia. Within each ethnic group, comparisons in recovery rates between the general population and alumni were mixed. Among alumni, there were no differences in recovery rates by race/ethnicity.

Discussion

Key findings

This paper has presented recent data about the mental, emotional, behavioural and substance abuse disorders of alumni of foster care and discussed why their life circumstances place them at higher risk for these disorders. Results indicated that many alumni served by Casey were experiencing mental health challenges. On average, alumni served by Casey experienced higher rates of past year and lifetime mental health disorders and higher recovery rates than a matched sample of the general population. Further, except for higher rates among American Indian/Alaska Native alumni on alcohol dependence prevalence rates (as is found in the general population), no ethnic differences were observed among alumni.

Practice and policy recommendations

Personal comments by alumni who have been interviewed (Bernstein 2000; Nicoll *et al.* under review) underscore how foster parents and staff can be agents of healing for them. However, we would be remiss if no similar discussion regarding the therapeutic effects, or lack of effects, of foster care affect the mental health outcomes among young people over the life course. In many cases, youth are not helped by the current services approach and it is unlikely that improvements in children's mental health services will have much effect unless foster care systems also become more therapeutic.

It is important to ask *under what conditions and for which children and adolescents is foster care therapeutic or not therapeutic?* For example, a recent Australian study asserts that foster care is a failure for children with conduct disorders and that the condition of these youth in foster care systems is 'wretched' (Delfabbro and Barber 2006). What can child

TABLE 9.4 Recovery rates for mental health diagnoses by race/ethnicity

MENTAL HEALTH DIAGNOSIS	CASEY NATIONAL STUDY						GENERAL POPULATION (NCS-R)					
	Hispanic/ Latino % (SE)	Black % (SE)	American Indian or Alaska Native % (SE)	White % (SE)	Other % (SE)	Total % (SE)	Hispanic/ Latino % (SE)	Black % (SE)	American Indian or Alaska Native % (SE)	White % (SE)	Other % (SE)	Total % (SE)
Major Depressive Episode	43.5 (8.6)	45.2* (9.2)	53.7 (6.1)	58.2* (3.5)	61.2 (11.9)	54.8* (2.7)	43.0 (8.6)	34.6 (6.9)	56.9 (9.6)	47.0 (2.8)	64.7 (15.0)	45.3 (2.3)
Panic Disorder	32.7 (12.5)	31.8* (9.4)	44.7* (7.4)	38.5* (4.8)	40.0* (15.2)	38.7* (3.5)	33.7 (13.7)	5.8 (3.4)	23.8 (15.9)	30.4 (6.7)	0.0 (0.0)	26.0 (5.6)
Modified Social Phobia	43.7* (11.0)	39.6 (13.0)	38.5 (8.2)	37.3 (4.4)	64.1 (18.0)	39.5* (3.4)	23.4 (7.8)	34.9 (10.5)	40.7 (12.6)	32.9 (4.3)	50.3 (25.0)	32.2 (3.8)
Generalized Anxiety Disorder	37.3* (12.6)	57.1* (10.2)	42.3 (7.8)	53.8* (4.8)	52.1 (20.7)	50.4* (3.6)	57.9 (15.7)	22.6 (9.9)	37.6 (19.1)	47.6 (5.9)	53.3 (35.2)	43.1 (5.2)
Alcohol Dependence	73.4* (13.1)	75.9 (9.5)	72.3 (6.3)	86.5* (3.4)	65.8* (15.9)	79.0* (2.9)	46.6 (19.2)	75.9 (21.6)	70.6 (22.1)	61.6 (8.3)	46.4 (35.2)	59.9 (6.2)
Drug Dependence	84.8 (8.4)	63.3* (12.2)	75.8* (6.3)	79.7 (4.3)	100.0 (0.0)	78.4 (3.1)	81.4 (12.4)	86.2 (16.9)	62.7 (29.5)	80.7 (5.5)	100.0 (0.0)	79.6 (6.8)
Post-Traumatic Stress Disorder	34.4* (8.2)	23.3 (7.8)	32.8 (5.6)	25.3* (3.4)	34.9* (14.5)	28.2* (2.6)	45.0 (14.1)	22.9 (8.6)	22.6 (14.1)	47.1 (5.9)	0.0 (0.0)	39.4 (5.2)
Anorexia	n/a	n/a	100.0* (0.0)	100.0 (0.0)	100.0* (0.0)	100.0 (0.0)	100.0 (0.0)	0.0 (0.0)	0.0 (0.0)	100.0 (0.0)	0.0 (0.0)	100.0 (0.0)
Bulimia	58.1* (34.5)	49.9* (35.4)	36.4* (14.6)	42.4* (8.7)	48.8* (25.2)	42.8* (7.0)	46.9 (12.1)	63.2 (32.9)	100.0 (0.0)	77.4 (16.9)	0.0 (0.0)	75.5 (11.6)
Sample size	127	140	195	556	50	1068	349	353	83	1632	76	2493

Comparing alumni to the general population: *Indicates a significant difference between alumni and the general population as tested by two-proportion z-test, p<.05 at the bivariate level.

welfare systems do with research-based interventions, training and professionalization of foster parenting to strengthen the capacity of foster
parents and residential care staff to deal better with conduct disorder,
affect regulation problems educational deficits? Child welfare, mental
health and social services systems should consider ways to reinvest
dollars, staff time and other supports to acquire and utilize some of
the innovative screening tools and intervention strategies developed
specifically to address the needs of youth in foster care and alumni of
care (for example, see the February 2009 special issue of the journal
Child Welfare). More specifically, we recommend the following: [5]

1. *Increase access to evidence-based mental health treatment for youth in care
    and alumni through the following strategies:*

    (a) Child welfare systems should develop procedures and train
        workers to assess children/youth upon entry into the foster
        care system to determine need and appropriate services for
        youth who have borderline/clinical indications of service
        need.

    (b) Reform systems to increase mental health insurance cover-
        age for alumni who have exited care. Governments should
        examine barriers to mental health care – including eligibility
        requirements that limit access to funding and worker capac-
        ity that may be insufficient to treat mental health problems
        (see McMillen and Raghavan 2009).

    (c) Provide specialized training to therapists to enable them to
        properly assess and treat PTSD, depression, social phobia
        and other disorders (see www.thereachinstitute.org.)

    (d) Expand early and ongoing evidence-based treatment de-
        velopment, evaluation and implementation to help alleviate
        mental health disorders (Kazdin and Weisz 2003; Landsverk
        2006).

    (e) Help youth in care access diverse opportunities and services
        that promote resiliency, coping skills and other aspects of
        healthy mental health functioning; this is a public health
        approach that is gaining support (National Research Council
        and the Institute of Medicine 2009).

---

5   Adapted from Pecora *et al.* (2009).

(f) As supported by a new US Federal law, P.L. 110–351 (Fostering Connections to Success and Increasing Adoptions Act) and current practice in other countries, extend foster care to age 21 or higher to help ensure that the mental health needs of young adults are met through state-funded mental health treatment.

2. *Improve non-relative foster parent and kinship care provider orientation and training with respect to youth mental health.* Agencies should provide foster parents with more comprehensive information about how to identify and address mental health difficulties that children in foster care experience (Pasztor *et al.* 2006; Price *et al.* 2008). Training areas include:

(a) Use a broad developmental context, informing foster parents about difficulties their child may encounter and about how they can help manage emotional and behavioural problems.

(b) Provide advocacy training so that youth and foster parents know what the youth's rights are regarding access to mental health services in their community.

(c) Increase the availability of respite care services so that foster parents can have a break from care-giving as well as timely crisis intervention services to help when problems arise.

3. *Provide comprehensive daily emotional support to youth in care.* Strategies include:

(a) Help reduce the stigma that youth in foster care feel by helping them understand what alumni have told us: that depression, anxiety and other mental health conditions are a 'natural reaction to an unnatural situation' and that mental health problems can be managed with proper support and intervention.

(b) Encourage youth to grieve at their own pace. Youth need to be allowed to discuss the positive aspects of their birth family and to process their grief over entering foster care.

(c) Systematically inform and involve youth in decisions concerning their mental health problems and involve them in developing their treatment regimen.

(d) Be vigilant about confidentiality concerns. Youth may feel that it is not safe to share because of information that is communicated between the therapist and caseworker and/ or foster parents. One of the key aspects of therapy involves supporting the fragments of the relationship that remains with the birth family or other family of origin. Upon reaching 18 (or 21 in some states) youth leave foster care, but their relationships – positive or less positive – will always be there with the family of origin.

4. *Address gaps in caseworker and other professional worker skills.*

(a) Provide group work and other evidence-based treatment approaches such as Cognitive-Behavioural Therapy or Trauma-Focused Cognitive-Behavioural Therapy to help youth grieve past losses, understand their thoughts and feelings and learn new ways of coping with mental health problems (Clarke, DeBar, and Lewinsohn 2003; Kazdin and Weisz 2003).

(b) Caseworkers and counsellors who are largely funded by Medicaid (the health program in the United States for low income families) need more adequately funded training, clinical supervision and quality improvement initiatives to improve diagnosis and treatment of PTSD, Generalized Anxiety and other common mental health disorders.

(c) Given the higher rate of unmet mental health needs among minority ethnic children (Ringel and Sturm 2001), develop, evaluate and integrate culturally responsive mental health services within foster care programmes, including kinship care.

Future directions

Two areas for further analysis and research—co-morbidity and gender differences—are not addressed in the current chapter due to space limitations.

Co-morbidity. Despite the significant risk of psychological and physiological trauma among alumni of foster care, few published studies describe the prevalence of specific co-morbidity in this population. There are a few exceptions. One exception is the Northwest Foster Care Alumni Study, a study that involved alumni served by public and voluntary foster care agencies, which demonstrated that nearly 20 per cent of alumni ages 20 to 33 had three or more current psychiatric problems, compared to only 3 per cent of the general population (Pecora *et al.* 2005). Jackson (2008) found similar rates of co-morbidity in a set of special analyses using Casey National Study data.

Gender differences. Gender differences in the mental health of alumni of foster care are rarely explored, especially with multivariate techniques that control for pre-placement and in-care experiences. In one of the few analyzes conducted to date, Jackson (2008) analysed data from a sub-sample of the Casey National Study and found that females had nearly twice the rate of depression as males (19% and 10%) and nearly three times the rate of PTSD (31% and 11%, respectively). The Midwest study has also reported rates by gender group (Courtney *et al.* 2007).

Replication of these youth and alumni mental health assessment studies will provide more information about the onset of disorders, course of treatment and recovery rates. With greater dissemination and implementation of research-based interventions for youth and their caregivers and more careful monitoring, more youth who are placed in care will make steady progress and have higher rates of sustained recovery.

References

Achenbach, T.M. (1991) *Manual for the Child Behaviour Checklist 4–18 and 1991 profile.* Burlington, VT: University of Vermont, Department of Psychiatry.

Auslander, W.F. McMillen, J. Elze, D. Thompson, R. Jonson-Reid, M. and Stiffman, A. (2002) 'Mental health problems and sexual abuse among adolescents in foster care: relationship to HIV risk behaviours and intentions.' *AIDS and Behaviour 6,* 4, 351–359.

Barth, R. Wildfire, J. and Green, D. (2006) 'Placement into foster care and the interplay of urbanicity, child behaviour problems and poverty.' *American Journal of Orthopsychiatry 76,* 3, 358–366.

Bernstein, N. (2000) *A Rage to Do Better: Listening to Young People from the Foster Care System.* San Francisco, CA: Pacific News Service.

Braitman, L.E. and Rosenbaum, P.R. (2002) 'Comparing treatments using comparable groups of patients.' *Annals of Internal Medicine 137,* 8, 693–695.

Brandford, C. and English, D. (2004) *Foster Youth Transition to Independence Study.* Seattle, WA: Office of Children's Administration Research, Washington Department of Social and Health Services.

Clarke, G.N. DeBar, L.L. and Lewinsohn, P.M. (2003) 'Cognitive-Behavioural Group Treatment for Adolescent Depression.' In A.E. Kazdin (ed) *Evidence-Based Psychotherapies for Children and Adolescents.* New York, NY: Guilford Press, pp.120–134.

Courtney, M.E. Dworsky, A. Cusick, G.R. Keller, T. *et al.* (2007) *Midwest Evaluation of Adult Functioning of Former Foster Youth: Outcomes at Age 21.* Chicago, IL: University of Chicago, Chapin Hall Centre for Children.

Delfabbro, P. and Barber, J. (2006) 'Psychosocial Well-Being and Placement Stability in Foster Care: Implications for Policy and Practice.' In R. Flynn, P. Dudding and J. Barber (eds), *Promoting Resilience in Child Welfare.* Ottawa: University of Ottawa Press, pp.157–173.

Egelund, N. and Lausten, H. (2009) 'Prevalence of mental health problems among children placed in out-of-home care in Denmark.' *Child and Family Social Work 14,* 2, 156–165.

Farruggia, S. Greenberger, E. Chen, C. and Heckhausen, J. (2006) 'Perceived social environment and adolescents' well-being and adjustment: comparing a foster care sample with a matched sample.' *Journal of Youth and Adolescence 35,* 3, 330–339.

Haro, J.M. Arbabzadeh-Bouchez, S. Brugha, T.S. de Girolamo, G. *et al.* (2006) 'Concordance of the Composite International Diagnostic Interview Version 3.0 (CIDI 3.0) with standardized clinical assessments in the WHO World Mental Health Surveys.' *International Journal of Methods in Psychiatric Research 15,* 4, 167–180.

Hosmer, D.W. and Lemseshow, S.L. (1989) *Applied Logistic Regression.* New York, NY: John Wiley and Sons.

Jackson, L.J. (2008) 'The co-morbidity problem: a deeper look at depression and PTSD in foster care alumni.' Unpublished doctoral thesis. University of Washington.

James Bell Associates (2004) *Preliminary Findings of the Child and Family Services Reviews in Fiscal Years 2001 and 2002.* Washington, DC: Author.

Kazdin, A.E. and Weisz, J.R. (eds) (2003) *Evidence-based Psychotherapies for Children and Adolescents.* New York, NY: Guilford Press.

Kendall-Tackett, K. and Giacomoni, S.M. (eds) (2003) *Treating the Lifetime Health Effects of Childhood Victimization.* Kingston, NJ: Civic Research Institute.

Kessler, R.C. Chiu, W.T. Demler, O. and Walters, E.E. (2005) 'Prevalence, severity and co-morbidity of twelve-month DSM-IV disorders in the National Co-morbidity Survey Replication (NCS-R)'. *Archives of General Psychiatry 62,* 6, 617–627.

Kessler, R.C. and Merikangas, K.R. (2004) 'The National Co-morbidity Survey Replication (NCS-R).' *International Journal of Methods in Psychiatric Research 13,* 2, 60–68.

Kessler, R.C. and Üstün, T.B. (2004) 'The World Mental Health (WMH) Survey Initiative Version of the World Health Organization (WHO) Composite International Diagnostic Interview (CIDI).' *International Journal of Methods in Psychiatric Research 13,* 2, 93–121.

Landsverk, J. Burns, B. Stambaugh, L.F. and Rolls-Reutz, J.A. (2006) *Mental Health Care for Children and Adolescents in Foster Care: Review of Research Literature.* Seattle, WA: Casey Family Programs.

McAuley, C. (2009) 'Emotional well-being and mental health of looked after children in the UK.' *Child and Family Social Work 14,* 2, 147–155.

McMillen, J. and Raghavan, R. (2009) 'Paediatric to adult mental health service use of young people leaving the foster care system.' *Journal of Adolescent Health 44,* 7–13.

Meltzer, H. Corbin, T. Gatward, R. Goodman, R. and Ford, T. (2003) *The Mental Health of Young People Looked After by Local Authorities in England.* London: The Stationery Office.

National Research Council and the Institute of Medicine (2009) *Preventing Mental, Emotional, and Behavioural Disorders among Young People: Progress and Possibilities.* Washington, DC: National Academies Press.

Nicoll, A. Holmes, K. Pecora, P.J. White, C.R. O'Brien, K. and Fain, A. (under review) 'In Their Own Words: Foster Care Alumni Talk about Transition Services to Prepare for Independent Living'. In *Child Welfare Research: An International Perspective.*

Pasztor, E.M. Hollinger, D.S. Inkelas, M. and Halfon, N. (2006) 'Health and mental health services for children in foster care: the central role of foster parents.' *Child Welfare, 85,* 1, 33–57.

Pecora, P.J. Kessler, R.C. Williams, J. Downs, A.C. *et al.* (2010) *What Works in Foster Care?* . New York, NY: Oxford University Press.

Pecora, P.J. Williams, J. Kessler, R.J. Downs, A.C. O'Brien, K. Hiripi, E. and Morello, S. (2003) *Assessing the Effects of Foster Care: Early Results from the Casey National Alumni Study.* Seattle, WA: Casey Family Programs. Available at www.casey.org.

Pecora, P.J. Kessler, R.C. Williams, J. O'Brien, K. Downs, A.C. English, D. *et al.* (2005) *Improving Family Foster Care: Findings from the Northwest Foster Care Alumni Study.* Seattle, WA: Casey Family Programs.

Pecora, P.J. White, C.R. Jackson, L.J. and Wiggins, T. (2009) 'Mental health of current and former recipients of foster care: a review of recent studies in the USA.' *Child and Family Social Work 14,* 132–146.

Price, J.M. Chamberlain, P. Landsverk, J. Reid, J.B. Leve, L.D. and Laurent, H. (2008) 'Effects of a foster parent training intervention on placement changes of children in foster care.' *Child Maltreatment 13,* 1, 64–75.

Ringel, J.S. and Sturm, R. (2001) 'National estimates of mental health utilization and expenditures for children in 1998.' *Journal of Behavioural Health Services and Research 28,* 3, 319–333.

Sparrow, S.S. Balla, D.A. Cicchetti, D.V. and Doll, E.A. (1984) *Vineland Adaptive Behaviour Scales: Interview Edition, Survey Form Manual.* Circle Pines, MN: American Guidance Service.

Stahmer, A.C. Leslie, L.K. Hurlburt, M.S. Barth, R. *et al.* (2005) 'Developmental and behavioural needs as predictors of service use for young children in child welfare.' *Paediatrics 116,* 4, 891–900.

US Department of Health and Human Services, Administration for Children and Families, Children's Bureau (2009) 'Trends in foster care and adoption: FY 2002–FY 2007'. Available from www.acf.hhs.gov/programs/cb/stats_research/afcars/trends.htm

Wittchen, H.-U. Üstün, T.B. and Kessler, R.C. (1999) 'Diagnosing mental disorders in the community: a difference that matters?' *Psychological Medicine 29,* 5, 1021–1027.

Commentary by Ian Sinclair on:
Rates of Mental, Emotional and Behavioural Disorders Among Alumni of Family Foster Care in the United States: The Casey National Alumni Study

Peter J. Pecora, Catherine Roller White, Lee Ann Murdock, Kirk O'Brien, Ronald C. Kessler, Nancy Sampson and Irving Hwang

As might be expected from its authors this is a very important study. Research in many countries has shown that 'children in care' have a high level of mental ill health. There is, however, much less evidence on the extent of this ill health among those who have left the care system. This careful study provides detailed evidence on this point and shows that what is true while children are in care remains true after they have left – compared with the rest of the population they are much more likely to suffer from mental ill health. As a bonus, it also shows the types of mental ill health from which they suffer, thus linking research evidence on effective treatments for, say, Post-Traumatic Stress Disorder to recommendations on what can be done for foster children.

Like all important studies this one raises further questions. To me the key ones are:

- Does the mental ill health of these 'fostering alumni' reflect their experiences in care or have to do with their heredity and experiences before and after care?

- What mechanisms maintain their different kinds of mental ill health?

- How far can interventions during or after 'care' improve their mental health?

British evidence suggests strongly that the poor mental ill health of these children is not the fault of 'care' itself. Aldgate and her colleagues[6] followed up a sample of children in care and a sample receiving 'preventive work'. There was no evidence that the 'care children' were deteriorating relative to their peers. Other studies have compared children remaining in care with others going home. So far the children going home have come out worse on mental health, 'failure to thrive' and difficult behaviour.

British studies have also shown that apparently similar children in care often behave 'well' in 'high quality' settings and badly in 'low quality' ones. The power of these settings is, however, limited. The behaviour of the children who move on reflects their new settings not their old ones. By contrast problems that have to do with 'attachment' or 'basic disturbance' have proved surprisingly consistent over time and across settings. So it seems likely that the mechanisms maintaining (say) 'behavioural problems' and 'attachment problems' – and hence the interventions needed – are different.

---

6   My colleagues and I have tried to summarize this evidence along with the evidence on what changes in foster care in Sinclair, I., Baker, C., Wilson, K. and Gibbs, I. (2005) *Foster Children: Where They Go and How They Get On*. London: Jessica Kingsley Publishers.

The evidence on the effectiveness of interventions with foster children comes mainly from the USA but is not presented here. To say this is not to criticize the chapter's detailed suggestions on what can be done. All these suggestions are highly sensible and some (e.g. on the need for counselling on the losses children experience and for treatment for PTSD) seem particularly important. But we also need to acknowledge how little we know about what works and in particular how far this depends on the basic quality of foster care or can rely on the skills of professionals outside it. And for some children the best we may be able to do is to give them the skills and support to survive demons that will be with them for the rest of their life.

Part Four:
Psychological Outcomes and
Correlates of Outcomes

CHAPTER 10

What Makes for Effective Foster Care: Some Issues

Ian Sinclair

Introduction

At any one time around 55 out of every 10,000 English children are officially 'looked after' by the state.[1] Most (at the latest count just over seven out of ten) of these children are fostered, but until the mid 1990s most British research in this field dealt with residential care or the care system in general. Recently, however, a number of British studies, many sponsored by government (Sinclair 2005), have variously focused on foster carers, fostered adolescents, kin care, contact between foster children and their families and children who were adopted or fostered long-term.

This chapter is based on one large study, the *Permanence Study* (Sinclair *et al.* 2007) and one group of studies, the *Fostering Studies* (Sinclair, Baker, Wilson and Gibbs 2005; Sinclair, Gibbs and Wilson 2004; Sinclair, Wilson and Gibbs 2005;). Taken together they allow us to give a broad picture of the English care system, place foster care within this context, compare its outcomes with those of other provision (e.g. adoption or residential care) and explore the factors that make this care more or less effective. There is no space to describe all this material and so we concentrate on four questions about effectiveness:

---

1   See official statistics on www.dcsf.gov.uk/DB/SFR/s00741.

- Are some categories of foster care (e.g. care by kin) more effective than others at providing placements that last as long as needed and promote well-being?

- What makes foster placements within these categories more or less effective?

- Can foster care effect outcomes after the children have left it and if so how does it do this?

- How far and in what ways can the departments that provide foster care ensure that it is effective?

Again for reasons of space, the chapter deliberately restricts its conclusions to what might be said on the basis of the author's own work rather than what can be drawn from the general body of work on these issues in the UK and elsewhere.

Method

The methodology has been described elsewhere (Sinclair *et al.* 2004; Sinclair, Wilson and Gibbs 2005; Sinclair, Baker, Wilson and Gibbs 2005; Sinclair *et al.* 2007). In broad outline, the methods were as follows.

The *Permanence Study* examined three questions:

- What kinds of children are looked after?

- How and why do they move into, out of and within the care system?

- How far do their chances of stability and well-being depend on (a) their own characteristics or (b) the particular placements, social work teams or councils they happen to have?

The researchers collected nationally representative data from the IT systems of 13 English councils. The basic sample consisted of all children looked after at any point in an agreed year (n=7399). There were further data from social workers on those looked after in the last six months of the year (n=4647, response rate 71%) and their team leaders (n=114, response rate 66%) and on foster households (n=1585) and residential units (n=315) used during the year.

The analysis was primarily statistical, with considerable use of descriptive statistics, estimates of the rate at which various changes (e.g.

return home) occurred and comparisons between children who took different routes or had different outcomes. Multi-level modelling was used to explore the effects of local authorities, teams and placements on outcomes. Case studies (n=95) were used to 'triangulate' the results and to illustrate and help explain the processes involved.

The *Permanence Study* looked at children in all kinds of placement. By contrast, the *Fostering Studies* were based on 596 foster children and their carers in seven local authorities. They aimed to determine:

- what foster carers liked or did not like about their role and why they stayed or left

- why some placements succeeded and others did not

- what happened to foster children over three years and why some 'did better' than others.

The foster children were first studied in 1998 when they had all been fostered for at least three months. They were followed up at three points in time over three years. The researchers collected data from foster carers (foster parents), the children's social workers, the foster carers' social workers and the children themselves. Comparisons between these sources of data suggested that the samples were broadly representative of children fostered in the seven authorities which in turn were nationally representative. Children fostered with relatives were under-represented but there was no reason to think that this invalidated the comparisons we made within the sample.

A key point about the sample is that almost all the children were 'long-stay'. In the course of a year many children come into care and leave quickly. Those who do not leave within six months are very unlikely to go home or otherwise leave the system in the near future unless they are very young children, who may wait for a while before adoption. It is these longer stay children who form the great bulk of any cross-section, particularly if, as in our sample, children who had been in care for less than three months are omitted. Our conclusions should be seen as applying to this 'long-stay' group.

Once again the analysis was primarily statistical with comparisons being made between children (and initially foster carers) who followed different routes or had different outcomes and after allowing for the differences between them at the point when they were first studied. However, considerable use was also made of the qualitative material in the questionnaires and of nearly 50 case studies. The aim here was to gain a deeper understanding of what was going on and produce a final account that fitted both the statistical and the qualitative data.

Finally, all the associations cited below are significant at p=.05 or beyond. The reasonable sample sizes mean that almost all the bivariate comparisons are significant at p<.001, as indeed are many of the others.

Do some types of foster placements do better than others?

The *Permanence Study* considered differences in outcome between three broad types of fostering: stranger fostering, fostering with relatives and friends and fostering in private or voluntary agencies.

Stranger foster carers carried out all fostering roles but kin carers and those in the independent sector had, to some extent, different roles and characteristics. Kin care was predominantly used for children who came into care when relatively young and stayed a long time. Evidence from the *Fostering Studies* supports other research in suggesting that kin carers were often poorer, worse housed and less well educated than stranger carers and that they also received less financial reward for fostering and commonly had disputes with the birth families.

In keeping with these findings 'placements with family and friends'[2] were typically seen by social workers as of lower quality than those with strangers. They were, however, more likely to be seen as achieving their purpose, they lasted longer than others and the children in them scored better on our measure of well-being. These advantages remained when we took account of what we knew about the children. Both the fostering studies and other research suggest that the greater length of kin care placements reflects their purpose rather than their greater ability to avoid breakdowns. The other advantages seem, on our evidence, to be real but have to be tested in other research.

Private or voluntary care was mainly provided outside the local authority area, had the advantages and disadvantages associated with

---

2   Officially all placements in this group are with 'family and friends'. In practice almost all are
     placed with kin and in this chapter the terms 'kin care' and 'family and friends care' are used
     interchangeably.

this[3] and sometimes included dedicated educational provision. Other research suggests that carers in this sector were better supported than those in the local authority one. Authorities, however, saw this provision as costly. They used it for specialist placements which they could not provide themselves, for example, placements for black and minority ethnic children in certain areas, difficult adolescents in most and needs arising from a simple lack of provision in others. After allowing for what we knew about the children, the *Permanence Study* failed to find any difference in outcomes between foster care provided by the independent and local authority sectors.

The study showed large differences between local authorities in their uses of kin care and care from the independent sector. Kin care in authorities that made much use of it did not seem to have worse results. There is therefore a case for increasing its use, thus at once reducing what is seen as a severe shortage of stranger carers and freeing these carers for roles other than long-term care. At the same time, kin care is not a 'free lunch'; its placements can go as wrong as any other and those who provide it have particular needs for support, many of which are not commonly met.

Are some foster care placements better than others?

There are differences within different kinds of foster placement as well as between them. Some foster children are 'easy', others are difficult. Some foster carers are warm, others seem colder. Some carers have hearts which go out to waiflike young children, while others enjoy the challenge of teenagers. For good reasons, much foster care research has ignored these differences between placements of the same general kind. By contrast, the *Fostering Studies* were centrally (although not exclusively) concerned with them and with the related question of which fostering placements were seen as being successful and which ones broke down.

The follow-up design helped with this task. Fourteen months after we first asked about the foster children, we sent out a second round of questionnaires. At this point we asked the foster carer, the child's social

---

3   The main disadvantages are the barriers to family contact, the costs of travelling for all parties and the difficulties of making educational arrangements outside the area. Children may also return home from distant placements to areas where they have lost all ties. On the other hand, placements outside the area can be more specialised (having a wider catchment area) and can break undesirable ties to delinquent groups, prostitution and so on.

worker and the foster carer's social worker whether the initial placement had broken down and whether it had gone 'very well', 'as well as could be expected' or 'not very well'. In each case we took the most 'pessimistic' of the answers and used it to form a measure of 'breakdown' or 'doing well'.[4] At follow-up three years after the first contact we looked at similar issues but also at changes in certain psychological scores and the apparent influences on the course of the child's career.

This approach allowed us to compare these outcomes taking into account what we knew of the children and the characteristics of their placements 14 or 36 months earlier (t1). In general, placements that tended to go well seemed to have similar characteristics to those that did not break down. They were alike in:

- the children's characteristics – children were more likely to stay and do well in their placements if at t1 they wanted to be fostered and did not have serious problems in their behaviour and their ability to relate to others

- the carers' characteristics – carers who at t1 were rated by the social workers[5] as seeing things from the child's viewpoint and as caring, accepting, encouraging, clear in their expectations and not easily upset by the child's failure to respond were more likely to have successful, lasting placements. So too were those who scored high on a self-completed test of 'child orientation'

- the 'fit' with the foster family – children who at t1 were accepted by the main carer, the other children in the family (if any) and the other foster children (if any) were much more likely to have successful, lasting placements

- family contact – children who had previously been abused and who had 'unrestricted' access to their current families were three times more likely to have breakdowns

- schooling – children who were described by their carers at t1 as 'enjoying school' were much more likely at follow-up to be doing well and much less likely to have had a breakdown

---

4   Potentially this introduces a bias as children for whom we did not receive a full set of questionnaires should be less likely to get a 'bad' rating'. We examined this issue in our original report and concluded that it did not affect our results. See Sinclair, Wilson and Gibbs (2005) p. 144.

5   These ratings were made by the child's social worker and also by the supervising social worker responsible for the support and professional supervision of the foster carer. For the statistical purposes we used the average of the two ratings.

- services – children who had contact with an educational psychologist were more likely to avoid breakdowns.[6]

The last five of these findings 'held' when we took account of the children's characteristics (i.e. their ages, lengths of time in placement, wishes and 'disturbance'). By contrast children who received any of a range of services (e.g. visits to a psychiatrist or clinical psychologists) other than educational psychology did worse than their fellows. These negative associations were no longer significant once we took account of the children's characteristics. The reasons for them almost certainly have to do with the way services are much more likely to be given when children are already in trouble and that most contacts are brief. That said, the results certainly did not suggest that these services when given as they now are have a good effect on the outcomes we measured.

Other analyses seeking to explain success were 'negative'. After allowing for previous characteristics, we did not find that success varied with the ages of carers and numbers and ages of other children in the placement, the presence of siblings in the placements or number of previous placements (as opposed to disruptions). These variables can be important in particular cases. Some children, for example, like babies in the house or want other children with whom to play, while others want to be on their own. Many children are distressed by not being placed with their siblings, but a few cannot tolerate being placed with them. The findings suggest a need to listen carefully to what both foster families and children want and to avoid 'rules of thumb'.

It is striking that the processes which did predict 'success' were not independent of each other. For example, children who were 'difficult' were more likely to be 'rejected' and to have placement breakdowns. However, the relationships between our measure of disturbance and disruption were not the same when there was a 'high' level as against a 'low' level of rejection. At low levels of rejection, the disruption rates of those with high and low levels of 'total SDQ score'[7] were equally low (13%). At higher levels of rejection, the rate of disruption was almost twice as high among those with 'high' scores on our measure of disturbance (Sinclair and Wilson 2003). So it seems that 'disturbance' both

---

6   The findings on educational psychology are statistically highly significant but also complex and unpredicted. They need further exploration (see Sinclair, Wilson and Gibbs 2005, p.218)

7   The total SDQ score is a summary score from the Strengths and Difficulties Questionnaire that we used as a general measure of 'disturbance'. The reference on which we relied was Goodman and Scott 2007. There is now a much wider literature on this measure.

makes rejection more likely and makes breakdown more likely among those who are rejected. If, however, a carer does not reject a disturbed child, the disturbance itself does not lead to placement breakdown.

One problem in 'teasing out' these relationships has to do with 'circular causation'. For example, skilled parenting may reduce problem behaviour but carers faced with problem behaviour may become less skilled. Another difficulty lies in the strong correlation between some key variables. So it could be that our measure of rejection is simply a proxy for the difficulty of the child on the one hand and the quality of the parent on the other.[8] In practice, we concluded that these complexities do not do away with the need to treat the key variables we have identified (child motivation and 'disturbance', carer quality, rejection, parental contact and schooling) as if they had a direct causal influence on placement outcome.

One reason for thinking this is that the *Permanence Study* built on and reinforced some of these findings. It showed that children were more likely to move from placements intended to last if they were older, had 'challenging behaviour' and did not want to be in care. Children were likely to be given higher ratings for 'well-being' if their carer was rated by another social worker as warm, clear in expectations and so on. However, carer characteristics only had an impact on stability if the child was over 11 and the placement was meant to last. Some younger children stayed in placements where they were acutely unhappy. Later, perhaps, they may be able to make their unhappiness known or bring about a breakdown that allows them to go elsewhere.

Other reasons for attributing causal significance to these findings come from the *Fostering Studies*. All of them hold true when we take account of the child's initial characteristics (i.e. motivation, behaviour and

---

8   These issues relate to our distinction between 'carer quality', which we saw as a general approach to parenting likely to be displayed to other foster children and 'fit', which was about the particular fit between an individual child and a family. In support of this distinction, we found that our ratings of carer quality were associated with previous 'breakdowns' with other foster children as well as predicting breakdown of current children. This finding supports the idea that the relationship between carer quality and breakdown does not simply reflect the fact that carers faced with difficult children become less skilled (a finding in keeping with the fact that the association holds after taking account of the child's 'disturbance'). By contrast, negative ratings of carer and family response to the current child were not more common among carers who had had other placement breakdowns. So it seemed that our ratings of carers were tapping some relatively stable attribute of the way that they parented foster children, but that our measures of family and carer acceptance represented the particular chemistry with a given child (see Sinclair, Wilson and Gibbs 2005, pp.180–195).

scores on measures of attachment problems). Our statistical modelling suggests that each makes an independent contribution to placement outcome.[9] Our qualitative data have shown that all the issues are important in their own right. Overall, our conclusion was that by far the safest assumption was that at least four issues (quality of fostering, 'fit or chemistry', school and contact) need attention if a placement is to go well. It would be very unsafe for practitioners to assume they do not.

Can foster care make a difference after the children leave it?

So far we have been concerned with the success of an individual placement. How far is this success enough to bring about a future good outcome? Sadly, it seems that a successful placement is no guarantee of long-term success. Indeed one of the major issues for residential work is that its ability to influence its residents' behaviour while they are in the home is bought at the cost of a great difficulty in influencing them when they leave. That which can change easily with a change of setting can change again when circumstances alter (Sinclair 2006).

The relatively large sample and three year follow-up meant that the *Fostering Studies* were able to look at what happened after foster care. We carried out case studies and some statistical work on what did or did not make for success in returning children to their homes, placing them for adoption and/or enabling them to move on to independent living. In what follows I have also drawn on statistics and case studies from the *Permanence Study*.

At first sight, the results from the fostering studies repeated those already familiar from studies of residential care. Behaviour and apparent success after leaving foster care did reflect what the children were like before they were fostered and their experience after fostering. This was true of all methods of leaving – going home, being adopted and

---

9   For example, one logistic model of 'avoiding breakdown' over three years was: in placement for two years at t1 (p=.012), low t1 'disinhibited attachment score' (p<.001), enjoys school at t1 (p<.001), high quality foster care at t1 (p=.027). It is possible to substitute a general measure of disturbance for the attachment variable and a rejection score for the parenting score to yield a similar model, whereas a model that is restricted to cases where there was prior abuse brings out 'unrestricted contact' as a predictor of breakdown although only at p=.05. Over three years, some children may move to new placements or have new restrictions placed on them – hence perhaps lowering the predictive power of quality of fostering or nature of contact at t1. But the most plausible interpretation of these equations is that contact, enjoying school and what goes on in the foster home all make an independent contribution to avoiding breakdown. (See Sinclair, Baker, Wilson and Gibbs 2005, pp.131–135).

moving to independent living. It was, however, very difficult to show that subsequent success depended on the type of fostering experienced. To give some examples:

- Children's well-being was greater on return home if they and their parent(s) wanted this and if the social worker gave higher ratings to the parenting they received at home and if they were doing well at school after return.

- Adopted children tended to do slightly better on some of our measures if their adoptive parents had good support networks and if their child's contact with their previous foster carers was not abruptly severed.

- Young people moving to independence were more likely to do well in their own eyes and those of others if they had scored low three years earlier on a measure of disturbance (total score on the Strengths and Difficulties Questionnaire (Goodman and Scott 1997) and if they were currently thought to have strong relationships with adults.

We were not able, however, to show that the experience of fostering affected the child's wish to return home, their parents' wish to have them, the networks of their adoptive parents or their scores on our personality measures. As we have seen, our foster carer measures did predict how well the child got on while fostered with that particular carer. They did not predict how they fared with the next carer (if they moved within the system). They did not appear to affect either long-term success or those variables that were related to this success.[10] And it was sobering that some variables concerned with 'basic personality' changed little over time, did not alter on change of placement or with quality of carer and were strong predictors of future well-being or otherwise.

At first sight it looks as if nothing the foster carer does has a long-term effect. However, this conclusion needs to be tempered in three ways.

First, it is logical to assume that careful assessment prior to discharge should contribute to later success. The reason for thinking this is that it does seem possible to identify factors in the next environment that

---

10   Young people who were now living independently were significantly more likely to feel that they were doing well if they also said that they had got on at school and with their carers. However, neither of these associations was significant if we took account of the level of the child's disturbance when measured while they were in foster care.

predict success. The *Permanence Study* showed that 'vulnerable children' – those who were younger, abused or neglected, or disabled were less likely to go back to their families. However, children displaying very difficult behaviour or who came from homes where there was domestic violence or the abuse of alcohol or drugs were more likely than others to have failed returns home but as likely as others to return there. As already discussed, the *Fostering Studies* were able to identify factors in adoptive homes, the child's own home and independent living that seemed to predict success or failure. By taking account of these factors it should be possible to avoid placing a child in a truly harmful environment or alternatively to make plans for reducing known risks.

Second, the *fostering studies* did yield some evidence that the way the transition was managed could be important. Adopted children whose previous foster carers stayed in touch were less likely than others to score high on a measure of 'inhibited attachment'. It would make sense to think that this association was causal and this would certainly fit our qualitative data, although we cannot be sure. Case studies in the *Pursuit of Permanence* suggested that successful returns home depended on good practice. We concluded that:

There was the need to consider a wide range of placements and not just return to mothers – placements with fathers, kin and friends could all 'work out'. There also needed to be clarity about what was planned and the conditions for its success. Social workers had to work purposefully, if possible with the agreement of all concerned, in order to achieve the plan at a measured but urgent pace. There had to be a realistic assessment of whether the conditions for return were met and a fall-back plan if they were not.

Other things also helped. These included continuity. The more the child was able to share the placement with their siblings, avoid a change of school, begin a longer term placement with known carers and maintain contact with the relatives to whom they were to return the better. 'Good' carers who were able to sympathize with the parent(s), support the child and work with the social workers were highly valuable. Overall, there was a need for adequate staffing to enable purposeful social work, avoid drift and allow thorough assessment (Sinclair *et al.* 2007).

There is a third reason for doubting the proposition that foster care cannot achieve long-term change. This is that the foster children themselves do not think so. Just over half the young people who answered our questionnaires and were now living independently agreed with the statement that 'I got a lot out of foster care' (the rest were more or less equally divided between those who said this was partly true and those who said it was untrue). Some also gave convincing accounts of how foster care had helped. One young woman, for example, had gained the qualifications to work in a unit for the Elderly Mentally Infirm. She reported with pride on her job, her dog, her baby, her partner and the fact that she was still in touch with her foster family, to whose encouragement she gave much of the credit.

Why is there this apparent conflict between the qualitative and statistical evidence? Three reasons, perhaps. First, we may have been looking for the wrong kind of change. As many excellent adoptive parents know, it may not be realistic to expect children who have entered care with such handicaps to lose their scars. This does not, however, mean that they cannot learn to manage their handicaps or achieve success despite them. Second, our measures of foster care are essentially measures of sympathetic, authoritative parenting. This may be a necessary condition for success, but other things (e.g. an interest in education and the presence of a good local school) may also be needed. Third, foster care may bring about changes that only bear fruit when the conditions are right. Children may learn in foster care about love or the value of education. The troubled families, lonely flats or dead end jobs for which many leave do not give them the chance to show what they have learnt. Later life may be more kind. To find if it is would require a longer follow-up than we were able to provide.

Overall the practical conclusion once again seems clear enough. First, we should strive to produce high quality placements. They are important in their own right and it is possible, although not proven, that they are needed for future success, even if they cannot ensure it. Second, we need to take very seriously the problems in the new environments (home, adoption or independent living) to which children move. It should be possible to ensure that children do not go to environments where they have very little chance, that any risks are calculated ones and that the transitions are well handled.

Decisions, outcomes and organization

The discussion so far suggests that we need to take the right decisions about where children should be and also ensure that their lives there are as good as possible. In England the decisions which shape the lives of children in care are taken by local authority social workers, their managers and the courts. The children's day to day life, however, takes place in classrooms, playgrounds and the foster or residential home. How they get on with the other adults and children in these settings is likely to have a large effect on their well-being. How far are English local authorities able to influence decisions and environments for the better?

In keeping with these distinctions, the *Permanence Study* found that decisions on where the child should be and how long they should stay there varied greatly by local authority and, within authority, by social work team. A mix of qualitative and quantitative data filled out the ways in which authorities were able to influence these decisions. For example, an authority that wanted to make more adoptive placements might insist that all plans for children in care under five explicitly considered adoption and had to be approved at a high level by someone committed to the policy. Other steps could include investing heavily in finding potential adopters, increasing the number of social workers in the relevant teams (since teams with low levels of staffing seemed to make fewer placements), making special efforts for children who were known to be hard to adopt, making it easier for foster carers to adopt[11] and ensuring that work was done to clear the way for a future adoption for children returning home in case the return did not work.

Although authorities differed over the key decisions that were taken on children, they did not differ over our measures of well-being or long-term stability.[12] Moreover, the *Fostering Studies* showed that whereas the arrangements for supporting foster carers differed greatly by local authority, the likelihood of breakdown did not. The chances of well-being and happiness seem to be determined much 'lower down' in the hierarchy and by those with whom the child has contact every day. In both the *Permanence* and *Fostering Studies,* well-being and stability did vary by our measures of quality of placement.[13]

---

11 At present there are disincentives to doing this as carers who adopt lose both financial and practical support.

12 These statements are based on multi-level models in the *Permanence Study* that took account of authority, team and child characteristics. The statement applies to the avoidance of breakdown which is by definition not intended. Authorities are almost certainly able to influence the likelihood of intended moves.

13 In the *Permanence Study*, we used multi-level modelling to determine the relative effects of departments, social work teams and placements. In general these models suggested that departments accounted for none of the variation in well-being and teams for about 2 per cent of it. By contrast, placement quality and child characteristics were both important. Teams and departments were, however, important determinants of the decisions that were taken.

Why did authorities apparently differ so little in their impacts on breakdown and immediate well-being? A plausible hypothesis is that they lacked effective methods of promoting 'good placements'. In theory these could be promoted by selection, training and providing support. There is no evidence that any of these methods are being used effectively. English authorities do not have validated ways of selecting carers. Our evidence from the *Fostering Studies* suggested that both the training and support provided by local authorities could raise the morale of foster carers and improve retention. Unfortunately neither, as currently provided, appeared to improve outcomes. Training is very likely part of the solution but in England we are not clear about how to train, or what else needs to go with training to make it work.

Although authorities may not be able to produce good carers, they should be able to identify those who are less effective. Our measures of carer quality were based on the observations of social workers and did predict outcomes. Other information on placements are potentially available through statistics on complaints and allegations and through interviews with children who leave placements. We could, however, find no evidence that any authority was making use of these sources of information in any systematic way. Furthermore external inspection concentrated on aspects of fostering which appeared to have no discernible effect on its outcomes and in this way concentrated local authority attention on organizational issues that had little, if any, influence on the children's day to day lives.

Conclusion

This chapter has looked at why some foster placements are more successful than others and at whether local authorities know how to produce these placements and ensure they lead to long-term success.

Findings include the following:

- Placements with kin typically have certain disadvantages, but in long-term placements these are usually outweighed by their advantages, so that the children are more settled and the placements more often seen as achieving their ends.

- Whatever the type of placement, carers who exercise 'child oriented' but 'authoritative' parenting have the best outcomes while the child is in placement.

- Other factors which contribute to the success of placements include the characteristics of the child, their experience of school, the nature of contact with home and the 'fit' or 'chemistry' between a child and a particular foster home.

- The success of a particular placement does not necessarily lead to long-term success. Some problems (e.g. over attachment) are intractable, whereas others that are resolved in placement may recur when a child moves to a new environment.

- Local authorities and, within them, social work teams have a major influence on the key decisions taken on children in care (e.g. on whether to use kin or stranger fostering) but appear to have much less influence on the quality of placement which seems to determine a child's immediate well-being.

Some of these findings may not easily translate to other countries, where, for example, the reasons for recruiting kin carers may be very different. However, the findings on authoritative parenting, for example, do seem to fit with a wide variety of international evidence on parenting in general. They need testing in other countries but should apply widely.

Certain broad recommendations flow from the findings:

- More use should be made of kin placements by those authorities that make little use of them, but care needs to be taken over their difficulties (poverty, quarrels between kin and so on).

- Much more attention needs to be paid to the problem of producing high quality placements – initially through quality assurance schemes and later through the development of effective selection, training and support.

- Similar attention needs to be paid to the problems around contact with parents, schooling and the 'poor fit' between some children and otherwise high quality placements.

- Much more attention needs to be paid to the transition between successful placements and subsequent adoptive placements, return home and independent living.

More detailed recommendations on these and other issues are to be found in the literature cited below, which should be of interest to two groups in particular: (a) those who are interested in examining the methods used in these studies and the strength or otherwise of the evidence produced and (b) those who want to think through the possible practical implications.

References

Goodman, R. and Scott, S. (1997) *Child Psychiatry.* Oxford: Blackwell.

Sinclair, I. (2005) *Fostering Now: Messages from Research.* London: Jessica Kingsley Publishers

Sinclair, I. (2006) 'Residential Care in the U.K.' In C. McAuley, P. Pecora, W. Rose (eds) *Enhancing the Well-Being of Children and Families through Effective Interventions: International Evidence for Practice.* London: Jessica Kingsley Publishers.

Sinclair, I. Baker, C. Lee, J. Gibbs, I. (2007) *The Pursuit of Permanence: A Study of the English Care System.* London: Jessica Kingsley Publishers.

Sinclair I, Baker, C. Wilson, K. and Gibbs, I. (2005) *Foster Children: Where They Go and How They Do.* London: Jessica Kingsley Publishers

Sinclair, I. Gibbs, I. and Wilson, K. (2004) *Foster Carers: Why They Stay and Why They Leave.* London: Jessica Kingsley Publishers.

Sinclair, I. and Wilson, K. (2003) 'Matches and mismatches: the contribution of carers and children to the success of foster placements.' *British Journal of Social Work 33,* 871–884.

Sinclair, I. Wilson, K. and Gibbs, I. (2005) *Foster Placements: Why They Succeed and Why They Fail.* London: Jessica Kingsley Publishers.

Commentary by Elizabeth Fernandez on:
What Makes for Effective Foster Care: Some Issues

Ian Sinclair

The mounting concern about the instability in living situations for children in care through multiple placement changes, the increasing use of foster care as a platform for the delivery of out of home care services and growing challenges in recruitment and retention of foster carers provide the context for the carefully crafted study reported in this chapter. Sinclair must be commended for this rich and informative synthesis of findings from a large scale study of children's pathways in the care system in the UK. A prospective longitudinal study conducted over three years, this inquiry into the outcomes of care draws on an extensive sample of 7400 children mapping their experience through different types of care. The various strands of the data collection strategy – administrative data from client information systems and questionnaires and interviews eliciting views of managers and social workers – enrich this study into the workings of the care system. A set of three further fostering studies based on a three year follow-up of 596 children provide further information on the pathways children follow and the reasons for their differing outcomes.

This richly detailed exploration of outcomes is a valuable addition to the empirical literature in child welfare providing important evidence on the variables that impact on positive outcomes for children in care. After cogently examining outcomes for different types of care – children in foster care, residential care, adoption and return home – Sinclair observes that many children in the sample experienced high levels of instability through planned and unplanned moves; that foster care performed as well as residential care; children in kinship care fared well on stability and welfare outcomes; that while the differences in the outcomes of fostering and adoption favoured the latter but, over the period studied, only marginally so if age and background were taken into account; that ages of carers, ages of other children in the foster care home and presence of siblings in the placement did not impact negatively on outcomes; that characteristics of both children and carers influenced outcomes as did the chemistry between them; that return home was not always planned and the outcomes for returned children were worse than those of apparently similar children who did not return; and that many young people transitioned out of care prematurely and received insufficient support.

While acknowledging the limitations of the study period and the complexities in the interaction between variables, Sinclair offers a set of thought provoking ideas for child welfare decision making including:

- extending the use and support of kinship carers to free stranger carers for specific roles

- reducing the traditional differences between adoption and long term foster care and the barriers to adoption by foster carers

- raising the expertise and morale of carers by investing in training and strategies for retention

- maximizing the potential of the schooling experience found to be a significant contributor to positive care outcomes and children's well-being

- ensuring children leave care at a pace that allows them to develop skills and relationships they need to transition to an environment that supports them and importantly

- listening to children and carers and respecting their insights without applying 'rules of thumb' in decision making.

Reflecting on the findings and recommendations some observations come to mind. The findings like those of Bada *et al.* (2008) and Rubin *et al.* (2007) underscore the importance of placement stability to child well-being outcomes. Emerging research on the impact of carer training interventions on placement stability (Price *et al.* 2008) add weight to the recommendations here to enhance carer knowledge and skills. The contribution of the unique chemistry between carer and child to positive outcomes, while a useful indicator for assessment and planning, reflects the vulnerability and fragility of foster care given such dynamics are likely to be evident retrospectively and the inherent difficulty in predicting how engagement between foster parent and child is likely to unfold over time.

There is a wide variation internationally in the language used to describe the phenomenon of placement instability. Terms including 'breakdown' (Berridge and Cleaver 1987; Egelund and Vitus 2009), 'movements' (James, Landsverk and Slymen 2004) 'trajectories' (Wulczyn, Kogan and Harden 2003), 'disruption' (Leathers 2006) feature in the research literature. Sinclair and his colleagues distinguish between intended moves, breakdowns that reflect the inability of carer and child to live together and permanence – a concept that includes an absence of movement but also a child's subjective sense of belonging to the family, an absence of conflicted loyalties and an enacted commitment of both carer and child to each other. Varying terminology and the implicit criteria for assessing stability and instability, present challenges for comparing trends from different studies nationally and internationally. Sinclair's chapter should stimulate critical conversations around the conceptual, definitional and methodological directions and advance future research in this important area of inquiry.

References

Bada, H.S. Langer, J. Twomey, J. Bursi, C. *et al.* (2008) 'Importance of stability of early living arrangements on behaviour outcomes of children with and without prenatal drug exposure.' *Journal of Developmental and Behavioural Paediatrics 29*, 3, 173–182.

Berridge, D. and Cleaver, H. (1987) *Foster Home Breakdown.* Oxford: Basil Blackwell.

Egelund, T. and Vitus, K. (2009) 'Breakdown of care: the case of Danish teenage placements'. *International Journal of Social Welfare 18*, 1, 45–56

James, S. Landsverk. J. and Slymen, D.J. (2004) 'Placement movement in out-of-home care: patterns and predictors.' *Children and Youth Services Review 26*, 185–206.

Leathers, S.J. (2006) 'Placement disruption and negative placement outcomes among adolescents in long-term foster care: the role of behaviour problems.' *Child Abuse* and *Neglect* 30, 3, 307–324.

Price, J.M. Chamberlain, P. Landsverk, J. Reid, J.B. Leve, L.D. and Laurent, H. (2008) 'Effects of a foster parent training intervention on placement changes of children in foster care.' *Child Maltreatment 13,* 1, 64–75.

Rubin, D.M. O'Reilly, A.L.R. Luan, X.Q. and Localio, A.R. (2007) 'The impact of placement stability on behavioural well-being for children in foster care.' *Paediatrics 119*, 2, 336–344.

Sinclair, I. Baker, C. Lee, J. and Gibbs, I. (2007) *The Pursuit of Permanence: A Study of the English Care System.* London: Jessica Kingsley Publishers.

Wulczyn, F. Kogan, J. and Harden, B.J. (2003) 'Placement stability and movement trajectories.' *Social Service Review 77*, 2, 212–236.

CHAPTER 11

Long Term Outcomes of Foster Care: Lessons from Swedish National Cohort Studies

Bo Vinnerljung, Eva Franzén,
Anders Hjern and Frank Lindblad

In this chapter we summarize results from five longitudinal national cohort studies on long term outcomes of foster care. First, we give a brief overview of Swedish child welfare, followed by a description of methods and data sources in our studies. Finally we suggest pathways toward improvements.

Child welfare in Sweden

In Sweden, 3 to 4 per cent of all children are placed in foster family/residential care before age 18 (Vinnerljung *et al.* 2007). In the capital, Stockholm, one in ten receives some form of child welfare intervention (Sundell *et al.* 2007). Half of all children who are placed in foster family care before age seven will remain in care for more than five years (Socialstyrelsen, non-published statistics). "Permanency planning", including adoption without parental consent, does not exist in Swedish legislation. For children in need of long term substitute parenting, foster family care is the only option. The great majority of child welfare interventions/services before adolescence—and even more so long term out-of-home care—are caused by parental problems or parental behaviour (Vinnerljung 1996a). "Long term care" is in practice the same as foster family care since residential care for young children is usually a temporary affair (e.g. while waiting for a foster home placement). Local child welfare authorities are responsible for care until the age of majority (18). Foster home placements are usually—but not always— extended one year after age 18 for youths who attend secondary school. Standardized "leaving care" or "emancipation" programs (as in the UK and the US) do not exist.

Methods

Sweden has a long tradition of maintaining national registers with high quality data regarding health and socio-economic indicators on the entire population. The key to all registers is a ten-digit personal identification number (PIN) that follows every resident from birth (or date of immigration) to death. The PIN enables us to link different registers with each other. The Swedish Multigeneration Register, containing data on first degree relatives of all inhabitants, enables linkages of children and parents (but not foster parents).

Details on methodological procedures are described in the original publications, but two background variables need to be clarified here. *Socioeconomic status (SES)* was defined according to a classification used by Statistics Sweden, which is based on occupation but also takes educational level, type of production and position at work of the head of the household into account (Statistics Sweden 1982). In two studies, estimates were also adjusted for episodes of parental hospital care for psychiatric illness or substance abuse (*indicators of psychosocial risk*). Data were obtained from the Swedish National Hospital Discharge Register. The variables were dichotomized (at least once/never) and defined according to the WHO International Classification of Diagnosis (ICD-9 and ICD-10; WHO 1989, 1992). By adjusting for these and other background variables, we were able to statistically simulate comparisons between foster youth and peers who had grown up in their parents care under similar socio-economic circumstances. We also used children who had received in-home care[1] or short term out-of-home care before their teens as comparison groups.

In Table 11.1, we list the national registers that have been used and the data retrieved.

---

1   "Contact families", corresponding to respite care (Andersson 1993).

TABLE 11.1 List of National Registers and data used in the studies

NATIONAL REGISTER	MAINTAINED BY	DATA RETRIEVED	STUDY				
			Mental health problems	Avoidable mortality	Teenage parenthood	Educational attainment	Self-support problems
Cause of Death Register	National Board of Health and Welfare	Date of death, cause of death		X			
Register of the Total Population	Statistics Sweden	Residency, birth country, immigration, and emigration	X	X	X	X	X
Multi-generation Register	Statistics Sweden	Identification of parents	X	X	X	X	
Housing and Population Census (1980 or 1990)	Statistics Sweden	Socio-demographic variables (e.g. SES)	X	X	X		X
Statistics on Income and Wealth	Statistics Sweden	Income, sources of income	X	X	X		X
The Education Register	Statistics Sweden	Formal education				X	X
Hospital Discharge Register	National Board of Health and Welfare	In-patient hospital care	X	X			
Child Welfare Register	National Board of Health and Welfare	Out-of-home and some in-home care	X	X	X	X	X
Register of Public Welfare Benefits	National Board of Health and Welfare	Recipiency of public welfare					X

Data were processed in logistic regression or Cox regression models. To simplify the presentation, results are shown as point estimates for relative risks (RR) and odds ratios (OR), without 95 per cent confidence intervals. All reported over risks in the tables are statistically significant (at least p<0.01). Percentages have been rounded off to full numbers without decimals and numbers in subgroups have been rounded off to hundreds.

Mental health problems in adolescence and young adult age

Background: International research has reported high prevalence rates for mental health problems among children in on-going care and among foster care leavers (e.g. Ford *et al.* 2007; Pecora *et al.* 2005). Since these studies lack such measures from the time of admission into care, it is not possible to estimate the impact of foster care on mental health. Our national register study, summarized below, shares that shortcoming.

We examined risks for hospitalizations due to a psychiatric disorder or suicide attempt at age 13–17 and 19–27 among 22,000 individuals who had received child welfare interventions before their 13th birthday, comparing them with 955,000 majority population peers (Vinnerljung, Hjern and Lindblad 2006). Here, we present results on:

- long term foster children, >5 years in care before age 18 (n=3900)

- youth who had received only in-home care before age 13 (n=6400)

Outcome measures were: (1) hospitalization for suicide attempt, ages 13–17 and 19–27 and (2) hospitalization for psychiatric disorder, ages 13–17 and 19–27.

Compared to majority population peers, long term foster children had five to sevenfold sex and birth year standardized over risks for both outcomes (see Table 11.2). But even after controlling for parental socioeconomic indicators and parental psychosocial risk indicators, substantial over risks remained. Risk estimates were lower for youth who had received in-home services. The same pattern emerged for different age spans at follow up (Table 11.2) and for diagnostic subgroups (depression, psychosis, etc.; not shown in tables). In both child welfare groups, age adjusted odds for all outcomes tended to be greater for boys than for girls but in the fully adjusted models there were no clear gender differences.

TABLE 11.2 Summary of Cox regression analyses. Relative risks (RR) for hospitalizations due to suicide attempt and psychiatric disorder at ages 13–17 and 19–27. Individuals born 1973–1982 who have received different child welfare interventions, compared to majority population peers

	AGE 13–17		AGE 19–27	
	MODEL 1 RR	MODEL 2 RR	MODEL 1 RR	MODEL 2 RR
Suicide attempt				
Majority peers	1	1	1	1
In-home care	4.0	2.1	3.7	1.9
>5 years in foster care	4.9	2.2	5.3	2.3
Psych disorder				
Majority peers	1	1	1	1
In-home care	5.0	2.9	4.1	2.4
>5 years in foster care	7.5	3.8	5.7	2.9

Model 1 is adjusted for sex and birth year. Model 2 is also adjusted for parental ethnicity, SES, geographical residence, recipience of public welfare and hospitalizations due to psychiatric disorder or substance abuse. All results are statistically significant at minimum $p<0.01$.

Suicide and other avoidable mortality

Background: Several Nordic studies have found high risks for premature death among young graduates of out-of-home care, but study groups have included many teenagers placed for antisocial behavior problems (e.g. Nygaard Christoffersen 1999).

We examined avoidable mortality (Hjern, Vinnerljung and Lindblad 2004) among two groups of former child welfare clients who had received interventions before their teens, comparing them with 955,000 majority population peers:

- youth who had been in foster care at least two years before age 13 (median seven years before age 18, mainly long term care; n=6500)

- youth who had received in-home interventions or had been placed in short term out-of-home care (<1 year) before their teens, but had otherwise lived with their parents ("other child welfare"; n=16,000).

Outcome measures were: (1) suicide and (2) other deaths that theoretically could have been avoided (e.g. deaths in accidents and diseases that normally do not lead to death).

In Model 1, adjusted for sex and birth year, the foster children from long term care had fourfold over risks for suicide during adolescence and young adult years, higher than the other child welfare group (Table 11.3). In the fully adjusted Model 2 (including birth parental socio-economic background and psychosocial risk indicators), twofold over risks remained for foster children, but were only slightly higher than for youth who had experienced less intrusive interventions. For other forms of avoidable death, over risks were lower among foster children and on the same level for both child welfare groups in both models.

TABLE 11.3 Summary of Cox regression analyses. Relative risks (RR) for suicide and other avoidable deaths at age 13–27. Individuals born 1973–1982 who have received different child welfare interventions, compared to majority population peers

	SUICIDE		OTHER AVOIDABLE DEATH	
	MODEL 1 RR	MODEL 2 RR	MODEL 1 RR	MODEL 2 RR
Majority peers	1	1	1	1
Foster children	4.3	2.2	2.5	1.4
Other child welfare	2.7	1.7	2.8	1.8

Model 1 is adjusted for sex and birth year. Model 2 is also adjusted for parental ethnicity, SES, geographical residence, recipience of public welfare and hospitalizations due to psychiatric disorder or substance abuse. All results are statistically significant at minimum $p < 0.01$.

Teenage parenthood

Background: Most risk factors predictive of teenage childbirth are also associated with high risks of entering out-of-home care (review in Vinnerljung, Franzén and Danielsson 2007).

We examined prevalence and risk for teenage parenthood in 50,000 former child welfare clients, born 1972–1982, in comparisons with 1.2 million majority population peers (Vinnerljung, Franzén and Danielsson 2007). Here we present results on youth that had been in:

- in-home care before teens, no out-of-home care before age of majority (n=8700)

- short term care (<2 years), entered care before age 13 (n=9900)

- long term foster care, 5–<12 years, median nine years before age 18 (n=4700)

- lifelong foster care, 12 years or more, median 16 years before age 18 (n=3500).

Due to age at the start of the intervention, it would have been exceptional if a girl had received child welfare interventions for reasons of early pregnancy.

Child welfare youth had three- to fourfold higher odds than majority population peers in age and birth year adjusted models (Table 11.4, Model 1). After adjusting also for parental sociodemographic factors and for a history of teenage parenthood among the birth parents (Model 2), over risks were lower. Youth who had grown up in lifelong foster care had moderately elevated odds (OR = 1.5), but for the other three child welfare group risks were higher.

TABLE 11.4 Summary of logistic regression analyses. Odds ratios for teenage parenthood among youth born 1972–1983 who have received child welfare interventions, compared to majority population peers

	MODEL 1 OR	MODEL 2 OR
Majority peers	1	1
In-home care before teens	4.0	2.1
Short term foster care (<2 years) before teens	4.1	2.1
Long term foster care (5–<12 years)	4.7	2.1
Lifelong foster care (≥12 years)	3.6	1.5

Model 1 is adjusted for sex and birth year. Model 2 is also adjusted for parental ethnicity, geographic residency, form of housing, SES, and familiar influences (birth mother or birth father a teenage parent).

Education

Background: International research has consistently reported that children/youth in foster care are low achievers in school and tend to enter adult life with a low education (review in Vinnerljung, Öman and Gunnarson 2005).

We examined educational attainments at age 20–27 for 30,000 former child welfare youth in eight birth cohorts of Swedish born individuals (1972–1979), comparing them to 745,000 peers who had never received child welfare interventions (Vinnerljung *et al.* 2005). Here we present results on comparisons with *majority peers whose mothers had only compulsory education*, for four child welfare groups:

- in-home care only before teens (n=4600)

- long term stable care, at least five consecutive years of foster family care (n=4500)

- long term instable care, at least five years in out-of-home care, but foster family placement disrupted by placement in residential care or by discharge followed by re-entry into care (n=1000)

- grown up in care, at least 12 years in care before age 18, in this analysis a subgroup of long term stable care (n=2400).

Outcome measures were: (1) compulsory education only (nine years) and (2) post secondary education.

Among comparisons, 12 per cent had only compulsory education at age 20–27. Among long term care alumni—regardless of their birth mother's education—the figures were over 40 per cent. For youth whose career had included disrupted placements, 55 per cent had only basic education. Among comparisons, 35 per cent had a college level degree, compared to 7–9 per cent in the long term foster care groups (not shown in tables).

In logistic regression models (Table 11.5), we adjusted results for sex and birth year but also for the statistical influence of (birth) maternal education (34–50% of the children in the child welfare groups had a birth mother with more than compulsory education) and ethnicity (Swedish, Nordic, or non-Nordic birth country) and recalculated odds ratios into relative risks (RR, see Vinnerljung *et al.* 2005). Long term foster care youth had at best a doubled risk of entering adult life with only a compulsory education, compared to peers with low educated mothers (Table 11.5). The latter peer group had three to four times better chances of having a post secondary education, compared to graduates from long term foster care. The educational attainments of former long term care foster children were on par with peers who had received in-home services (but no out-of-home care) before their teens.

TABLE 11.5 Summary of logistic regression analyses. Odds ratios recalculated into relative risks (RR) for having only primary education at age 20–27 (cohorts born 1972–1979) and for having post secondary education at age 24–27 (cohorts born 1972–1975) among individuals who have received different child welfare interventions, compared to majority population peers

	PRIMARY EDUCATION ONLY	POST SECONDARY EDUCATION
	RR	RR
Majority peers, mother only primary education	1	1
In-home care before teens	2.7	0.30
Long term stable foster care	2.4	0.33
Long term instable foster care	3.6	0.23
Grown up in care	2.2	0.35

Model is adjusted for sex, birth year, birth mother's ethnicity, and education.

Self-support problems

Background: Several European and US studies have found high rates of self support problems among adult foster care leavers (e.g. Clausen and Kristofersen 2008; Courtney and Dworsky 2006).

We assessed prevalence and risk for receiving public welfare at age 23–25 for over 23,000 former child welfare clients, comparing them with 576,000 majority population peers. Here we focus on three child welfare groups:

- in-home care only before teens (n=2800)
- long term care, at least five years before age 18 (n=2500)
- grown up in care, at least 12 years in care before age 18 (n=1900).

Outcome measures were: (1) welfare at least one month during ages 23–25 (occurrence of welfare), (2) welfare at least one month each year at age 23–25 (recurring welfare) and (3) welfare exceeding 50 per cent of disposable income for at least one year (had lived on welfare). Frequencies for each group are presented in Table 11.6.

TABLE 11.6 Prevalence of public welfare recipience age 23–25 among individuals born 1972–1977 who have received different child welfare interventions and among majority population peers

	≥1 MONTH AT AGE 23–27	≥1 MONTH EACH YEAR AT AGE 23–27	>50% OF DISPOSABLE INCOME AT LEAST ONE YEAR
In-home care before teens	55%	16%	10%
Long term foster care	51%	23%	20%
Grown up in foster care	43%	18%	16%
Majority peers	14%	3%	2%

Odds for all outcomes were high in sex and birth year adjusted models (Table 11.7). In Model 2, former foster children had three- to four-fold odds for recurring welfare or for having lived on welfare, compared to majority population peers from similar socioeconomic backgrounds. Odds adjusted for parental socioeconomic background factors tended to be on par—or higher—for graduates of long term care compared to peers in the in-home care group.

TABLE 11.7 Summary of logistic regression analyses. Odds ratios (OR) for public welfare recipience at age 23–25 among individuals born 1972–1977 who have received different child welfare interventions, compared to majority population peers

	MODEL 1			MODEL 2		
	≥1 MONTH AT AGE 23–25	>1 MONTH EACH YEAR AT AGE 23–25	>50% OF DISPOSABLE INCOME AT LEAST ONE YEAR	≥1 MONTH AT AGE 23–25	>1 MONTH EACH YEAR AT AGE 23–25	>50% OF DISPOSABLE INCOME AT LEAST ONE YEAR
	OR	OR	OR	OR	OR	OR
In-home care before teens	5.5	6.9	5.8	2.8	2.7	2.3
Long term care	6.5	10.0	12.6	3.1	3.8	4.9
Grown up in care	4.8	7.0	9.7	2.3	2.8	4.0
Majority peers	1	1	1	1	1	1

Model 1 is adjusted for sex and birth year. Model 2 is also adjusted for mother's ethnicity, residency, form of housing, and SES.

Discussion

Compared to majority population peers, young adults who were in foster care for the better part of their formative years had striking over risks for:

- mental health problems
- suicide and other forms of avoidable deaths
- teenage parenthood
- entering adult life with only compulsory education
- self-support problems.

The same factors that propel children into out-of-home care are also associated with increased risk for negative long term outcomes. Subsequently, conclusions about causal effects of long term foster care are difficult to reach, since experimental studies usually are impossible for legal or ethical reasons. But when we compared foster care youth with peers who received in-home services before their teens, or had been in short term foster care before age 13, outcomes were mostly similar. Our results and earlier research with comparison groups (including birth siblings in their parents' care; review in Vinnerljung 1996b), suggest that long term foster care has at best weak compensatory power over time. Regardless of causality issues, an inevitable question is: must it be so?

Pathways to improvement
Taken together with previous Scandinavian reports on increased risks of future medical problems (e.g. Kristofersen 2005) and severe delinquency (Vinnerljung 1999), as well as reports on extreme mortality rates of birth parents (Franzén and Vinnerljung 2006), our results provide arguments for the US and UK policy of "permanency planning". But today, foster care is the only way of providing Swedish children with a long term substitute family. Given this, raising the quality of foster care is an obvious approach. In their landmark study, Kessler and colleagues (2008) have convincingly demonstrated that high quality care has a positive impact on mental and somatic health.

Several pathways toward improvements appear promising. They all involve a partnership between agencies/local authorities and foster carers, a moving away from the model of "placing out" that has been the base of foster care for many decades. Our three proposals below also outline a "minimum standard" in foster care, defined in legislation or in binding agreements between agencies, foster carers and birth families.

1. *Make agencies accountable for assessing health, for health monitoring during placement and for providing easy access to health services.* In the US, the American Academy of Pediatricians (1994) and The Child Welfare League have for many years recommended that all foster children should have their somatic and mental health assessed at time of placement, or shortly thereafter. Many US foster care agencies currently have such routines (e.g. Hansen *et al.* 2004) and in the UK children in out-of-home care receive annual medical check-ups (e.g. Hill and Watkins 2003). In Sweden, such routines do not exist. Making agencies—not foster parents—accountable for health issues should be tried and evaluated. Studies showing a high prevalence of psychiatric disorders among children and youth in foster care suggest that this may be most important in the area of mental health (e.g. Ford *et al.* 2007).

2. *Make agencies accountable for assessing children's cognitive potential, for identifying obstacles to school progress, for monitoring progress in school, and for accessing/providing services aimed at promoting school achievements.* Again, the first step is establishing routines where standardized instruments are used for assessing cognitive capacity and for identifying obstacles for good school achievements (Evans, Scott and Schulz 2004). In a Swedish pilot project aimed at improving foster children's school achievements (n=25), three out of four children aged 8–12 were initially substantially underachieving in school, compared to their tested cognitive capacity (Tideman *et al.* submitted). We believe school/education should be an area of priority, considering the strong links between low education and self support problems for foster care alumni (Reilly 2003; Vinnerljung *et al.* 2010). Our own on-going register analyses suggest that around half of the high risks for a number of negative outcomes (e.g. serious crime and substance abuse) in this group can be statistically explained by low educational attainment. In fact, one of the main conclusions of our national register studies is that poor school performance and low educational attainment seem to be key factors in explaining—*and for improving*—the dismal outcomes for foster

care alumni in many life areas. Agencies can and should act as champions for the educational rights of foster children and youth. According to US and Norwegian experiences, programs that allow foster youth to remain in care several years after age of majority seem to be a simple but promising additional path to improvement (Courtney *et al.* 2007; Clausen and Kristofersen 2008). Systematic use of mentors to support foster children's school work during time in care also seems to be worth trying and evaluating (compare Rhodes and Dubois 2006).

3. *Make agencies accountable for sex education and for provision of birth control to adolescent foster youth.* Looking at the high over risks for teenage childbearing among foster children, it would be unethical not to try to do something about it. Improving access to mainstream services would be a first step. Meta-analyses, based mainly on US studies, suggest that effective prevention strategies employ a combination of education and provision of contraceptives (Ferrer-Wreder *et al.* 2004). A second step may be trials where evidence based risk group interventions are adapted to the needs of foster care youth (e.g. Allen and Philliber 2001).

References

Allen, J. and Philliber, S. (2001) 'Who benefits most from a broadly targeted prevention program? Differential efficacy across populations in the Teen Outreach Program.' *Journal of Community Psychology 29*, 6, 637–655.

American Academy of Pediatrics (1994) 'Health care of children in foster care.' *Paediatrics 93*, 2, 335–338.

Andersson, G. (1993) 'Support and relief: the Swedish contact person and contact family program.' *Scandinavian Journal of Social Welfare 2*, 2, 54–62.

Clausen, S.-E. and Kristofersen, L. (2008) *Barnevernsklienter i Norge 1990–2005* [Child welfare clients in Norwau 1990–2005]. Oslo: NOVA, Rapport 3/2008.

Courtney, M. and Dworsky, A. (2006) 'Early outcomes for young adults transitioning from out-of-home care in the USA.' *Child and Family Social Work 11*, 3, 209–219.

Courtney, M. Dworsky, A. Cusick, G.R. Havli.e, J. Perez, A. and Keller, T. (2007) *Midwest Evaluation of the Adult Functioning of Former Foster Youth: Outcomes at Age 21*. Chicago, IL: University of Chicago, Chapin Hall Centre for Children.

Evans, L. Scott, S. and Schulz, E. (2004) 'The need for educational assessment of children entering foster care.' *Child Welfare 83*, 6, 565–580.

Ferrer-Wreder, L. Stattin, H. Lorente, C.C. Tubman, J. and Adamson, L. (2004) *Successful Prevention and Youth Development Programs. Across borders.* New York, NY: Kluwer Academic.

Ford, T. Vostanis, P. Meltzer, H. and Goodman, R. (2007) 'Psychiatric disorder among British children looked after by local authorities: comparison with children living in private household.' *British Journal of Psychiatry 190*, 319–325.

Franzén, E. and Vinnerljung, B. (2006) 'Foster children as young adults: many motherless, fatherless or orphans. A Swedish national cohort study.' *Journal of Child and Family Social Work 11*, 3, 254–263.

Hansen, R. Mawjee, F.L. Barton, K. Metcalf, M. and Joye, N. (2004) 'Comparing the health status of low-income children in and out of foster care.' *Child Welfare 83*, 4, 367–380.

Hill, C.M. and Watkins, J. (2003) 'Statutory health assessments for looked-after children: what do they achieve? *Child: Care, Health and Development 29*, 1, 3–13.

Hjern, A. Vinnerljung, B. and Lindblad, F. (2004) 'Avoidable mortality among child welfare recipients and intercountry adoptees: a national cohort study.' *Journal of Epidemiology and Community Health 58*, 5, 412–417.

Kessler, R. Pecora, P. Williams, J. Hiripi, E. *et al.* (2008) 'Effects of enhanced foster care on the long term physical and mental health of foster care alumni.' *Archives of General Psychiatry 65*, 6, 625–633.

Kristofersen, L. (2005) *Barnevernbarnas helse. Uførhet og dödelighet i perioden 1990–2002* [Health of child welfare children. Impairment and mortality 1990–2002]. Oslo: NIBR, Rapport #2005:12.

Nygaard Christoffersen, M. (1999) *Risikofaktorer i barndommen* [Childhood risk factors]. Köpenhamn: SFI, Rapport 99:18.

Pecora, P. Kessler, R. Williams, J. O'Brien, K. *et al.* (2005) *Improving Family Foster Care. Findings from the Northwest Foster Care Alumni Study.* Seattle, WA: Casey Family Programs.

Reilly, T. (2003) 'Transition from care: status and outcomes of youth who age out of foster care.' *Child Welfare 82*, 6, 727–746.

Rhodes, J. and DuBois, D. (2006) 'Understanding and facilitating the youth mentoring movement.' *Social Policy Reports 20*, 3, 3–19.

Statistics Sweden (1982) *Socio-Economic Classification (SEI).* Stockholm: SCB.

Sundell, K. Vinnerljung, B. Löfholm, C. and Humlesjö, E. (2007) 'Child protection in Stockholm: a local study of childhood prevalence of investigations and service delivery.' *Children and Youth Services Review 29*, 2, 180–192.

Tideman, E. Vinnerljung, B. Hinze, J. and Aldernius Isaksson, A. (submitted) *Improving Foster Children's School Achievements: Promising Results from a Swedish Intensive Small Scale Study.*

Vinnerljung, B. (1996a) *Svensk forskning om fosterbarnsvård – en översikt* [Swedish foster care research – a review]. Stockholm: Liber Utbildning/CUS.

Vinnerljung, B. (1996b) *Fosterbarn som vuxna* [Foster children as adults]. Lund: Arkiv Förlag.

Vinnerljung, B. (1999) 'Förekomst av adoptivbarn och långtidsvårdade fosterbarn bland placeringar av tonåringar i dygnsvård' [Prevalence of adoptees and long term care foster children among new placements of teenagers in out-of-home care]. *Socialvetenskaplig Tidskrift 6*, 4, 313–328.

Vinnerljung, B. Berlin, M. and Hjern, A. (2010) 'Skolbetyg, Utbilding och risker för ogynnsam utveckling hasbam' [School achievements, education and risks for unfavourable development among children]. In Socialstyrelsen *Social Rapport 2010*, 227–266. Stockholm: Socialstyrelsen.

Vinnerljung, B. and Franzén, E. (forthcoming) 'Indicators of self support problems among former child welfare clients.'

Vinnerljung, B. Franzén, E. and Danielsson, M. (2007) 'Teenage parenthood among child welfare clients: a Swedish national cohort study of prevalence and odds.' *Journal of Adolescence 30*, 1, 97–116.

Vinnerljung, B. Hjern, A. and Lindblad, F. (2006) 'Suicide attempts and severe psychiatric morbidity among former child welfare clients – a national cohort study.' *Journal of Child Psychology and Psychiatry 47*, 7, 723–733.

Vinnerljung, B. Öman, M. and Gunnarson, T. (2005) 'Educational attainments of former child welfare clients – a Swedish national cohort study.' *International Journal of Social Welfare 14,* 4, 265–276.

Vinnerljung, B. Tideman, E. Hinze, K. and Aldenius-Isaksson, A. (forthcoming) 'Improving foster children's school achievements. Promising results from a Swedish pilot project.'

Vinnerljung, B. Hjern, A. Ringbäck Weitoft, G. Franzén, E. and Estrada, F. (2007) 'Children and young people at risk. Social Report 2006.' *International Journal of Social Welfare 16,* Supplement 1, S163–S202.

WHO (1989) *International Classification of Disorders. Ninth Edition.* Geneva: WHO.

WHO (1992) *International Classification of Disorders. Tenth Revision.* Geneva: WHO.

Commentary by Fred Wulczyn on:

Long Term Outcomes of Foster Care: Lessons from Swedish National Cohort Studies

Bo Vinnerljung, Eva Franzén, Anders Hjern and Frank Lindblad.

Although it may seem odd to say so, the issue of child well-being is for all intents and purposes an emerging theme in policy and practice debates in the child welfare field. The main issue concerns the distinction between child protection and child welfare. Child protection, with a primary focus on child safety, is the narrower and more well-established of the two constructs. In contrast, child welfare draws upon the broader notion of child well-being and references health, cognitive functioning and social emotional well-being as well as life outcomes such as lifelong social connections, employment, social assistance and criminal history. With respect to policy and practice, the central tension has to do with when and how the *state* intervenes within families on behalf of children when it appears their well-being is threatened.

As this chapter makes abundantly clear, the issue of child welfare—i.e. well-being—is unlikely to recede from the debate any time soon. The incidence of suicide attempts, psychiatric disorders, teenage child birth, educational outcomes and receipt of public assistance are all greater among children with at least some contact with the child welfare system and particularly so for children placed away from home for long periods. When children are involved with the state, the state has a duty to make sure children are safe and to attend to their long-term well-being.

The paper also makes clear, although in a less direct way, how difficult the policy and practice issues are. As public child welfare agencies around the world face greater accountability, the question becomes the extent to which child welfare services influence developmental outcomes, either positively or negatively. When compared with the general population, children touched by the child welfare system are at a significant disadvantage. However, the risk of contact with the child welfare system is not spread evenly throughout the population, so discerning the developmental impact of child welfare services requires a carefully constructed counterfactual, particularly if, in the end, the goal of collecting such data is to discern the benefits (or harm) of having been involved with the child welfare system for purposes of holding public agencies accountable. Given some of the policy recommendations, the authors clearly favor this direction.

This chapter also shows the benefit of having population-based longitudinal data. Any effort to understand how the child welfare system affects life course outcomes demands data capable of providing a longterm view. To that end, however, few countries have the good fortune of having register data, so it will be hard to move forward without specialized data collection strategies and the methodological sophistication needed to isolate the impact of child welfare services from the myriad other influences (e.g. schools, neighborhoods, peer groups and families) that directly affect life course trajectories.

When contrasted with efforts to keep children safe, no small achievement under the best of circumstances, engaging families to promote well-being of children is the taller order. As this chapter suggests, the logic of well-being and the life course perspective require a view of childhood that invites holistic service networks that integrate a full range of services within family and community contexts. Though it is in many respects an obvious strategy, welfare traditions around the world are not necessarily aligned with a developmental approach to service organization. Designing such service structures is one of the great challenges. The lessons from Sweden highlight why the challenge is worth taking on.

CHAPTER 12

Foster Care in Denmark: Comparing Kinship and Non-Kinship Forms of Care

Lajla Knudsen, Tine Egelund and Anne-Dorthe Hestbæk

Out-of-home care generally produces poor outcomes for socially disadvantaged children. Although the Danish Consolidation Act on Social Services aims at compensating the children for the deprivations that led to the placement, out-of-home care has been capable of compensating these children only at the level of the most socially disadvantaged of their contemporaries. As adults previously cared-for children are disproportionately unemployed and poor; mentally and physically ill; substance abusers, etc. (Christoffersen 1993; Vinnerljung 1996a). In Denmark, the public costs of out-of-home care have risen dramatically during the last two decades and, therefore, social service authorities are encouraged to develop and test new forms of out-of-home care to meet the extraordinary needs of children in care.

Foster care has been the preferred care environment in Denmark for the past 25 years (Figure 12.1). Changes, however, have recently occurred with the Care Reform, now formalizing kinship care. The Care Reform stresses the responsibility of parents, other relatives and social networks for participating in solving the problems of troubled children. Whereas kinship care previously had limited application, the Reform now requires municipal child protection authorities to consider whether kinship care is a useful option whenever they place a child.

This chapter compares foster children, foster carers and caring environments for children in kinship care and ordinary foster care. *Kinship care* refers to placements with carers related to the foster child. *Ordinary foster care* refers to carers with no previous relationship to the child. Throughout this chapter, for the sake of comparison, we will refer to ordinary foster care as non-kinship care.

The Danish out-of-home care landscape for children and adolescents

Over the past 40 years constantly about 1 per cent of the child population, 0–17 years of age, has been placed in out-of-home care in Denmark. About 15,000 children were placed in care at the beginning of 2008. More than 6000 (44 per cent) of these children were placed in foster care.

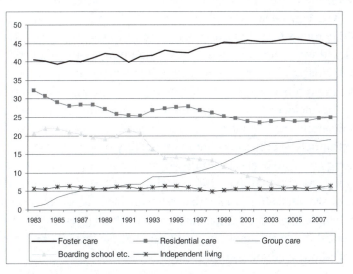

FIGURE 12.1 The development in out-of-home care environments in Denmark 1983–2008

Including children and adolescents 0–22 years of age.

For up to 6 per cent of placements in recent years (2005–2008) the specific care environment does not yet appear from registers. These cases are not included.

Source: Statistics Denmark; Statistik Danmarks – www.statistikbanken.dk.

The Danish child care landscape is highly diversified, however. As Figure 12.1 shows, 25 per cent are placed in residential institutions, which are either public institutions or private foundations with public funding. Residential institutions often have specific mandates, e.g. institutions specializing in handling school problems or antisocial behaviour, or offering therapy to children with severe emotional or behavioural problems. Nineteen per cent are placed in group care ('socio-pedagogical homes'), which are privately owned, often highly professionalized and specialized units, caring for 5–10 children or adolescents and 12 per cent are placed in either boarding schools[1] or some kind of independent living (Egelund and Hestbæk 2003).

The vast majority of children in foster care are placed in non-kinship care. Only about 2 per cent of all children in care are placed in either kinship or network care.[2]

Throughout the last two decades, only a small number of children have been placed with relatives. In a national study Christoffersen (1988) found that 18 per cent of the foster children were placed with relatives, equivalent to 7–8 per cent of all children in care. Nielsen (2002) found in a study from Copenhagen that 10 per cent of foster children were cared for by relatives (amounting to 4% of all children in care). Finally, in a national pilot study Lindemann and Hestbæk (2004) found that 5 per cent of all children in care were placed with relatives.

The incidence of placements in kinship care has been scarce in all Scandinavian countries. Several researchers explain this fact as practitioners' skepticism about the suitability of kinship care, especially among social workers deciding which care milieu is the most beneficial for the child (Holtan 2002; Mehlbye 2005; Vinnerljung 1996b). Social workers often doubt that relatives have adequate resources or can handle being both foster carers and relatives (Mehlbye 2005). This skeptical discourse among practitioners has facilitated a preference for (professionalized) non-kinship care.

Research on kinship care

Despite reservations of practitioners about the suitability of kinship care, research has revealed a number of positive outcomes: children in

---

1   It is customary in Denmark to place some older children in boarding schools also serving 'ordinary' adolescents if the cared-for children are not severely troubled and if Child Protective Services expect the children to profit from ordinary schooling.

2   'Network' carers know the child before the placement, but are not related to the child. We do not deal with 'network care' in this chapter as very few (19) of the children were placed in this type of care.

kinship care experience continuity in family relations (Holtan 2002). Kinship care is often a lasting relationship generating more stability and fewer breakdowns (Dubowitz and Feigelman 1993; Geen and Berrick 2002; Vinnerljung, Sallnäs and Kyhle-Westermark 2001). Children in kinship care develop relatively well. The break from the child's home is not as traumatizing (Holtan 2002) when the child is placed with relatives, and the child often manifests a more frequent contact with her or his parents and siblings (Ehrle and Geen 2002; Gleeson and O'Donnell 1997; Holtan 2002). Moreover, kinship carers tend to have taken care of the child informally before the foster care decision is formally made. The few Nordic studies on this subject support these international results (Lindemann and Hestbæk 2004; Holtan 2002; Nielsen 2002; Vinnerljung 1996b).

Methods

Data were collected in 2007 by standardized questionnaires to foster carers. Children and adolescents aged 4–22 years, who according to official registers were in kinship or network care at the end of 2006, were included. A control group – a random sample of children in non-kinship care matched by age – was also included. Of 617 question-naires sent to foster carers of children meeting these criteria 444 were returned, yielding a response rate of more than 70 per cent.

We consider a foster relation 'kinship care' when the foster carers, themselves, state that they are related to the child. We do so because kinship care was introduced with the Care Reform implemented only two years before we collected our data. Long-term placements with kinship carers initiated before this time, therefore, may still – legally – be defined as ordinary (non-kinship) foster care.

Kinship foster families are defined by one of the foster carers be-ing related to the child. Considering the fluidity of the nuclear family, however, we do not limit kinship to consanguinity. Former step parents and their relatives are also considered kinship carers.

We use two-sided Fisher's exact test when testing differences be-tween proportions. Distributions in tables larger than $2*2$ are tested with Chi^2-tests. Associations between discrete variables are tested using gamma-coefficients.

Results

Gender, age and ethnic background of children and adolescents in care
As regards *gender*, significantly more girls than boys are placed in kinship care than non-kinship care. Fifty-seven per cent of the children in kinship care are girls, compared to 45 per cent in non-kinship care.

The foster children in this study are 14 years old on average. Given the age matching of the control group, we cannot offer findings on age differences between children in the different kinds of foster care.

Last, no significant differences in *ethnic background* appear between the groups. Few ethnic minority children are placed in foster care (2% and 5% of children in kinship and non-kinship care, respectively).

Reasons for placing children in out-of-home care
According to the foster carers' assessments there is no doubt that both the children placed in non-kinship care and their families of origin are more severely troubled than children in kinship care (Tables 12.1 and 12.2).

TABLE 12.1 Proportion of children cared for because of diverse reasons associated with the child herself or himself, distributed by type of foster care (per cent)

REASONS FOR PLACEMENT	KINSHIP CARE	NON-KINSHIP CARE	
One or more reasons associated with the child herself/himself	52.7	69.8	**
School problems	15.5	28.0	**
Problems connected to leisure activities and/or peer relations	11.3	24.9	**
Behavioural problems	31.0	42.9	*
Mental health problems	4.2	11.1	*
Mental disability	4.9	12.6	*
Physical disability	3.5	5.0	
Other health problems	9.9	13.4	
Substance abuse	2.8	1.5	
Delinquency	3.5	2.3	
Other problems	3.2	7.5	
N	142–158	261–266	

*p < 0.05, **p < 0.01, ***p < 0.001.

Table 12.1 shows that children in non-kinship care are significantly more often than children in kinship care placed in foster care on the basis of their own problems. About two-thirds of the children in non-kinship care (70%) and half of the children in kinship care (53%) are placed because they, themselves, have problems. School problems, difficulties in peer relations, behavioural and mental health problems are significantly overrepresented among children in non-kinship care.

Table 12.2 shows that parents of children in non-kinship care face a worse situation than do parents of children in kinship care.

TABLE 12.2 Proportion of children cared for because of diverse reasons associated with the parents of the child, distributed by type of foster care (per cent)

REASONS FOR PLACEMENT	KINSHIP CARE	NON-KINSHIP CARE	
One or more reasons associated with the parents of the child	98.7	99.6	
Conflict/severe disharmony in the home	32.5	43.4	*
Violence between parents	9.7	21.5	**
Substance abuse	55.8	54.0	
Mental illness	27.3	32.1	
Mental disability	6.5	12.8	*
Physical disability	3.9	3.4	
Child neglect	18.8	39.6	***
Physical child abuse	4.5	15.8	***
Sexual child abuse	1.3	4.9	
Other criminal activities – the mother	10.4	6.0	
Other criminal activities – the father	8.4	9.8	
Poverty/dangerous physical environment	14.3	20.4	
Parents are dead/lack of family relations	24.5	16.6	
Other serious illness or death in the family	11.7	8.3	
Parents are absent or do not care for the child (parents in prison, the child is thrown out of home)	4.5	11.3	*
Other problems	13.3	13.5	
N	154–158	265–266	

*p < 0.05, **p < 0.01, ***p < 0.001.

Almost all parents have one or more problems contributing to the child's placement. Parents of children in non-kinship care significantly more often, however, live in mutual conflict, disharmony and violence. Moreover, these parents are significantly more often perpetrators of physical child abuse and neglect, or they are mentally disabled, or absent. In contrast, parents of children in kinship care are (nearly significantly) more often deceased ($p < 0.056$).

School performance

Children in non-kinship care have more school problems than children in kinship care. Table 12.3 makes clear that children in kinship care significantly more often receive mainstream instruction in ordinary schools, whereas children in non-kinship care more often attend special education.

TABLE 12.3 Type of instruction of foster children of school age, distributed by type of foster care (per cent)

	KINSHIP CARE	NON-KINSHIP CARE	
Ordinary school education	71.6	59.4	*
Mainly ordinary school education/special education in some disciplines or at some times	4.9	5.9	
Special education	15.7	27.3	*
Other	7.8	7.5	
N	102	187	

Three children not offered any instruction or currently not using the instruction offered are not included.

'Other' includes boarding schools, internal schools in residential care settings, etc.

*$p < 0.05$.

Non-kinship carers assess the performance of their foster children more pessimistically than kinship carers do. Table 12.4 shows that more than half of the non-kinship carers assess the level of knowledge of their foster children as lower than that of their contemporaries. The same assessment applies to one-third of children in kinship care.

TABLE 12.4 Foster carers' assessment of the level of knowledge of their foster child compared to that of the child's contemporaries, distributed by type of foster care (per cent)

	KINSHIP CARE	NON-KINSHIP CARE
Lower level	32.4	52.2
The same level	61.8	41.4
Higher level	5.9	6.5
N	102	186

Gamma = −0.319, p < 0.01.

Moreover, kinship carers to a higher degree expect their foster children to finish compulsory schooling (nine years of instruction), as almost two-thirds (63%) of these carers are very certain of the success of the child in primary school. By contrast non-kinship carers expect that half (48%) of the children will complete primary school. Nonetheless no significant difference between kinship and non-kinship foster children appears in the proportion finishing primary school and starting secondary education. Most foster children, however, enjoy going to school. Ninety-three per cent of children in kinship care and 87 per cent of children in non-kinship care highly or to some extent enjoy going to school.

Health and well-being of children in care
MENTAL HEALTH PROBLEMS AND DISABILITIES

The high incidence of somatic and mental health problems among children in care, compared to their 'ordinary' contemporaries, is well documented (Egelund *et al.* 2008). Table 12.5 shows that the morbidity rate is higher among non-kinship foster children than among kinship foster children.

TABLE 12.5 Proportion of children who have been diagnosed by a medical doctor or a psychologist, distributed by type of foster care (per cent)

	KINSHIP CARE	NON-KINSHIP CARE	
Mental disability	7.5	17.8	**
Attention Deficit Hyperactivity Disorder (ADHD) etc. (hyperactivity and/or attention problems)	8.8	15.4	
Child psychiatric illness	2.8	7.2	
Locomotive disability	3.4	2.1	
Severely reduced sight	3.4	2.1	
Serious hardness of hearing	1.4	1.3	
Severe impediment of speech	0.7	4.6	*
Serious dyslexia	1.4	5.1	
Other major disability	2.7	6.8	
N	144–147	235–242	

*p < 0.05, **p < 0.01.

Table 12.5 shows that differences between children in kinship and in non-kinship care predominantly concern mental health problems, of which only mental disabilities are significant.

SDQ-SCORE OF THE CHILDREN IN CARE
We used the Strengths and Difficulties Questionnaire (SDQ) to screen children younger than 17 years for socio-emotional problems (Goodman 1999). We find an equivocal association between type of foster care and the children's total SDQ-score, as well as their scores on all sub-scales of the SDQ.

TABLE 12.6 Total SDQ-score of 4–16-year-old foster children, distributed by type of foster care (per cent)

	KINSHIP CARE	NON-KINSHIP CARE
Normal	69.6	44.8
Borderline	11.6	12.8
Abnormal	18.8	42.4
N	112	203

Gamma = 0.461, p < 0.001.

Table 12.6 shows that 70 per cent of children in kinship care score within the normal range compared to less than half of the children in non-kinship care. The proportions of non-kinship foster children within the normal and abnormal range of the total SDQ-score are almost identical. This result indicates that a large proportion of all foster children – and especially children in non-kinship care – may need mental health interventions in order to cope with their daily challenges.

Core characteristics of the foster carers
AGE, ETHNIC BACKGROUND AND MARITAL STATUS OF CARERS
Carers in both types of foster care are 51 years old on average. However, a large difference exists in the distribution of age groups between kinship carers and non-kinship carers. Among kinship carers 44 per cent are either below 40 years old or above 59 years old, compared to only 12 per cent of non-kinship carers.

TABLE 12.7 Difference between the foster child's and the foster carer's age, distributed by type of foster care (per cent)

	KINSHIP CARE	NON-KINSHIP CARE	
Under 27 years	19.9	4.2	***
27–46 years	54.5	92.3	***
47 years and more	25.6	3.4	***
N	156	261	

*p < 0.05, **p < 0.01, ***p < 0.001.

The foster children are 37 years younger on average than the carers, with no significant difference between the two types of foster care. The difference between the child's and the carer's age, however, varies considerably more in kinship than in non-kinship care. Table 12.7 shows that both relatively low and high age differences are more common in kinship care than in non-kinship care. Nearly all non-kinship carers are between 27 and 46 years older than their foster child, compared to approximately half of the kinship carers. Almost all the carers are from ethnically Danish families. Very few carers have an ethnic minority background. Kinship carers relatively often are singles (17%), compared to non-kinship carers (5%). Two-thirds (68%) of the singles are women and one-third (32%) men.

CARERS' EDUCATION, EMPLOYMENT AND ECONOMICAL
CONDITIONS

Kinship carers are less educated than non-kinship carers. Forty-one per cent of kinship carers have no schooling beyond primary school compared to 22 per cent of non-kinship carers. Not surprisingly, then, more kinship carers (18%) lack vocational training than do non-kinship carers (12%). Significantly more non-kinship carers (40%) than kinship carers (29%) have medium-cycle higher education (e.g. nurses).

Three major differences in the labour market participation are apparent. First, a significantly higher proportion of non-kinship carers (40%) work as full-time carers, probably caused by differences in remuneration. Non-kinship carers receive a regular wage for their work allowing them to take care of the child at home. Kinship carers, in contrast, are only reimbursed for specific expenses and relatively few (8%) can afford to stay at home with the child. Second, a vast difference exists between the proportion of carers living on pensions or disability benefits: 19 per cent of kinship carers and 4 per cent of non-kinship carers have retired. Finally, more kinship carers (25%) than non-kinship carers (12%) are unskilled or skilled workers.

Kinship carers report an average taxable gross income of approximately 525,000 DDK and non-kinship carers of 690,000 DKK per family in 2006, which is a highly significant difference. The income of non-kinship carers is similar to that of families with children in the Danish population as a whole. The higher proportion of single-parent households, and more kinship carers provided for by pensions or disability benefits, contribute to this difference in income. Also, non-kinship carers tend to be more satisfied with their family income than kinship carers.

Support to foster carers

Support to tackle the caring for troubled children has both material and non-material dimensions.

FINANCIAL SUPPORT

Kinship carers do not receive remuneration for their work in contrast to non-kinship carers. A few of them do, however, get paid – possibly because they started as foster carers before the Care Reform. The wage (including regular payment and compensation for expenses) of those kinship carers who receive a wage at all, however, is significantly lower (on average approximately 9000 DKK a month) than that of non-kinship carers (19,000 DKK a month). Kinship carers, who do not receive regular payment but are only reimbursed for expenses, on average receive a monthly compensation of approximately 7000 DKK.

EDUCATION OF CARERS

Training is considered a major support to foster carers. Participation in training programmes has, therefore, been statutory since 2006. Still, as appears from Table 12.8, more than half of the kinship carers have not received any training at all.

TABLE 12.8 Proportion of foster carers who have participated in diverse kinds of training courses, distributed by type of foster care (per cent)

	KINSHIP CARE	NON-KINSHIP CARE	
No training programmes at all	56.2	24.8	***
Standard introductory course for foster carers	19.0	39.5	***
Network programmes for foster carers	18.3	29.5	*
Specific programmes for kinship and network carers	13.1	3.1	***
Programmes concerning conflict mediation, specific therapeutical methods, the use of life histories, diaries, etc.	11.1	43.8	***
Participated in talks about co-operation	16.3	22.5	
Other training	9.2	45.7	***
N	153	258	

$*p < 0.05$, $**p < 0.01$, $***p < 0.001$.

There is a highly significant difference where non-kinship carers attend training more often and participate in more different courses (on average 3.2) than do kinship carers (on average 1.8 courses).

INSPECTION

Inspection of foster care is compulsory according to law. Inspection has an element of control but also of help to cope with difficult situations. Inspectors are also supposed to talk to the foster child separately during visits. Data show that inspectors pay more visits to non-kinship foster homes than to kinship foster homes. Half the kinship homes and 67 per cent of the non-kinship homes are visited at least once every half year.

There is also a (non-significant) tendency that inspectors more often have talks with children in non-kinship care. Thirty-eight per cent of kinship foster children and 46 per cent of children in non-kinship care talk with an inspector at least once every half year. The lower level of inspection of kinship families is paradoxical as child protection social workers often express scepticism with this type of care (Lindemann and Hestbæk 2004; Mehlbye 2005).

The caring environment

Nearly all foster carers have biological or adoptive children of their own. Most of them, however, have left home. A third of the foster children, no matter the type of care, live in homes with at least one biological or adoptive child of the foster carer.

Nine out of ten kinship carers view the foster child as a fully integrated family member. The same applies to 71 per cent of the non-kinship foster children. Most kinship carers experience no or few conflicts (78 %) in their daily life with the foster child compared to 68 per cent of the non-kinship carers.

Parental contact and co-operation

Many foster children have no contact with their biological fathers. We, therefore, focus on contact with birth mothers. It depends on the type of care how frequently foster children visit their mothers. The proportion of children in kinship care visiting their mother once a week or more often is twice as large as the proportion of children in non-kinship care. In contrast, twice as many children in non-kinship care as in kinship care visit their mothers about once a month. However, irrespective of the type of care, more than half of the children never visit their mothers, visit irregularly or visit less frequently than once a month.

Most foster carers, irrespective of the type of care, find their co-operation with the child's parents tolerable, good or even very good. This is the case for 74 per cent of kinship foster carers and 84 per cent of non-kinship foster carers . Our data, thus, indicate, that co-operation may be more difficult for kinship carers than for non-kinship carers, although parents of children in non-kinship care have a higher extent of problems.

Discussion

Contrary to American studies (e.g. Berrick 1997; Berrick, Barth and Needell 1994; Dubowitz and Feigelman 1993; Ehrle and Geen 2002; Gebel 1996; Gleeson and O'Donnell 1997; Hegar 1999; Scannapieco, Hegar and McAlpin 1997) our Danish study does not confirm that ethnic minority children are more often placed in kinship care. Very few ethnic minority children are placed in any type of foster care. This result corresponds with other Danish studies (e.g. Egelund *et al.* 2008), finding that ethnic minority children are disproportionately often placed in residential care.

International results on the severity of problems among children in kinship care are inconclusive as some studies report problems similar to non-kinship foster children's, while others point to less serious problems in kinship foster children (Cuddeback 2004). Danish children placed in kinship care, however, have fewer and less severe problems than children placed in non-kinship care. Antisocial behaviour, for instance, is significantly less frequent in kinship foster than in non-kinship foster children. This result resembles the findings of Keller *et al.* (2001), showing that children in non-kinship care had significantly more frequent behavioural problems than children in kinship care. Berrick *et al.* (1994), in contrast, documented that children in both types of placement have a similar high occurrence of behaviour and health problems. The probability of being placed in kinship care is, however, not lower for Danish children with health problems as documented in some studies (e.g. Grogan-Kaylor 2000). Furthermore, non-kinship foster children have lower school performance, poorer mental health and more SDQ-scores within the abnormal range than kinship foster children.

Moreover, the family background of non-kinship foster children presents more developmental risks than that of kinship foster children (e.g. violence in the family, child neglect, physical child abuse and mental disability). We do not, however, like Cuddeback (2004), find parents' substance abuse and mental health problems more frequent among kinship foster than non-kinship foster children.

Kinship care has no tradition in Denmark. Even after promoting kinship care in the law, Child Protective Services have shown marked reluctance to place children with their grandparents. It is our hypothesis that the relatively less troubled situation of the kinship foster children mirrors this scepticism as the authorities are not willing to place highly disadvantaged children with kin.

Regarding the carers, our findings are similar to those of many other studies (e.g. Berrick 1997; Cuddeback 2004; Geen and Berrick 2002, Ehrle and Geen 2002) documenting that kinship carers are poorer, less educated and more often single than non-kinship carers. Kinship carers are not more unemployed but more frequently hold a position as a worker or are supported by different pensions.

Like other studies (e.g. Berrick *et al.* 1994; Cuddeback 2004; Dubowitz and Feigelman 1993; Egelund and Hestbæk 2003; Flynn 2002; Gebel 1996; Ehrle and Geen 2002; Gleeson and O'Donnell 1997; Nielsen 2002) we also find that the support to kinship carers is sparse. In a research review Triseliotis (1989, p.14) finds that when foster parents are well prepared, trained and supported during placement, a successful placement is more likely. Kinship care in Denmark is, nevertheless, legally designed as a 'discount' model of care as regards remuneration and – in practice – also as regards training and inspection.

The impact of other children's presence in the foster home has been the focus in some studies (e.g. Berridge and Cleaver 1987). Triseliotis (1989) concludes that positive outcomes of the placement are more likely when the foster parents are either childless or have no children of the same age and sex as the foster child at home. Consequently, it seems that Danish kinship foster children have a more favourable position than non-kinship foster children as a larger proportion of them is placed in homes with no other children present.

Kinship foster carers generally evaluate the situation of their foster children more positively than non-kinship foster carers (whether it concerns school performance, integration in the family, etc.). Information from different kinds of foster carers may, however, imply a potential bias to the results. (Professionalized) non-kinship carers meet the child as a result of the child's problematic situation and may focus more on this. Kinship carers having had positive relations with the child before the placement may consider the problems secondary when evaluating the child's situation. A pilot project for this study, however, to some extent supports our results. In the pilot project caseworkers were asked to evaluate the severity of problems of children in kinship care compared to children in other care environments. Approximately half of the caseworkers found that the children in kinship care had as many problems as other children placed in care while approximately the other half found that children in kinship care were less troubled than children placed in other care environments (Lindemann and Hestbæk 2004). This finding to some extent supports that the evaluations of the two groups of foster carers are based on objective differences rather than on different stances towards the children when evaluating them.

These analyses are based on the first of two data collections for a longitudinal study following a panel of children and adolescents in foster care. At the follow-up we will compare the outcomes of children placed in kinship and non-kinship care taking into account that the seriousness of their problems was dissimilar at entry into care. Therefore, we cannot yet discuss the relative advantages and disadvantages of the two types of foster care vis à vis each other. If, however, kinship carers seem to succeed as well as non-kinship carers despite their worse socioeconomic and demographic point of departure and failing support to their efforts there will certainly be reason to reconsider the widespread scepticism among practitioners towards kinship care.

Acknowledgement
The Danish Ministry of Welfare has generously financed the data collection for this study.

References
Berridge, D. and Cleaver, H. (1987) *Foster Home Breakdown.* London: Blackwell.

Berrick, J.D. (1997) 'Assessing quality of care in kinship and foster family care.' *Family Relations* 46, 3, 273–280.

Berrick, J.D. Barth, R. and Needell, B. (1994) 'A comparison of kinship foster homes and foster family homes: implications for kinship foster care as family preservation.' *Children and Youth Services Review 16,* 1/2, 33–63.

Christoffersen, M.N. (1988) *Familieplejen: En undersøgelse af danske plejefamilier med 0–17–årige plejebørn.* København: Socialforskningsinstituttet, Rapport 88:11.

Christoffersen, M.N. (1993) *Anbragte børns livsforløb: En undersøgelse af tidligere anbragte børn og unge født i 1967.* København: Socialforskningsinstituttet, Rapport 93:11.

Cuddeback, G.S. (2004) 'Kinship family foster care: a methological and substantive synthesis of research.' *Children and Youth Services Review, 26,* 623–639.

Danmarks Statistik *Børn og unge anbragt uden for eget hjem (31.december) efter område, anbringelsessted, alder og køn.* Available at www.statistikbanken.dk/statbank5a/default.asp?w=1280, accessed on 11 March 2009.

Dubowitz, H. and Feigelman, S. (1993) 'A profile of kinship care.' *Child Welfare 73,* 2, 153–169.

Egelund, T. and Hestbæk, A.-D. (2003) *Anbringelse af børn og unge uden for hjemmet. En forskningsoversigt.* København: Socialforskningsinstituttet, Rapport 03:04.

Egelund, T. Andersen, D. Hestbæk, A.-D. Lausten, M. *et al.* (2008) *Anbragte børns udvikling og vilkår. Resultater fra SFI's forløbsundersøgelser af årgang 1995.* København: SFI – Det Nationale Forskningscenter for Velfærd, Rapport 08:23.

Ehrle, J. and Geen, R. (2002) 'Kin and non-kin foster care – findings from a national survey.' *Children and Youth Services Review 24,* 1/2, 15–35.

Flynn, R. (2002) 'Research review: kinship foster care.' *Child and Family Social Work 7,* 311– 321.

Gebel, T.J. (1996) 'Kinship care and non-relative family foster care: a comparison of caregiver attributes and attitudes.' *Child Welfare 75,* 1, 5–19.

Geen, R. and Berrick, J.D. (2002) 'Kinship care: an evolving service delivery option.' *Children and Youth Services Review 24,* 1/2, 1–14.

Gleeson, J.P. and O'Donnell, J. (1997) 'Understanding the complexity of practice in kinship foster care.' *Child Welfare 76,* 6, 801–826.

Goodman, R. (1999) 'The extended version of the strengths and difficulties questionnaire as a guide to child psychiatric caseness and consequent burden.' *The Journal of Child Psychology and Psychiatry 40,* 791–799.

Grogan-Kaylor, A. (2000) 'Who goes into kinship care? The relationship of child and family characteristics to placement into kinship foster care.' *Social Work Research 24,* 3, 132–141.

Hegar, R.L. (1999) 'The Cultural Roots of Foster Care.' In, R.L. Hegar and M. Scannapieco (eds) *Kinship Foster Care. Policy, Practice and Research.* Oxford: Oxford University Press.

Holtan, A. (2002) *Barndom i fosterhjem i egen slekt.* Doktorgradsavhandling. Universitetet i Tromsø.

Keller, T.E. Wetherbee, K. Le Prohn, N.S. Payne, V. Sim, K. and Lamont, E.R. (2001) 'Competencies and problem behaviours of children in family care: variations by kinship placement status and race.' *Children and Youth Services Review 23,* 12, 914–940.

Lindemann, A. and Hestbæk, A. (2004) *Slægtsanbringelser I Danmark. En pilotundersøgelse.* København: Socialforskningsinstituttet, Rapport 04:21.

Mehlbye, J. (2005) *Slægtsanbringelse – det bedste for barnet? – En pilotundersøgelse.* København: AKF Forlaget.

Nielsen, F. (2002) *'Som plejeforældre ser det' – kortlægning og analyze af foranstaltningen 'familiepleje' i Københavns Kommune.* Copenhagen: Institut for Statskundskab, Københavns Universitet.

Scannapieco, M. Hegar, R.L. and McAlpin, C.M. (1997) 'Kinship care and foster care: a comparison of characteristics of outcomes.' *Families in Society 78,* 5, 480–488.

Triseliotis, J. (1989) 'Foster care outcomes: a review of key research findings.' *Adoption and Fostering 13,* 3, 5–17.

Vinnerljung, B. (1996a) *Fosterbarn som vuxna.* Lund: Arkiv.

Vinnerljung, B. (1996b) *Svensk forskning om fosterbarnsvård. En översikt.* Stockholm: Centrum för utvärdering av socialt arbete, Liber utbildning.

Vinnerljung, B. Sallnäs, M. and Kyhle-Westermark, P. (2001) *Sammenbrott vid tonårsplacering: om ungdomar i fosterhem och på insitution.* Stockholm: Socialstyrelsen, Centrum för utvärdering av socialt arbete.

Commentary by June Thoburn on:

Foster Care in Denmark: Comparing Kinship and Non-Kinship Forms of Care

Lajla Knudsen, Tine Egelund and Anne-Dorthe Hestbæk

The place of kinship care within the range of options for children needing out of home placement is an increasing focus for descriptive, process and outcome research. What is becoming very clear is that there are important differences in the way in which it is used in different jurisdictions. This chapter is essentially descriptive but flags up that outcome data will follow. It explains that in Denmark, despite increased emphasis in policy and legislation on foster family care, as in most European countries there is still a heavy reliance on group care. The recognition that the care system does not succeed as well as hoped in compensating for earlier adverse experiences is leading, as elsewhere, to a search for more effective options. One such option is kinship foster care, but, unlike the situation in Southern European countries including Spain and Italy, this has not, to date, been taken up in any large measure – only around 2 per cent of Danish children in care are placed with kinship or network foster carers.

Having set the scene, the authors describe their sample and report that in important respects the 'kin' and 'non-kin' samples differ. They recognize that these differences will need to be allowed for when they move on to compare outcomes for the two groups. The methodology attempts to ease these problems by selecting broadly matched age groups. However, given that *age at placement* is recognized as a key variable impacting on outcome, it will be important to bring this into the analysis by providing data on age at joining the foster or kinship families. From studies in other countries, it may be that those in kinship care were younger when they joined their families: if this is so, it will go towards explaining why those in non-kinship care were, on average, more troubled.

Other interesting questions come to mind. Is the small number in kinship care explained in part by more comprehensive support than is available in some other countries for family members who care for their young relatives outside the care system? In England, for example, alternative approaches are being used to provide help to kinship carers without the need for the children to enter or remain in care and it is anticipated that numbers in formal kinship foster care will stabilize and then fall. Another question is around the possible impact of much lower maintenance payments for kinship than non-kin in England; this discrimination has been held to be unlawful.

Access to data from Nordic and mainland European countries in the English language research literature is greatly to be welcomed. The statistics on which this article is based are more detailed than is often the case with large data sets and therefore especially welcome. We look forward eagerly to the publication of data on outcomes for those in both kin and non-kin foster family care.

CHAPTER 13

Selected Educational Outcomes for Young People Aged 17–19 Years in Long Term Foster Care in Ireland

Fiona Daly and Robbie Gilligan

Introduction

This chapter presents selected results from a follow up study to *Lives in Foster Care: The Educational and Social Support Experiences of Young People Aged 13–14 Years in Long Term Foster Care* (Daly and Gilligan 2005). This Phase 2 study was carried out in 2007/2008 and involved returning to the same foster carers who took part in the 'Lives in Foster Care' (Phase 1) report to gather data on the same young people in their care.[1] The main aim of the Phase 2 study was to establish how the same group of young people were doing, as regards their current living arrangements, education and economic activity. The results presented in this chapter focus on selected aspects of young people's educational history and current economic status. In particular, this chapter considers the following:

- the age at which young people left school
- whether young people sat State examinations at school

1   Funding for the Phase 1 study and part of the Phase 2 study was given by the Office of the Minister for Children and Youth Affairs, which is part of the Department of Health and Children.

- the highest school educational level achieved by young people
- what young people are doing now, e.g. employed, further education or training.

One of the key questions to be addressed in the chapter is what factors are associated with young people continuing their education beyond secondary school?

Foster care in Ireland

In 2006, there were a total of 5247 children and young people in the care of the State in Ireland, which represented 0.5% of the 0–18 year population (Health Service Executive 2009). The majority of young people in care in Ireland are in foster care, 88 per cent (4631), which includes young people in relative foster care (1482). Almost three quarters of young people in State care have been in care for more than one year, 73 per cent (3833). Furthermore, one third of children, 34 per cent (1764), have been in care for five years or more. These statistics point to two trends in the State care system in Ireland: first, the predominance of foster care as the primary means for looking after children in care; and second, out of the total number of children and young people in care at a particular point in time, a significant proportion are likely to have been in care on a long term basis.

Before discussing how the present study was carried out, the following section considers some of the findings from international research on the educational outcomes of young people in care.

Literature on educational outcomes

Research findings from a number of countries point to the inferior educational attainment of children in public care, when compared to those not in care. Importantly, there is also evidence that doing well in education is associated with doing well more generally for young people in care. Thus educational failure or under-performance has particular implications for young people, for their social as well as educational progress.

Consistent findings across a number of countries for young people in care show that there is a greater likelihood for young people in care to have no educational qualification on leaving school, compared to those never in care. For example, a British study found that 42.5 per cent of those ever in care had no educational qualification as compared to16.6 per cent of those never in care (Cheung and Heath 1994). In the US, Courtney and Dworsky (2006) report on a comparison of the progress of a sample of 19 year olds who had left (or were still in) care with results for 19 year olds from the nationally representative National Longitudinal Study of Adolescent Health. Over a third of the care group had no high school of Graduate Equivalency Diploma, as against less than 10 per cent of their peers in the general population.

Another common theme that emerges from international research is a greater tendency for young people in care to have less education/ lower attainment or leave the educational system earlier when compared to young people not in care. For example, a Danish study found that 12 per cent of young adults formerly in care had completed gymnasium (high level) (school leaving certificate) as compared to a rate of 17 per cent in a 'risk' group (whose parents were long term unemployed and had received welfare assistance for a specified period) and 39 per cent in a general control group (Christofferson 1996). In the same study, the care group had a school drop out rate of 10 per cent as compared to 7 per cent for the risk group and 2 per cent for the control group. In their Swedish study, Vinnerljung, Öman and Gunnarson (2005) found that young people who had grown up in care were over twice as likely (2.2 times) as their majority population peers with least educated mothers (considered by the authors to be a relevant comparison group) to have nine years or less of basic compulsory education, or three times as likely as their majority population peers overall. In a study in Chicago, Smithgall *et al.* (2004, p.28) found that those in care (n=692) were more likely than the majority not in care (n=21,672) to have dropped out: 55 per cent versus 36 per cent and as a corollary to be less likely to have graduated: 32 per cent versus 59 per cent. Thirty five per cent of the young care leavers in an Australian study were found to have completed high school (end of year 12) compared to 80 per cent of the 'at-home' comparison group and 10 per cent of the more risk-exposed 'early home leavers' (Cashmore and Paxman 1996, pp.172–173)

The lack of standardized data collection in relation to educational attainment across a range of different countries means that we must be cautious in generalizing from the evidence cited here. Nevertheless it is striking how convergent the messages are from the different studies.

Methodology

Selection of participants

The participants in the Phase 2 study were drawn from the same population studied in Phase 1. There were three main selection criteria for the Phase 1 study: first, young people were aged 13–14 years; second, they had been in foster care for more than one year;[2] and third, they had been with their current foster carer at the time for more than six months. A list of all the young people in the Republic of Ireland who met these three criteria were drawn up by the former health boards[3] and released to the research team after legal and data protection issues had been resolved.

Foster carers were the key informants for the Phase 2 study (as in Phase 1). It was decided that they remained the people best placed to be able to provide comparable information on the current circumstances of this group of young people who were the focus of the study.[4]

Research method

The main research instrument used in Phase 2 was a structured questionnaire, which was administered to carers during a telephone interview. The topics covered included the young person's current foster care status, their current economic status (e.g. employment, full-time education, etc.) and aspects of their educational history.

Response rate

There were a total of 205 interviews with foster carers carried out in Phase 1. In Phase 2, contact was made with a total of 168 of the original foster carers in Phase 1. Fully completed interviews were done with 118 of these foster carers and partially completed interviews were carried out with a further 23 foster carers. Therefore, substantial information was collected from just over two thirds of the same foster

---

2   This was the definition used for the purpose of the research to indicate that young people were in *long term* foster care.

3   The former health boards were replaced by the Health Service Executive in 2004. The Health Service Executive is a statutory body and provides health and personal social services to all people living in the Republic of Ireland. This includes taking responsibility for the placement and welfare of children/young people in the care of the State.

4   As some of the young people were under 18 years of age, interviewing them directly would require their own personal consent as well as consent from their foster carer, the relevant Health Service Executive area responsible for their care and a birth parent. The practical implications of this for a national study prevented direct access with young people themselves.

carers who were involved in Phase 1, giving a response rate of 68.8% (n=141). Limited interviews were carried out with a further 27 foster carers.[5] Therefore, including these limited interviews means that basic information at the very least was available for a total of 168 young people, representing 81.9% of all cases in Phase 1.

It was not possible to carry out interviews in the case of 37 carers from Phase 1.[6] In almost half of these cases (n=17), this was due to foster carers being uncontactable despite attempts to obtain updated contact details for these foster carers from the relevant Health Service Executive region (formerly health board areas). There were ten refusals and eight non-respondents.[7] In addition, two carers had passed away since Phase 1 (both grandparent relative carers).

Characteristics of young people in the study

Before presenting some of the main findings, a profile of young people in the study is given, which includes gender, age, current living arrangements and care histories.

Gender: 53.6 per cent (90) of young people were female and 46.4 per cent (78) were male

Age group: The majority of young people were aged 18–19 years old – 40.5 per cent (68) were aged 18 and 45.8 per cent (77) were 19 years old.

Current living arrangements: 55.4 per cent (93) were still living with the same foster carer (from Phase 1). Out of these 93 young people:

- 78 were categorized as being in after care (aged 18 years or over) [8]

---

5   The main reason for partially completed and limited interviews was that these tended to involve cases where young people had aged out of foster care and were no longer living with the same foster carer, as in Phase 1. Also, some of these cases represented situations where the foster carer and the young person were no longer in contact with each other and the foster carer could not answer some of the questions asked.

6   It is reasonable to suggest that at least some of the 37 missing cases may have experienced relatively poor outcomes. One of the main reasons for some refusals by foster carers was that the placement had broken down and the carer found it extremely difficult to talk about the circumstances surrounding this. Where placements had broken down, there was unlikely to be any contact at present between the foster carer and the young person. The potential impact of non-response is acknowledged by the authors and will be considered later in the chapter.

7   Non-respondents had originally agreed to do the interview but then did not participate despite several call backs.

8   When a young person reaches 18 years of age, they have gone beyond the legal age limit of State care.

- 11 were still in foster care (aged 17 years old)
- four young people had been adopted by the same carer.

Where young people were not living with the same foster carer (n=75), information was available on the living arrangements of 69 young people:

- 28 were 'living independently', typically living by themselves or with a partner/friends
- 18 had returned to live with their birth family or another relative
- nine were in residential care or another foster care placement (excluding relative care)
- 14 were categorized as having 'other' living arrangements, where they were in situations that could be deemed as being short term or indicating some degree of vulnerability.[9]

Young people's care histories

Age first placed in care: on average 4.2 years old, which ranged from a few days old to 13 years of age; 54.1 per cent (73) of young people were first placed in care when aged three years of age or younger (n=135). Therefore, young people in this study were found to have spent a fairly extensive part of their young lives in care.

Previous care placements: 47.5 per cent (67) had previous care placements prior to their placement with the foster carer (from Phase 1) (n=141); on average, these young people had 2.2 previous care placements. However, almost one out of 10 of all young people in the study, 8.9 per cent (15) had three or more previous care placements.

Relative/non-relative care placement: 22.0 per cent (37) of young people were related to their foster carer (from Phase 1) (n=168).

Main results

The main results of the Phase 2 study aim to provide some insight into aspects of young people's lives at a time when many of them were at an age where they are likely to be maturing out of foster care and starting to lead independent lives. As stated earlier, the main focus here is on

---

9   This category included young people living in sheltered accommodation (three), with a friend's family (three), in a hostel/B&B (two), homeless (one) or in prison (one).

two areas: selected aspects of young people's educational history; and their current economic status.

Selected aspects of young people's educational history
Three main areas are explored here:

- the age at which young people left school
- examinations taken prior to leaving school
- highest educational level achieved in school.

The following results are based on all 168 young people in Phase 2.[10]

School leaving age
Based on the young people who had left school by the time of interview and for whom information was available (n=147), it was found that the average age of leaving school was 17.1 years.[11]

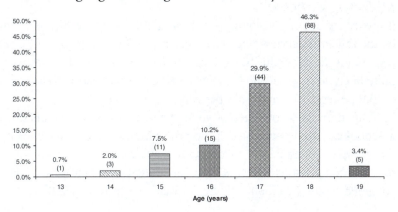

FIGURE 13.1 Age at which young people left school (n=147)

Figure 13.1 shows that young people were most likely to leave school at 17 or 18 years of age – 29.9 per cent (44) at age 17 years and 46.3 per cent (68) at age 18 years, which represents just over three quarters of young people. Early school leaving is defined as leaving school before

---

10 Questions on young people's education were a priority in the questionnaire and the main education questions were asked during all interviews with foster carers, including interviews where only limited information was obtained.

11 This is based on the mean (SE = 0.097).

the legal school leaving age of 16 years. One in ten young people left school early, 10.2 per cent (15), mostly at the age of 15.

School examinations

Given the age of young people in Phase 2, it was appropriate to collect some information on the State examinations that young people had taken at school – both the Junior Certificate and Leaving Certificate exams.

(1) Junior Certificate[12]

The vast majority of young people sat the Junior Certificate exam – 89.5 per cent (145).[13] There was little difference in the per centage of boys and girls who sat the Junior Certificate exam – 89.2 per cent (66) of boys compared to 91.9 per cent (79) of girls.

(2) Leaving Certificate[14]

Just over six out of ten young people sat the Leaving Certificate exam by the time of interview with foster carers, 64.0 per cent (103).[15] Corresponding to trends in the national student population, females were more likely to have sat the Leaving Certificate examination than males – 70.9 per cent (61) and 56.8 per cent (42) respectively.[16]

The information on whether young people took State examinations at school was used to produce data on the educational level achieved by this group of young people in long term foster care. It was then possible to make comparisons with the national student population using data compiled by the Economic and Social Research Institute (ESRI).[17]

---

12   The Junior Certificate is a national State examination taken at the end of the junior cycle (third year) in secondary school, typically at age 15 or 16.

13   This result is based on 162 young people as it was missing for the remaining six.

14   The Leaving Certificate is a national State examination taken two to three years after the Junior Certificate, usually when young people are aged 17 to 18. Where young people go on to further education or third level education, the results of this exam tend to determine which course they are accepted for.

15   The result is based on 161 young people

16   This association was of borderline statistical significance using chi-square – $x^2 = 3.484$, df = 1, p<.10.

17   The ESRI carry out an annual survey of school leavers across the country. The Institute conducts economic and social research to inform policymakers, including national government.

Highest educational level reached in school

TABLE 13.1 Highest educational level of school leavers (n=136) compared to the national student population

HIGHEST EDUCATIONAL LEVEL	FOSTER CARE STUDY %(n)	ESRI REPORT %
No formal qualifications	6.6 (9)	2
Junior Certificate	25.7 (35)	12
Leaving Certificate	67.6 (92)	86
Total	**100.0 (136)**	**100.0**

Source for ESRI data: Byrne, McCoy and Watson 2008, p.7.

Table 13.1 shows that young people in the foster care study were less likely to have taken the Leaving Certificate compared to those in the national population – 67.6 per cent (92) compared to 86 per cent nationally. The most common reason for young people not sitting the Leaving Certificate was because they had already left school (n=43) in the time between the Junior Certificate and Leaving Certificate examinations. The number of young people who left with no formal qualifications was higher than the national population – 6.6 per cent (nine) compared to 2 per cent.[18] Young people in the foster care study were more likely to have reached a lower educational level in their schooling than their peers in the national population. However, it is certainly noteworthy that almost two thirds of young people in the research had remained at school to take the Leaving Certificate exam.

During telephone interviews, foster carers were keen to point out the significance of young people's achievements in their education, particularly when considered in the context of their family circumstances. For example, in three instances, foster carers stated that the young person was the first member of their birth family to have sat the Leaving Certificate exam (while other siblings had left school early). In addition, six out of ten foster carers, 63.1 per cent (89) felt that being in foster care had had a positive impact on the young person's education. Some carers said that being in foster care meant that young people received the adequate supports and encouragement needed to do well at school (13), were more likely to attend school (15) and were more likely to stay on at school and complete their exams (19).

---

18   Out of the 15 young people in the study, four were male and five were female.

Current economic status

Foster carers were asked what young people were doing now in terms of whether they were still at school, were in employment or had gone onto further education or training. Table 13.2 shows the results.

TABLE 13.2 Young people's current economic status

ECONOMIC STATUS	%	N
Still at school or recently finished school	17.4	28
Student in further education	24.8	40
Student in higher education	11.2	18
Training course/apprenticeship	7.4	12
Employed	14.3	23
Unemployed	13.7	22
Child care duties	5.0	8
Other	6.2	10
Total	**100.0**	**161***

*Data were missing for seven young people.

Table 13.2 shows that just over one half of young people, 53.4 per cent (86), are still participating in education in some form (first three categories combined), whether it is in secondary school – those who are still at school or just recently finished – further education or higher education.[19] In addition, 7.4 per cent (12) of young people were doing a training course, typically an apprenticeship, examples of which include training to qualify as a plumber, electrician or hairdresser.

How do the findings in Table 13.2 on young people's economic status compare to the national student population?

The *School Leavers Survey Report 2007* (Byrne *et al.* 2008) carried out by the Economic and Social Research Institute (ESRI) contains information on the current economic status of school leavers nationally in the academic year 2004/2005. It is based on a random stratified sample of a 'reference cohort' of 2025 young people who have *finished* their school education. In order to be comparable with this national dataset, Table 13.3 shows the current economic status of young people in the foster care study who had left school by the time of interview, i.e. it excludes those who were still at school or recently just finished school in Table

---

19   Further education tended to involve post-Leaving Certificate courses, e.g. certificate level courses. Higher education represented young people on diploma and degree courses.

13.3 (n=28). Therefore, the foster care data are based on a total of 133 young people. In addition, it reports the results on the current economic status of school leavers in the ESRI school leavers report.[20]

TABLE 13.3 Current economic status of school leavers in the foster care study and the ESRI School Leavers Survey Report 2007

ECONOMIC STATUS	FOSTER CARE STUDY % (n)	ESRI REPORT %
Student (further or third level education)	43.6 (58)	41.6
Training/apprenticeship	9.1 (12)	10.5
Employed	17.3 (23)	37.7
Unemployed	16.5 (22)	4.8
Unavailable for work/inactive	13.5 (18)	4.8
Total	**100.0 (133)**	**100.0**

Source for ESRI data: Byrne *et al.* 2008, p.44

Table 13.3 shows where differences in current economic status emerge between young people in the foster care study and the national population based on the ESRI report. Young people in the national population were more than twice as likely to be employed than those in the foster care study – 37.7 per cent compared to 17.3 per cent respectively.

Young people in the foster care study were three times more likely to be unemployed (16.5 per cent compared to 4.8 per cent in the national population) and unavailable for work/inactive (13.5 per cent compared to 4.8 per cent in the national population). Therefore, some of the potential routes after completing secondary education can be different for this group of young people formerly in long term foster care compared to young people in the national population. However, young people in foster care were as likely to be currently studying (43.6% compared to 41.6%) or doing a training course/apprenticeship (9.1% compared to 10.5%) as young people in the national population, despite the earlier finding that young people were less likely to have taken the Leaving Certificate exam compared to the national student population.[21]

---

20   There are likely to be some differences in the definition of categories in both studies and the relatively small population size of young people in the foster care study should also be borne in mind when considering these results. Also, respondents in the ESRI study were young people themselves and they were interviewed/surveyed between 20 and 26 months after leaving school. However, a comparison with the ESRI data should provide some indication of any major differences in the current economic status of young people who are maturing out of foster care compared to trends in the overall population.

21   The results of the Leaving Certificate exam are typically used to gain entry to many further education and third level courses.

Participation in education beyond secondary school

The issue of remaining in education beyond secondary school was considered in more detail to establish if there were any circumstances under which it was found to be more prevalent. One factor was found to be significant and related to the level of stability in young people's living circumstances. Young people in foster care who were still living with the same foster care household as in the Phase 1 study were significantly more likely to continue with their education beyond school, as Table 13.4 shows.

Tht table shows that young people who were still living with the same foster carer (as in Phase 1) were twice as likely to be participating in education beyond school, compared to those who were not living with the same foster carer – 57.1 per cent (40) and 28.6 per cent (18) respectively. When this result is compared to the rate of participation in education beyond school in the national student population, 41.6 per cent (see Table 13.3), this is particularly noteworthy. Also young people who did not live with the same foster carer were found to be three times more likely to be unemployed or unavailable for work/inactive compared to those who did – 47.6 per cent (30) and 14.3 per cent (10) respectively. These results are statistically significant.

TABLE 13.4 Current economic status by whether young people are living with the same foster carer (as in Phase 1)

CURRENT ECONOMIC STATUS	YP LIVING WITH FOSTER CARER		TOTAL
	Yes % (n)	No % (n)	
Education beyond school	57.1 (40)	28.6 (18)	43.6 (58)
Employment or training	28.6 (20)	23.8 (15)	26.3 (35)
Unemployed or unavailable for work/inactive	14.3 (10)	47.6 (30)	30.1 (40)
Total	100.0 (70)	100.0 (63)	100.0 (133)

$X^2 = 18.743$, df = 2, p<.005.

Living with the same foster carer was also found to be associated with certain positive aspects of young people's final year schooling in secondary school; in particular, where young people left school at an older age and also where they had sat the State examinations at school (both factors were significant). Therefore, it could be argued that stability in young people's foster care placements can contribute to more favourable educational outcomes both during and beyond secondary school. However, given the nature of the data in the study, a direct causal link cannot be established, but these findings suggest possible conditions which are more conducive to better outcomes for young people, particularly when they have aged out of foster care.[22]

Note of caution on the results

It should be remembered that the young people aged 17–19 years on whom this research is based could be considered to be the most advantaged of young people in State care in terms of the relative stability that many of them have experienced in their foster family placements. In addition, there are no data on 37 young people who were part of Phase 1. Therefore, the findings could be overly positive relative to the general picture of children in care. Further work was done to take account of missing data and to address this possibility.

In the worst case scenario, it could be assumed that all 37 young people for whom data were missing in Phase 2 did not continue with their education after leaving secondary school. In addition, current economic status was missing for a further seven young people whose foster carers participated in Phase 2. If this group of 44 young people were assumed to have experienced less positive outcomes and did not continue their education beyond secondary school, the per centage of young people who were currently students would fall from 43.6 per cent (see Table 13.3) to an estimated per centage of 28.3 per cent (n=205). Therefore, at the very least, it could be argued that one in four young people from the Phase 1 study remained in some form of education after they finished their schooling. As this estimated calculation is based on the very worst case scenario, the correct figure is likely to be somewhere between 28.3 per cent and the actual result based on cases where information was available, 43.6 per cent.

---

22   Most of the data in the study consisted of categorical data, which has implications for the nature of statistical testing that can be employed. The chi-square statistical test of significance was used in the data analysis, which can be used to establish an association between variables but not a causal link between the variables.

Conclusions

The primary aim of this research was to provide evidence about the educational outcomes of a group of young people who were ageing out of long term foster care. Young people tended to leave school at the age of 17 or 18 years and there was a fairly low rate of early school leaving (one in ten). However, they were found to have achieved a lower educational level with fewer sitting the traditional school leaving examination, the Leaving Certificate, compared to their peers in the national population. So, while early school leaving was not found to be a major issue for this group of young people, based on the official definition of leaving before the age of 16 years, it was clear that a substantial proportion of young people in the study left school during the period between sitting the Junior Certificate exam and the time they would have been due to sit the Leaving Certificate. So, leaving school prior to taking the Leaving Certificate appears to be an issue. Nevertheless, after taking account of missing cases, it is estimated that at least 27.9 per cent of all young people from the Phase 1 study had continued with their education beyond secondary school.

Continuing their education beyond secondary school was significantly more likely for young people who still lived with the same foster carers, with whom they had been placed in the Phase 1 study. Stability in family circumstances, sitting the Leaving Certificate and having a care history with minimal changes to placements were found to be associated with a more positive economic status. Where young people had experienced instability in family circumstances, had not taken the Leaving Certificate and experienced many placement changes in care, they were found to be more likely to have a vulnerable economic status, where they were unemployed or categorized as 'other', which often indicated some degree of social exclusion. The association found between stable living arrangements and educational progress in the research should help to inform policy and practice in promoting the educational welfare of children and young people in care. It is important to recognize the value of education in the progress of young people in care.

Based on the results presented here, the majority of young people in the study can be deemed to be in a fairly similar position to that of their peers, who are emerging into young adulthood. They have similar decisions to make about their lives in terms of continuing their education, taking up employment or participating in further training. However, the group of young people in this study are very different to young people in short term foster care or in other categories of State care by virtue of their experiences of being in *long term* foster care. In some cases, it may not be fair to make direct comparisons between their educational outcomes and those of the national student population. As some foster carers themselves were keen to point out, the young people in their care had made significant achievements in their education in their own right.

Future research in the area will contribute more to our understanding of educational outcomes for young people in care. It is important to have access to data that make it possible to track young people's progress over time, as well as research being carried out to facilitate international comparisons. The perspectives of young people themselves are also crucial to provide greater knowledge and awareness. It is hoped that a third phase of this study will be carried out, where a group of the young people will be given the opportunity to tell their own story about their educational experiences as a young person in long term foster care. This will provide a rich insight into some of the issues discussed here in terms of the factors that may contribute to positive educational outcomes for young people with a care background and ensure that young people's own voices are represented in the research.

References

Byrne, D. McCoy, S. and Watson, D. (2008) *School Leavers Survey Report 2007*. Dublin: Economic and Social Research Institute and Department of Education and Science.

Cashmore, J. and Paxman, M. (1996) *Wards Leaving Care: A Longitudinal Study*. Kensington, New South Wales: Social Policy Research Centre, University of New South Wales.

Cheung, S.Y. and Heath, A. (1994) 'After care: the education and occupation of adults who have been in care.' *Oxford Review of Education 20*, 361.

Christofferson, M.N. (1996) 'A follow-up study of out-of-home care in Denmark: long-term effects on self-esteem among abused and neglected children.' *International Journal of Child and Family Welfare 1*, 25–39.

Courtney, M.E. and Dworsky, A. (2006) 'Early outcomes for young adults transitioning from out-of-home care in the USA.' *Child and Family Social Work 11*, 209–219.

Daly, F. and Gilligan, R. (2005) *Lives in Foster Care*. Dublin: Children's Research Centre.

Health Service Executive (2009) *Preliminary Analysis of Child Care Dataset 2006* (unpublished).

Smithgall, C. Gladden, R. Howard, E. Goerge, R. and Courtney, M. (2004) *The Educational Experiences of Children in Out-of-Home Care*. Chicago, IL: Chapin Hall Center for Children.

Vinnerljung, B. Öman, M. and Gunnarson, T. (2005) 'Educational attainments of former child welfare clients – a Swedish national cohort study.' *International Journal of Social Welfare 14*, 265–276.

Commentary by Paul Delfabbro on:
Selected Educational Outcomes for Young People Aged 17–19 Years in Long Term Foster Care in Ireland

Fiona Daly and Robbie Gilligan

Although there are a number of international studies that have examined the effect of out-of-home care on children's safety, psychosocial well-being and relationships with their birth families, relatively few studies have examined how being placed into care affects children's long-term employment prospects and their engagement, performance and stability in formal education. For this reason, Fiona Daly and Robbie Gilligan's study of 168 young people in Ireland makes an important contribution towards enhancing our understanding of this neglected topic. A positive feature of their findings is that the experience of being in care appears to have given most disadvantaged young people an opportunity to undertake their studies in a relatively stable home environment. Two thirds received their Leaving Certificate and a further 26 per cent received their Junior Certificate. The findings showed that those young people who remained with their foster families beyond the age of 18 and who were relatively stable in care had the best educational and employment outcomes. These findings underscore the fundamental importance of stability and continuity of connections in out-of-home care and the potentially damaging effects of placement instability as well as failures to provide ongoing support once young people 'graduate' from the care system.

Daly and Gilligan's work also highlights the extent to which socioeconomic disadvantage persists within out-of-home care populations and especially amongst those who are unable to remain with their foster families as adults. Although favourable, the level of educational attainment in this sample was still significantly lower than in normative populations and there were much higher levels of unemployment in the 'leaving care' sample. Many of these results mirror similar findings in Australia from studies of leaving care populations (Cashmore and Paxman 1996) as well as studies (Barber and Delfabbro 2004) that have examined the educational fortunes of children during their time in care. In South Australia, for example, our findings suggest that the situation for young people in care is likely to be more dire than described in the Irish research. Children would appear to change placement at a much higher rate in Australia and in Daly and Gilligan's sample. For example, in contrast to Daly and Gilligan who report that one in ten children had three or more placements, we found that almost 25 per cent of children sampled for our longitudinal study in 1998–1999 had experienced ten or more previous placements and that over 40 per cent had to change school as a result of the first placement we observed. Many of the Australian placement changes coincided with changes in schools and often to locations that were geographically removed from the previous school. Our studies also found very high rates of suspension and exclusion amongst children in statutory care and this also contributed to the ongoing pattern of school changes.

Research of the nature described by Daly and Gilligan should be undertaken more regularly and arguably on an ongoing basis by government departments around the world. The stability and adequacy of schooling is fundamental for the future employment prospect of care-leavers, but also provides the principal way in which young people can develop social networks, sport and leisure interests as well as a clear sense of identity within a particular geographically confined area.

References

Cashmore, J. and Paxman, M. (1996) *Wards Leaving Care: A Longitudinal Study*. Kensington, New South Wales: Social Policy Research Centre, University of New South Wales.

Barber, J.G. and Delfabbro, P.H. (2004) *Children in Foster Care*. London: Taylor and Francis.

CHAPTER 14

Can Tutoring by Foster Parents Improve Foster Children's Basic Academic Skills?

A Canadian Randomized Field Trial

Robert J. Flynn, Marie-Pierre Paquet
and Robyn A. Marquis

International research consistently indicates that the educational achievement of many young people in foster care lags behind that of their age peers in the general population (e.g. Trout *et al.* 2008; Jackson 2007; Flynn *et al.* 2004). This educational gap is attributable to pre-care factors such as early abuse, neglect, or extreme poverty and to in-care influences such as placement disruptions or changes in schools. The present chapter examines the problem of low educational achievement among young people in care and summarizes the methodology and first-year results of a two-year randomized field (RFT) trial that we are conducting in Canada. The RFT is a "real-world" effectiveness trial rather than a lab-based efficacy trial of tutoring by foster parents as a means of improving the basic academic skills in reading and mathematics of primary-school aged foster children. The chapter provides a selective overview of international research on the academic status of young people in care, reviews the literature on adult volunteer tutoring as an intervention to improve academic skills among young people in the general school population and summarizes the first-year results of our RFT. (A more detailed and technical paper on the evaluation of the RFT will be submitted to a peer-reviewed archival journal.)

International research on the academic status of young people in care

US research

Trout *et al.* (2008) provided a thorough and informative synthesis of US research conducted during a 66-year period (1940–2006) on the academic status of young people in care. It is telling that although Trout and her colleagues originally planned to include in their review a summary of research on educational interventions aimed at improving the academic functioning of young people in care, they were unable to do so because they found too few such studies to summarize.

From an initial pool of 203 articles, only 10 (6%) of which had been conducted outside the United States, Trout *et al.* (2008) reviewed only those 29 articles that had met their screening criteria: studies conducted in the US, published in a US journal and containing data on the academic status of school-age children and adolescents served in out-of-home placements. The 29 articles reported on 36 data sets that had been based on a total of 13,401 students.

Trout *et al.* (2008) found that young people in care were three times as likely to be involved in special education as students in the general school population. Teachers reported that as many as four-fifths of the young people in care were academically at risk and performed below grade level, with most in the low to low-average range on measures of academic achievement. Trout and her colleagues were of the opinion that many young people in care would require intensive educational assistance to address their difficulties. They also recommended that future research test evidence-based academic interventions and use standardized achievement tests to provide information on the gains experienced by young people in care in specific academic areas, such as receptive or expressive language, reading comprehension, or math calculation.

UK research

Jackson (2007) noted that improved educational achievement has become a key policy issue in the UK, where the situation remains one of widespread under-performance. She noted that the proportion of young people in care in England whose academic results in secondary school would allow them ready access to postsecondary education had increased only slightly in recent years. She also lamented the fact that little or no research was being conducted in the UK on the basic reasons for the "huge and persistent gap in attainment between care leavers and others" (Jackson 2007, p.4). She felt that much more attention needed to be paid to the pivotal role of foster parents in enhancing the educational performance of young people in care. Also, according to Jackson (2007), the failure of the UK to put sufficient emphasis on the education of young people in care is also characteristic of other English-speaking countries, such as Canada, the US and Australia.

Canadian research

We limit attention here to our own research, most of which has been carried out over the last decade as part of the Ontario Looking after Children (OnLAC) project (Flynn, Dudding and Barber 2006). Our work owes a great deal to the original Looking After Children initiative in the UK (Ward 1995), which has had an important impact in a number of countries. In our earliest published Looking After Children study (Flynn and Biro 1998), we found that young persons in foster care had considerably higher rates of suspension and grade retention than their age peers in the general population. Subsequently (Flynn *et al.* 2004), we compared the educational performance of 340 Ontario 10–15 year olds and 132 5–9 year olds in care with that of nationally representative samples of the same age from the general Canadian population (Statistics Canada and Human Resources Development Canada 1999). Ratings by the foster parents of these young people on a composite measure of reading, spelling, math and overall educational performance indicated that 80 percent of the 10–15 year olds in care scored in the same performance range as the lowest third of 10–15 year olds in the general population, who had been rated on the same composite measure by their own parents. Similarly, 78 percent of the 5–9 year olds in care were rated by their foster parents as in the same educational performance range as the bottom third of 5–9 year olds in the general population.

With data from year 6 (2006–2007) of the OnLAC project (Miller, Flynn and Vandermeulen 2008), we found that a likely contributor to educational difficulties among young people in care was the frequency of moves from one school to another, other than those involved in the child's natural progression through the school system. Although most of the younger children, aged 5–9 years, had changed school less than three times, fully 68 percent of those aged 10–15 years and 77 percent of those aged 16–20 had changed schools three or more times. Also, a higher proportion of children in care than in the general population had missed significant amounts of school, often for health-related reasons (e.g. appointments with physicians). The proportion of the children who had repeated a grade increased with age, with 16 percent of the 5–9 year olds, 27 percent of the 10–15 year olds and 32 percent of the 16–20 year olds having repeated a grade (Miller *et al.* 2008).

In the most recent provincial report from the OnLAC project (Miller, Vincent and Flynn 2009), based on the year 7 (2007–2008) data, we described the educational performance and preferences of 2470 young people in care aged 10–15. The percentage rated by their caregivers as doing poorly or very poorly was 28 percent in math, 25 percent in science, 22 percent in reading and 20 percent overall. The proportion saying they liked various school subjects a lot varied considerably: 69 percent in the case of gym or physical education, 35 percent for science, 34 percent for English, 31 percent for math, 20 percent for arts (including music and drama) and only 18 percent for French. The percentage rating various school-related activities as very important was 67 percent for getting good grades, 66 percent for always showing up to class on time, 65 percent for handing in assignments on time, 62 percent for making friends, 42 percent for expressing their opinions in class, 38 percent for learning new things and for participating in extracurricular activities and only 14 percent for taking part in student council or other similar groups. Thirty-two percent of the young people in care aspired to obtaining one or more university degrees and 33 percent wanted a college or apprenticeship diploma. Only 10 percent aspired to getting only a secondary school diploma.

Overall, the girls in the year 7 OnLAC sample had better educational results than the boys. The girls were less likely to have been assessed or placed on an assessment waiting list for possible learning-related problems (58% vs. 79%), to have received special academic help at school (49% vs. 69%), or to have had an individual education plan (51% vs. 73%). The young people's caregivers also rated the girls' school performance more highly, with 41 percent seen as doing very well or well in reading compared with 28 percent of the boys. The caregivers rated 24 percent of the girls, versus 13 percent of the boys, as performing very well or well in written work such as composition and 29 percent of the girls versus 20 percent of the boys as doing very well or well overall. Only in math were a similar proportion of the girls (24%) and boys (23%) seen as doing very well or well. Not surprisingly, the caregivers had different educational aspirations for the two genders: they hoped that 37 percent of the girls (vs. 25% of the boys) would go to university and that 33 percent (vs. 23%) would complete community college or nursing school. On the other hand, they hoped that 34 percent of the boys would complete trade, technical school, or business college but held the same aspirations for only 15 percent of the girls. The young people's child welfare workers were somewhat more likely to rate the girls' educational results as matching their ability (64% vs. 58%) and also felt that a higher proportion of the girls were acquiring special skills and interests (34% vs. 26%).

The girls' self-reported results also tended to be more positive than the boys'. The girls were more likely to report reading for fun every day (37% vs. 28%) and had higher educational aspirations, with 40 percent (vs. 26%) hoping to obtain one or more university degrees. Regarding their teachers and caregivers, however, the girls and boys had similar perceptions: 89 percent versus 86 percent, respectively, said that, all or most of the time, their teachers treated them fairly and 89 percent versus 83 percent said their teachers gave them extra help when needed. Concerning their caregivers, most of the girls and boys (82% vs. 84%, respectively) said that, all or most of the time, their caregivers were willing to help them with problems at school and 94 percent vs. 95 percent reported that their caregivers encouraged them to do well in school.

Tutoring by adults as an intervention to improve children's basic academic skills

Given the lack of well validated, evidence-based interventions to improve the educational outcomes of young people in care (Trout *et al.* 2008), Jackson's (2007) emphasis on the role of foster parents in enhancing foster children's educational outcomes and the willingness of the caregivers in our OnLAC data to help their foster children with school work, we decided to explore tutoring by foster parents as a potentially promising intervention. We thought that this would be especially timely in Ontario, given that the provincial government and child welfare organizations are currently placing great emphasis on improving educational outcomes as a strategic priority. We also felt that a home-based educational intervention would complement the systems-change initiatives now being undertaken by several local Children's Aid Societies, in which the agencies are collaborating with primary, secondary and postsecondary educational systems in their geographic areas to improve educational outcomes among young people in care.

Tutoring in the general population

Our literature search uncovered an encouraging systematic review and meta-analysis that found volunteer adult tutoring to be effective for improving reading among children of primary-school age in the general population (Ritter *et al.* 2006). Ritter and his colleagues synthesized the results from 21 randomized field trials, including 28 cohorts, in which an intervention group had been compared with a control group. The 21 studies had appeared between 1985 and 2005. Ritter *et al.* (2006) concluded that volunteer tutoring by adults had a positive influence on children's progress in language and reading, with statistically significant effect sizes in the small to moderate range: 0.30 on overall reading outcomes, 0.26 on reading-global, 0.41 on reading letters and words, 0.30 on reading oral fluency and 0.45 on writing. The mean effect size on reading comprehension (0.18) was not statistically different from zero, nor was the effect size for mathematics-global (0.27), for which only five studies had been available, however.

High-structure programs that presented tutors with specific materials and lessons to cover or else specified the amount of time to spend on various reading activities had a significantly higher mean effect size (0.59) on the outcome of global reading than low-structure programs (0.14), which were either non-directive or simply had the tutor and tutee read together (Ritter *et al.* 2006). The amount of program structure, however, did not have significantly different effects on the other reading outcomes. Moreover, there were no significant differences in effectiveness between programs that used different types of tutors (i.e. parent, college-age, or community tutors) or that had appeared in journals rather than dissertations or unpublished studies.

Tutoring of young people in care

In the only evaluation of tutoring of young people in care that we found, Courtney *et al.* (2008) carried out a randomized evaluation of the Early Start to Emancipation Preparation (ESTEP)-Tutoring Program in Los Angeles County. The ESTEP-Tutoring program was intended to improve the reading and math skills of foster youths aged 14 and 15 and from one to three years behind grade level in reading or math. The program included a mentoring relationship with the tutor and workshops on other independent-living topics and was offered through 12 community colleges. College-age tutors met with the foster youths, usually in the students' homes. Curriculum materials were pitched to the foster youth's level in reading, spelling and math and each young person was eligible for 65 hours of tutoring.

In the evaluation, 226 foster youths were randomly assigned at baseline to the ESTEP-Tutoring group and 209 to the control group. Approximately two years later, 212 (94%) of the ESTEP-Tutoring group and 190 (91%) of the control group were re-interviewed at the final follow-up. Overall, only 62 percent of the ESTEP-Tutoring foster youths had become engaged in the tutoring program, receiving an average of 18 hours in math and 17 hours in reading. Unexpectedly, but reflecting the evaluators' lack of complete control over the study, 12 percent of the control group had somehow succeeded in receiving the tutoring intervention, at about the same dosage level as the experimental youths.

The most important finding at the two-year follow-up was that the ESTEP-Tutoring program had no differential impact on any of the educational outcomes. There were no statistically significant differences between the experimental and control groups. Both groups experienced a statistically significant gain on passage comprehension between the baseline and two-year assessments, but both groups also lost a significant amount of ground on letter-word identification and math calculation. Moreover, no significant change was reported for the sample as a whole on either school grades or school behavior.

In summary, despite the disappointing results of the ESTEP-Tutoring program (Courtney *et al.* 2008), the systematic review by Ritter *et al.* (2006) suggested that tutoring by adult volunteers can help children in the primary grades to improve the basic academic skill of reading. We were also encouraged by the fact that parents were found to be as effective as other types of adult volunteer tutors.

Our randomized field trial of tutoring by foster parents

Our RFT is a three-year (2007–2010) project that is testing the effectiveness, under real-world conditions, of tutoring by foster parents in improving the basic academic skills in reading and math of foster children in primary school. The project title—the *Registered Education Savings Plans (RESPs) for Kids in Care Project*—reflects the fact that educational funds in the form of RESPs are being provided by the nine collaborating local Children's Aid Societies (CASs) in Ontario for the future postsecondary education of the 77 children in the research sample. The money deposited in RESP bank accounts will be augmented by a 40 percent match from the Canadian government, garnering interest on a tax-free basis until eventually used to pay for postsecondary educational expenses.

Participants

The project sample was composed of 77 young people (51% female, 49% male) who were residing in family foster care. All gave their informed assent to participate. At the pre-intervention assessment in September–October, 2008, the young people were aged 6 to 13 years ($M = 10.7$; $SD = 1.6$) and were in grades 2–7. In recruiting the children, we had asked staff members in the nine collaborating CASs to nominate children whom they thought would be likely to benefit from foster-parent tutoring and likely to remain in the same foster home for the next two school years. We also asked the CAS staff members not to nominate any children whom they deemed so academically weak (e.g. because of pronounced intellectual disabilities) or so behaviorally disturbed that the children would be unlikely to benefit from tutoring.

A total of 68 foster parents gave their informed consent to participate in the study as tutors. We preferred that the foster parents tutor only one foster child in their respective homes but allowed them to tutor a maximum of two, in order to increase recruitment. We chose foster parents as tutors because they are a widely available resource, interested in seeing their foster children do well in school and likely to be as effective as tutors as other adult volunteers (Ritter *et al.* 2006).

Evaluation design

The study is being carried out in three phases. Phase one (2007–2008) included the recruitment of local CASs, foster parents and foster children, the random assignment of the foster parent–foster child pairs to the experimental and control groups, the baseline (i.e. pre-intervention) assessment of the foster children and foster parents and the training as tutors of the foster parents in the intervention group. Phase two consisted of intervention year one (2008–2009), during which the 35 foster parents in the intervention condition were to offer 30 weeks of tutoring, three hours per week, to the 42 foster children who had been randomly assigned to the intervention group. Their results on the post-intervention assessment (June 2009) that brought intervention year one to a close were to be compared with those of the wait-list control group of 35 foster children who were in the care of 32 foster parents. Phase three consists of intervention year two (2009–2010), now underway, which will provide a second period of 30 weeks of foster-parent tutoring for the original intervention group and 30 weeks of tutoring for the year-one wait-list control group. The two groups will be compared again at the end of intervention year two (June, 2010) to assess the effects of two years of tutoring versus one year only.

Tutoring intervention

The individual, one-to-one tutoring approach that we are evaluating is based on Michael Maloney's (1998) *Teach Your Children Well* educational model. Developed over the last 20 years in Belleville, Ontario, Canada, the Maloney model employs the method of direct instruction, an educational approach that uses clearly structured and well organized teaching materials. In Project Follow Through, which compared the relative effectiveness of a wide range of instructional methods for educationally disadvantaged children in the US, direct instruction was consistently found to be the most effective method (Bereuter and Kurland 1981–1982). *Teach Your Children Well* also includes a behavior management component, in which foster parents award points to their children for positive behaviours during tutoring sessions.

Michael Maloney trained the intervention foster parents in his tutoring method during phase one and the control foster parents at the beginning of phase three, in one-day, 6-hour workshops. During both intervention years, he has also provided ongoing coaching to the foster parents in the form of individual telephone consultations, group teleseminars and newsletters. Each foster parent agreed to provide three hours of individual tutoring per week to one foster child (or, in a few cases, two foster children), for 30 weeks in a given year. The weekly three-hour tutoring period includes two hours of instructing the child in reading, using the step-by-step *Teach Your Children Well* instructional manuals. The weekly tutoring also includes 30 minutes of listening to the child read out loud and 30 minutes of supervising the child's independent work on the computer with math software that comprises 225 step-by-step lessons. Each foster parent also agreed to collect data on the child's performance during each tutoring session and to send the data each week by e-mail or telephone to the project team. These performance data are monitored by Michael Maloney. The research team also prepared a letter that the foster parent was to distribute, as needed and feasible, to the foster child's teacher. The letter informed the teacher that the child was receiving tutoring in reading and math and encouraged the teacher to consider adjusting the amount of the child's homework accordingly.

Outcome measures

On three occasions—at baseline, the end of intervention year one and the end of intervention year two—we (i.e. the three authors of the present chapter) administer the fourth edition of the *Wide Range Achievement Test* (WRAT4; Wilkinson and Robertson 2006) to the foster children in the intervention and control groups. The WRAT4 is a well known standardized measure of basic academic skills. It consists of five subtests: Word Reading, Reading Comprehension, Spelling, and Math Calculation. The three waves of assessments enable us to compare, at the end of intervention year one, the level of reading and math skills attained by the foster children who have had a year of tutoring (the year-one experimental group) based on the Maloney model, versus those who have had none (the year-one wait-list control group). Also, at the end of intervention year two, we will be able to compare the level of academic skills of the foster children who have had two years of tutoring (the original experimental group) versus those who have had only 30 weeks (the original wait-list control group).

On the same three occasions, the foster parents in both groups complete two standardized behavioral measures, the Conners' *ADHD/ DSM-IV Scales-Parent* (*CADS-P;* Conners 1999), which assesses the foster children's level of attention and hyperactivity and the *ASEBA Child Behavior Checklist for Ages 6 to 18* (*CBCL/6–18;* Achenbach and Rescoria

2001), which assesses the foster children's degree of internalizing and externalizing behavior. These instruments will allow us to evaluate the impact, if any, of the tutoring intervention on the foster children's mental health and relationship with their foster parents (a topic that we do not address in the present chapter).

The year-one results of the field trial

Baseline measures of basic academic skills

As mentioned at the outset, we present here only a summary account of the first-year results of our RFT. A more detailed and technical version of the evaluation will be submitted to a peer-reviewed archival journal. Randomization was successful in terms of creating intervention and control groups that were equivalent at baseline on our demographic, academic-skill and behavioral measures. The baseline scores of our sample of foster children on our standardized measures of academic skills were similar to the standardized pre-test scores presented by Trout *et al.* (2008). In both instances, the children in care were about one-fifth to one-third of a standard deviation below the population mean on reading, but a full standard deviation below the population mean on math calculation.

Outcomes at the end of intervention year one

We based our evaluation of the year-one impact of the tutoring intervention on the 30 (out of 42) foster children in the intervention group who had received the tutoring intervention and been reassessed at the end of intervention year one and on the 34 (out of 35) control group children who had been reassessed at the end of year one. As recommended by Gliner (2003), we used multiple linear regression to carry out an analysis of covariance (ANCOVA) on the data from our pre-test-post-test comparison group design, thus maximizing the statistical power of our small-sample study. The use of ANCOVA via regression enabled us to adjust the foster children's post-test scores on each of the four WRAT4 subtests (Word Reading, Sentence Comprehension, Spelling and Math Calculation) for their pre-test scores and for their chronological ages (the latter covariate was used because the children's ages at the pre-test spanned a large range, from 6 to 13 years).

The results of *t*-tests on the adjusted post-test scores showed that the foster children who had received foster-parent tutoring during year one had made significantly greater gains than those in the control group on two important WRAT4 subtests, namely, Sentence Comprehension and Math Calculation. On both of these measures of key academic skills, the effects (respectively, Cohen's ds of .39 and .46) were closer to the level that Cohen (1992) considers to be moderate ($d = .50$) rather than small ($d = .20$) in size. These same effect sizes were also very close to or even slightly above the level ($d = .41$) that Ferguson (2009) defines as practically (and not merely statistically) significant in social science data. On the other hand, on the two remaining WRAT4 subtests, Word Reading and Spelling, the gains of the tutored foster children were not significantly different from those of the foster children in the control group.

Conclusion: lessons from year one of the field trial

Overall, we view the results of the tutoring intervention as encouraging, especially in light of the current dearth of rigorously evaluated educational interventions for children in out-of-home care. The tutoring provided by the foster parents enabled the foster children in the intervention group to make substantively important gains in reading and math that went well beyond the progress that they would have experienced had they been exposed only to an additional year of primary schooling.

When we rated the fidelity with which the foster parents had implemented the Maloney (1998) tutoring model, we found that 48 percent (20 out of 42) of the foster parent–foster child pairs had implemented the intervention well (i.e. with high fidelity). On the other hand, 24 percent (10 out of 42) had implemented the tutoring model less well and 29 percent (12 out of 42) had not implemented it at all. This suggests that roughly half the foster parents and foster children who say they want to engage in what is a demanding tutoring regime of three hours a week for 30 weeks will be able to carry through on their commitment at a high level. We also learned that if the foster parents and foster children do not begin the tutoring process shortly after the training of the foster parents takes place, they may not begin at all.

We learned during intervention year one that implementation of the tutoring model needs improvement. In particular, the foster parents need to be induced to participate more regularly in the monthly coaching teleseminars that are part of the model and the child reward system also needs to be implemented more systematically. Improvements such as these may call for more intensive training of the foster parents than was provided in the six-hour, one-day training format used in the present evaluation. We also think that a group tutoring model would be worth evaluating. Compared with the individual, one-to-one, in-home model that we evaluated, the group model would offer several advantages, at least for some foster parents. The group model would take a good deal of pressure off the foster parents by having more intensively trained adult volunteers (e.g. university students or retired adults) tutor groups of four or five children in care, perhaps at the local CAS or in a more neutral setting, on a twice-a-week basis. If the group model were to prove promising, after a randomized evaluation, it would represent a useful complement to the individual tutoring model that we evaluated. Local CASs would have the option of offering both the individual and group models, to meet the needs and preferences of different subgroups of foster parents and foster children.

In practice and policy circles in child welfare in many countries, improving the educational outcomes of young people in care has become a high priority. Our results to date suggest that tutoring by foster parents is a feasible and economical way of improving key academic skills of foster children in reading and math. Tutoring also complements the system-change efforts now being initiated in Ontario by child welfare organizations and school boards. We look forward to evaluating, in 2010, the results of the second year of direct-instruction tutoring that our original intervention group is currently receiving from their foster parents, to see whether additional tutoring adds meaningfully to the gains made during the first year. As Trout *et al.* (2008) have insisted, effective educational interventions are urgently needed by many young people in care.

Acknowledgements
Our work on this chapter was supported by grant no. 5292099, *Evaluation Study on Improving the Educational Achievement of Children in Care,* awarded to Robert J. Flynn and Tim D. Aubry (2007–2010), by the Canada Education Savings Program, Human Resources and Social Development Canada. This support is gratefully acknowledged, but the opinions expressed herein are attributable only to the authors.

References

Achenbach, T.M. and Rescoria, L.A. (2001) *ASEBA Child Behavior Checklist for Ages 6–18 – Parent (CBCL 6–18)* Burlington, VT: Achenbach System of Empirically Based Assessment.

Barth, R.P. and Berry, M. (1988) *Adoption and Disruption,* New York, NY: Aldine de Gruyter.

Bereuter, C. and Kurland, M. (1981–1982) 'A constructive look at Follow Through results.' *Interchange 12,* 1, 1–22.

Cohen, J. (1992) 'A power primer.' *Psychological Bulletin 112,* 155–159.

Conners, C.K. (1999) *Conners' ADHD/DSM-IV Scales-Parent (CADS-P)* Toronto, ON: Multi-Health Systems.

Courtney, M.E. Zinn, A. Zielewskiu, E.H. Bess, R.J. *et al.* (2008) *Evaluation of the Early Start to Emancipation Preparation-Tutoring Program, Los Angeles County.* Final report. Washington, DC: US Department of Health and Human Services, Administration for Children and Families.

Ferguson, C.J. (2009) 'An effect size primer: a guide for clinicians and researchers.' *Professional Psychology: Research and Practice 40,* 532–538.

Flynn, R.J. and Biro, C. (1998) 'Comparing developmental outcomes for children in care with those of other children in Canada.' *Children and Society 12,* 228–233.

Flynn, R.J. Dudding, P.M. and Barber, J.G. (eds) *Promoting Resilience in Child Welfare.* Ottawa, ON: University of Ottawa Press.

Flynn, R.J. Ghazal, H. Legault, L. Vandermeulen, G. and Petrick, S. (2004) 'Use of population measures and norms to identify resilient outcomes in young people in care: an exploratory study.' *Child and Family Social Work 9,* 65–79.

Gliner, J.A. (2003) 'Pretest-posttest comparison group designs: analysis and interpretation.' *Journal of the American Academy of Child and Adolescent Psychiatry 42,* 500–503.

Jackson, S. (2007) 'Progress at last?' *Adoption and Fostering 31,* 1, 3–5.

Maloney, M. (1998) *Teach Your Children Well: A Solution to Some of North America's Educational Problems.* Belleville, ON: QLC Educational Services.

Miller, M. Flynn, R. and Vandermeulen, G. (2008) *Looking After Children in Ontario: Good Parenting, Good Outcomes: Ontario Provincial Report (Year Six)* Reports for 0–4, 5–9, 10–15 and 16–20 year olds. Ottawa, ON: Centre for Research on Educational and Community Services, University of Ottawa.

Miller, M. Vincent, C. and Flynn, R. (2009) *Looking After Children in Ontario: Good Parenting, Good Outcomes. Ontario Provincial Report (Year Seven).* Report for 10–15 year olds. Ottawa, ON: Centre for Research on Educational and Community Services, University of Ottawa.

Ritter, G. Denny, G. Albin, G. Barnett, J. and Blankenship, V. (2006) 'The effectiveness of volunteer tutoring programs: a systematic review.' *Campbell Systematic Reviews 7.*

Statistics Canada and Human Resources Development Canada (1999) *National Longitudinal Survey of Children and Youth, Cycle 3 Survey Instruments 1998–99.* Ottawa, ON: Statistics Canada and Human Resources Development Canada.

Trout, A.L. Hagaman, J. Casey, K. Reid, R. and Epstein, M.H. (2008) 'The academic status of children and youth in out-of-home care: a review of the literature.' *Children and Youth Services Review 30,* 979–994.

Ward, H. (ed.) (1995) *Looking After Children: Research into Practice.* London: HMSO.

Wilkinson, G.S. and Robertson, G.J. (2006) *Wide Range Achievement Test 4 (WRAT4)* Lutz, FL: Psychological Assessment Resources.

Commentary by Johan Piet Strijker on:

Can Tutoring by Foster Parents Improve
Foster Children's Basic Academic Skills? A
Canadian Randomized Field Trial

Robert J. Flynn, Marie-Pierre Paquet, Robyn A. Marquis

Foster children lag behind their peers in academic skills due to such things as having to change schools. They go to special schools more often and also repeat years more often. Between 20 per cent and 30 per cent does poorly across the various teaching areas. The figures reveal that foster children are a vulnerable group in need of extra attention to prevent them from lapsing into poverty, with all its associated problems. Researchers in the US, the UK, and Canada are convinced that improving school performance is necessary. Among the promising interventions is tutoring by foster parents. Meta-analytical research results reveals a positive effect size of adult tutors on language and reading skills that is small to fair, with highly structured programs having greater effect than less structured ones.

This chapter describes program theory for interventions with foster children who are underachieving at school. The underpinning program theory is the "educational learning model", a method of direct instruction with which the authors have 20 years' experience. In order to test the effectiveness of the intervention, a randomized field trial was conducted with 42 foster children assigned to the intervention group and 35 foster children to the control group. Wide Range Achievement Test (WRAT4) pre-test scores showed that children in both groups scored below average. After a year of intervention by foster parents providing three hours tutoring weekly, small but significant changes in effect size were found, with the intervention group yielding a higher average. One of the problems encountered in the field research was that slightly more than half of the foster parents had not implemented the intervention properly, which probably had a negative influence on the effect size. This research shows that tutoring by foster parents as a structured intervention model can improve foster children's academic skills, thus providing them with a better foundation for leading an independent life.

CHAPTER 15

Growing Up in Care
An Australian Longitudinal Study of Outcomes

Elizabeth Fernandez

Background

Research on the experience of children growing up in care has identified important trends. These include concerns about instability in care placements (James 2004; Sinclair *et al.* 2005); failure of care systems to ensure optimal educational outcomes (Harker *et al.* 2004; Pecora *et al.* 2006); children's vulnerability to emotional difficulties and mental health concerns while in care (Burns *et al.* 2004; Clausen *et al.* 1998; Rubin *et al.* 2006). There is widespread concern about children in care who experience instability. The disruption and insecurity engendered by repeated moves is unsettling for children and compounds the effects of the instability characteristic of their pre care experience. There is also consistent evidence in the studies cited that the rate of emotional and behavioural found in children in care is substantially higher than the general population. Children experiencing instability in care placements have been described as having more behavioural problems and health problems and delayed educational attainment than peers who experienced more stability (Fanshel, Finch and Grundy 1989). Contact maintained between children in care and their birth families and its impact on placement outcomes has also received considerable attention in the research and practice literature. A link has been noted between parental contact and various domains of child wellbeing (Cantos, Gries and Slis 1997). Placement instability accentuates the sense of loss experienced through initial and subsequent separations threatening children's evolving sense of identity and belonging (Cleaver 2000).

There is emerging emphasis on extending the limited focus of research on placement stability and permanence to researching measurable developmental outcomes and overall child wellbeing (Parker *et al.* 1991; Wulczyn *et al.* 2006). Current research also points to the limitations of cross sectional studies in capturing developmental sequences advocating longitudinal research (Farrington 1991). Increasing recognition is also accorded to the need to give a central place to the voices of children in research and practice concerning them. (Gilligan 2002 Grodin and Glantz 1994). This chapter reports selected findings from a longitudinal study of outcomes of the experience of care from the perspective of children, their carers and caseworkers. Outcomes are analysed from three successive waves of data collection focusing on children's family and social relationships, emotional and behavioural development, self esteem and their overall adjustment in care placements.

Theoretical orientations guiding the study include conceptual frameworks of attachment and resilience. The importance of attachment in providing children with a secure relational base is acknowledged (Howe, 1995 Children's resilience is nurtured by development of attachments to caring parents, caregivers and supportive adults in their social world (Gilligan 2002; Howe 1995; Masten and Coatsworth, 1998). That resilience can be nurtured at any time in the life cycle is supported by researchers. Rutter's (1990) work on risk and protective factors affecting development suggests that despite effects of risk factors cumulative protective factors may have disproportionate positive effects. This underlines the role that carers and significant adults can play in enhancing children's sense of self esteem and self efficiency.

Context

In the Australian context most children in out of home care are placed under Care and Protection orders. The number of children placed under such orders rose by more than 100 per cent in the last decade. The rate of children entering care has risen from 3.1 per 1000 at June 1998 to

6.2 per 1000 at June 2008 (Australian Institute of Health and Welfare 2009). The proportion of children in long term care ranges between 25 to 64 per cent in all state jurisdictions. Relative to the USA and UK, use of adoption has been very limited. The introduction of time frames for legal termination of parental rights is only recent. The programme site of the current research is unique in its emphasis on permanent placement and adoption from care.

Data collection and analysis

The research used a prospective longitudinal, repeated measures design. Children and young people's needs, strengths and difficulties were assessed at different stages of care: at four months after entry to care and at 24 month intervals thereafter. Quantitative and qualitative methods were combined to elicit perceptions of children, caseworkers, carers and teachers on care outcomes. Personal semi-structured interviews with children over eight years of age and interviews with caseworkers and foster carers of children of all ages are the main sources of data. Interviews explored children's reasons for entering care, care history, attachment to foster families, experience of birth family contact, educational attainment, emotional and behavioural development, identity, self esteem and overall adjustment in placements. Standardized measures used in the study included: the Achenbach Child Behaviour Checklist (CBCL) (Achenbach 1991) with versions completed by carers, caseworkers and teachers (the CBCL assesses 113 problem behaviours and is scored using a computerized program to produce three summary scores and eight further subscales); the Hare Self Esteem Scale (HSES) (Hare 1985) (assesses Home, School and Peer self-esteem); and the Interpersonal Parent and Peer Attachment Scale (IPPA) (Armsden and Greenberg 1987) (measures a child's level of attachment to his or her caregiver/s and friends or peers on three subscales – trust, communication and alienation). The research also drew partially on the Looking After Children Framework (LAC) which plots children's wellbeing through various developmental domains along which children are expected to progress to realize their potential (Parker *et al.* 1991).

Qualitative interviewing was used as an important medium for sourcing meaningful accounts of children's and carers' experience and their social reality (Babbie 2001). The interviews were recorded and transcribed in order to allow analysis to be informed by methods derived from Grounded Theory (Strauss and Corbin 1998). With the assistance of computer based software the qualitative data was analysed thematically to identify patterns of thought and meaning emerging from the texts. By employing peer checking of codes applied and themes developed the subjectivity of isolated analysis was kept in check (Padgett 1998). Qualitative data cited in the chapter are drawn from pools of data grouped by themes.

The children

The sample included 59 children, 29 boys and 30 girls drawn from the Barnardos Australia *Find a Family Program* operated by a non Government, not for profit organization which places children in need of long term care with foster and adoptive families. The sample was recruited over a two year period and included all children aged 4–14 entering care with a long term care plan. At this point in the study four children have exited from the study following transfers to another agency and return to birth family. All children were placed with non related foster families with the exception of one child placed with kin. Nineteen per cent are adopted since the study began. The most frequently cited reason for care relating to the birth mother was drug or alcohol dependence (29%). The mother's mental health was a factor in 22 per cent of cases and lack of financial support, housing and social support represented 18 per cent of cases. Physical abuse, neglect and inadequate parenting were identified in 36 per cent of cases. Thirty-nine per cent of the children were abandoned by the birth father. In 39 per cent of cases, the child experienced either physical or sexual abuse by the father. Domestic violence was identified in 22 per cent of the cases. The ethnic composition of the sample included Anglo-Australian (70%), Indigenous Australian (2%), European (17%), Fijian, Tongan, Thai (9%) and Sri Lankan (2%). The average age of children at third wave of data collection is 12 years. Children have been in care for 8.5 years on average. The majority are in foster placements. Children have had on average 4.4 placements. Seventy-three per cent have been in their current placement for three years or more. Girls have had longer placements with their current carer than boys (p=0.05).

Cohesion with foster family

The children in the study were asked to rate the level of cohesion they experienced with the current foster family using a study developed measure. They were asked about their relationship with their foster mother, foster father and foster siblings using response categories of 'very well', 'quite well', 'not very well' and 'badly'. All but one respondent indicated that they got on with their foster mother 'very well' or 'quite well'. Almost nine out of ten respondents were positive about their relationship with their foster father, rating 'very well' or 'quite well'. However, one in ten respondents indicated that they got on with their foster father 'not very well' or 'badly'. Forty-eight per cent of respondents indicated they got on 'very well' both with their foster mother and their foster father. Eighty-six per cent of respondents were positive about their relationship with their first foster sibling, rating 'very well' or 'quite well'. However, 8 per cent indicated that they got on 'not very well' or 'badly' with their eldest foster sibling. A similar pattern is shown for the relationship with a second foster sibling, 89 per cent rating 'very well' or 'quite well'; 11 per cent rating 'badly'. In interviews children elaborated on the valued aspects of their relationship with carers. In the quotations below extracted from their narratives, two children reflect on their perception of the foster carers' commitment to them:

- 'They cuddle me and they say that they love me, they take care of me all the time. They take me to the doctors if I look sick. They give me food on a plate. They give me my room, my own room. They take me to friends' houses and drop me off at school and pick me up and they say that they love me' (male, 11 years).

- 'She's understanding, she's nice. She helps me with lots of things. She's just a very kind person she's got a nice heart…sometimes I give a hug to (carer) before I go to bed…I don't know what's the most important thing. When I go shopping with her, just me and her by ourselves we just talk you know. I like how we have time by ourselves sometimes' (female, 17 years).

Relationship with birth family

Birth parent contact was measured by asking the children to estimate how often they see their birth mother, father or siblings. For these analyses the frequency ratings were collapsed into at least monthly, every few months, yearly or less. Nine in ten (90%) respondents report they have had some contact with their siblings who are not living with them. Half have had less than monthly contact with these siblings and just under one in three (30%) have had contact either monthly or fortnightly with them. Nine in ten (92%) respondents report that since the last interview (two years ago) they have had some contact with their birth mother. Two thirds (67%) reported either monthly (31%) or quarterly (36%) contact. Nearly two in five respondents (38%) had not seen their birth father. One quarter had seen their birth father on holidays and one quarter had seen him quarterly.

Children were also asked to rate how often they would like to see birth family members, the options provided being 'more often', 'less often', 'never' or 'same'. Almost all children nominated either 'more often' or 'same', with only two children wanting less paternal contact and one child wanting less maternal contact. When asked whether they would like to see their siblings, birth mother and birth father either 'more often', 'less often', 'not at all' or 'the same amount' respondents consistently responded with 'more often' (birth mother: 63%; birth father: 78%; siblings: 62%) or 'the same' (birth mother 34%; birth father: 15%; siblings: 38%).

Qualitative analysis of the children's interview transcripts reflect the strong connections children felt towards their birth parents. Many children expressed clear and positive connections with their birth parents while also evaluating the positive aspects of the foster home.

- 'I want to live with my mum but I like the school and that... And Mum couldn't pay for the school, so I'll live here, but I probably want to live with my mum' (male, 12 years).

- 'I'm always missing my mum. It doesn't happen that much now, cause I see her every month' (male, 13 years).

Some of the children expressed concern that they rarely see their birth fathers and were keen to establish a connection.

- 'I feel happy and normal when I see him. I look forward to seeing him' (female, 11 years).

- '...I'd like to see him (father) a lot more, heaps and heaps and heaps more times, it makes me feel happy' (female, eight years).

- 'I don't have a real dad, I never did. I only have false dads' (female, eight years).

Cohesion with foster family analysis
The level of cohesion with the foster family was examined in relation to birth family contact. There is no evidence that contact with the birth father or siblings is related to cohesion with the foster family. However, contact with the birth mother is negatively correlated with foster mother cohesion (p=0.05) and foster father cohesion (p=0.05). The lower the birth mother contact, the greater the cohesion score for the foster mother and the foster father. Given that 97 per cent of respondents would like either more contact (63%) or the same amount of contact (34%) with their birth mother and that cohesion scores were high for foster mothers it is likely that new attachments and established ones are being sustained concurrently.

Emotional and behavioural outcomes

Incorporated in the children's interview schedule in each wave of data collection was the children's self assessment of their relationship building skills, anxiety and concentration and behaviour problems using the 30 item domain on emotional and behavioural development from the LAC Assessment Framework (Parker *et al.* 1991). The children's self assessment of their feelings and interpersonal skills based on the 30 item child version of this tool was analysed in terms of Quinton and Murray's (2002) six subscales. It is important to note that all LAC subscales, except pro-social skills, are scored to indicate that a higher score means more problems. The value of each subscale and the total score appears to decrease across the three waves, suggesting emotional and behavioural difficulties diminished with time (Table 15.1).

The scores reported for each of the subscales at interview 3 are within the same range or less than those reported by Quinton and Murray (2002) based on 100 children aged 10–18 in the UK. Statistically significant differences to note are the decrease in peer subscale ratings from interviews 1 to 3 (p=0.001) and the decrease in the emotional subscale from interviews 1 to 3 (p=0.002).

Analysing relationships between cohesion and LAC subscales it is noted that the greater the foster mother cohesion the fewer relationship problems with carers (carer subscale p=0.006). The greater the foster father cohesion the fewer the conduct problems (p=0.05).

TABLE 15.1 Children's scores on LAC subscales at Interviews 1 and 3 and data from a comparable group of 100 children in care (UK)

	INTERVIEW 3		INTERVIEW 1		UK	
	Mean	sd	Mean	sd	mean	sd
Conduct	2.98	2.51	4.08	2.9	3.4	2.7
Emotional	3.86*	4.03	7.13	5.1	3.8	3.4
Overactive	4.71	2.68	6.22	2.4	4.7	2.9
Peers	2.43*	1.88	4.85	2.3	2.9	2.0
Pro social	6.52	1.97	7.50	2.2	8.4	2.4
Relationship with carers	2.95	2.35	4.73	2.4	3.4	2.4
Total score	21.10	8.90	27.29	10.1	19.2	1.0

*Significantly different from Interview 1 ($p<0.05$).

The children's self assessment of the emotional and behavioural health is complemented by carer and caseworker assessments on the Child Behaviour Checklist (CBCL 4–18) for children aged 4 to 18 (Achenbach 1991) used in the present study. The measure was completed at three successive waves of data collection. In this study comparisons have been made with the findings of the Australian Government's Mental Health of Young People in Australia (Sawyer *et al.* 2000), based on a national representative sample of children aged 4–17. The statistic for comparison is the per centage of children falling in the 'clinical range' of the survey, derived by using the per centage of children having 't-scores' above the recommended cut-offs of 64 for the three summary scores, Internalizing problems, Externalizing problems and Total score and 70 for the subscales.

TABLE 15.2 Percentage of children in 'clinical range' of problems on Achenbach CBCL summary scales, compared to the Mental Health of Young People in Australia (MHYPA) Survey (n=3870)

CBCL SCALE	ASSESSMENT 1	ASSESSMENT 2	ASSESSMENT 3	MHYPA SAMPLE
SUMMARY SCALES	%	%	%	%
Total problems	43.4	38.2	35.3	14.1
Internalizing problems	35.8	21.8	26.0	12.8
Externalizing problems	34.0	37.3	22.4	12.9

The data in Table 15.2 indicate that at the first wave of assessments 43.4 per cent of children were in the clinical range for total problems, 35.8 per cent for internalizing problems and 34.0 per cent for externalizing problems. Total problems, internalizing and externalizing problems exceeded the MHYPA community norms.

At the third assessment 36 per cent of the children, for example, were above the clinical range cut-off for total problems, compared to only 14 per cent of the Australian youth sample. Comparison of scores from first, second and third waves of data using t-tests revealed the following trends:

- Fewer children in the study sample fell into the clinical range of total problems at the third assessment compared to the first assessment.

- There was a significant decrease between interviews 1 and 2 on the internalizing scores ($p<0.05$) and the anxiety and depression subscale ($p<0.000$).

- There was a significant difference between the externalizing ratings at interview 1 and the externalizing ratings at interview 3 ($p<0.000$).

A further indicator of the clinical spectrum of the group is the number of subscale problems that each child had over the clinical threshold. Children could have between zero and eight such problems. Over the first two assessments carer ratings indicated that between 7.5 to 28 per cent demonstrated clinically significant problems. Attention problems, social problems, delinquent behaviour and anxiety and depression were frequently in the clinical range. At the third interview social problems and anxiety and depression were the main problems outside the Australian community sample subscale figures. In relation to the subscales the general pattern over time indicates that the percentage of children problem free or with one problem for example, was 48 per cent at interview 1 and 62 per cent at interview 3, while those with multiple problems (between two and eight problems) was 30 per cent at interview 1 and 16 per cent at interview 3.

Patterns by gender and age group

The percentage of girls with a clinical range of 'Total Problems' was 38.9 per cent at interview 1 and 18.8 per cent at interview 3. Boys showed a similar pattern in relation to the per centage in the clinical range on total problems. Prevalence above the clinical threshold on 'Total Problems' at interview 1 was 41 per cent, compared to 27 per cent at interview 2. Much of the problem behaviour for the girls is attributed to the internalizing spectrum, specifically anxiety and depression, whereas the boys had a broad distribution of problems with only thought problems not represented.

Teachers completed the Achenbach Teachers Report Form (TRF), a companion to the CBCL on two occasions. The TRF is norm referenced and assesses key problem subscales and overall problem scores and includes an Adaptive Functioning Scale that provides an assessment of norm referenced attributes relating to Academic Performance and Adaptive Functioning. A full discussion of results from this analysis is available in Fernandez (2008).

Parent and peer attachment

The Interpersonal Parent and Peer attachment was completed by the study children at the second and third waves of data collection (interviews 2 and 3). Table 15.3 presents results on the three subscales, trust communication and alienation and the total score. The alienation scores are reversed, so a higher score means less alienation. With the other subscales and total scores a higher score indicates greater attachment.

Children reported stronger maternal attachment, trust and communication and overall peer attachment at interview 3 than at interview 2. This indicates that children are feeling more settled in their relationship with their foster mother and same aged children. There was no progression or deterioration in the children's feelings of attachment toward their foster fathers. Boys reported improved scores on three material attachment scores, including alienation, trust and total score. They also showed significantly improved scores on all the peer attachment scores. In terms of age, younger children had a stronger maternal trust and better peer communication at interview 3. Teenage children had improved maternal trust and total maternal attachment scores. Additionally older children had significantly better peer communication scores. There were no changes in paternal attachment scores. In general across the two assessments the changes in score were in the positive direction not signalling deterioration and lend some support to the benefits of children's time in care. The strongest changes were observed for boys and for older children who appeared to be 'catching up' to the girls and younger on some of these variables.

TABLE 15.3 Changes in IPPA scores from interview 2 to interview 3 for all children

	INTERVIEW 2		INTERVIEW 3		
	Mean	sd	Mean	sd	sig
Maternal attachment					
Alienation	22.5	3.4	25.8	3.4	p=0.001
Communication	23.1	3.5	23.9	4.3	ns
Trust	28.2	4.0	33.2	5.0	p=0.000
Total	91.2	12.6	102.7	15.8	p=0.008
Paternal attachment					
Alienation	23.0	3.6	23.7	5.4	ns
Communication	23.3	3.0	22.7	5.9	ns
Trust	28.5	4.3	31.0	6.9	ns
Total	91.3	12.4	95.3	22.4	ns
Peer attachment					
Alienation	22.1	4.7	24.0	5.2	ns
Trust	33.5	6.1	37.6	6.1	p=0.023
Communication	27.0	5.0	31.3	5.8	p=0.002
Total	85.7	15.7	96.7	15.4	p=0.013

ns=not significant.

A further trend in the IPPA is that children's responses to the maternal and peer subscales were closely interrelated. Responses to the paternal attachment questions, however, were only related to each other and not to the other two sets of subscales. Children's attachment to their foster mothers and peers appeared to be based on similar judgements but children thought in a different way when considering their attachment to foster fathers. One possible explanation for responding differently to fathers is the likelihood these children have had a little opportunity to develop a paternal relationship given the high proportion of absent birth fathers at entry to care, whereas most of the children have had previous experiences of a mother figure and siblings in their birth families.

The children's ratings on the IPPA were analysed for relationships with the LAC scores. Table 15.4 presents matrices, showing relationships between the LAC and either the maternal, paternal or peer IPPA attachment ratings.

TABLE 15.4 IPPA maternal attachment and LAC scores at interview 3

	TRUST	ALIENATION	COMMUNICATION	TOTAL
Conduct	−0.3965			−0.3308
	p=0.010			p=0.037
Peers			0.3586	−0.3256
			p=0.021	p=0.040
Relationship with carers		−0.3397		−0.3123
		p=0.030		p=0.050
Total LAC score	−0.3488		−0.3078	−.3397
	p=0.025		p=0.050	p=0.032

There were a range of significant correlations observed between the LAC and maternal attachment scores, most frequently between the total scores for each instrument. In each case the correlations were small and inverse, indicating that the greater the attachment score, the lower the LAC score. For example, greater maternal trust was associated with lower conduct problems and greater maternal communication was associated with lower peer problems. Compared to the maternal attachment scores the paternal attachment scores and LAC showed greater consistency and some were stronger in magnitude. Lower paternal attachment on any of the IPPA subscales was associated with greater relationship problems with carers (Table 15.5). This was also indicated in the Total LAC scores and in particular between paternal trust and the total LAC problem score.

TABLE 15.5 IPPA paternal attachment and LAC scores at interview 3

	TRUST	ALIENATION	COMMUNICATION	TOTAL
Relationship with carers	−0.4133	−0.3609	−0.3705	−0.3884
	p=0.008	p=0.022	p=0.019	p=0.013
Total LAC score	−0.4841	−0.3473	−0.4081	−0.4100
	p=0.002	p=0.028	p=0.009	p=0.009

The LAC and IPPA peer scores also indicated stronger associations than had been found for the maternal scores (Table 15.6). Not surprisingly, lower peer attachment scores had low–moderate correlations with peer problems on the LAC, where greater attachment was associated with fewer problems. Peer attachment was positively correlated with pro-social scores on the LAC. The strongest relationship observed was between the IPPA communication subscale and the total LAC score, such that those with greater communication scores had lower LAC scores.

TABLE 15.6 IPPA peer attachment and LAC scores at interview 3

	TRUST	ALIENATION	COMMUNICATION	TOTAL
Emotional problems			−0.5124	−0.3544
			p=0.001	p=0.023
Conduct			−0.3805	
			p=0.014	
Overactivity			−0.3674	−0.3408
			p= .018	p=0.029
Pro-social	0.4060	0.3485		0.3520
	p=0.008	p=0.026		p=0.024
Peer	−0.4762	−0.4535	−0.4703	−0.5248
	p=0.002	p=0.003	p=0.002	p=0.000
Total LAC score	−0.4186	−0.3150	−0.6094	−0.4946
	p=0.006	p=0.045	p=0.000	p=0.001

Self esteem

Children's self esteem was assessed using the Hare Self Esteem Scale (HSES) at the second and third waves of data collection (interviews 2 and 3). The HSES has three subscales to assess different aspects of self esteem: peer self esteem, home self esteem and school self esteem. The scores on the HSES for the children at interviews 2 and 3 are set out in Table 15.7.

TABLE 15.7 Interview 3 Hare self esteem scores, including gender breakdown

	MEAN	SD	RANGE
All children			
School	29.8	5.2	19–40
Peer	30.0	5.1	20–38
Home	33.6	4.7	20–40
Total	93.2	12.4	68–115
Girls			
School	28.8	5.5	21–40
Peer	30.4	5.4	22–38
Home	32.5	5.1	20–40
Total	91.4	14.0	68–110
Boys			
Peer	29.6	4.9	20–38
School	30.8	4.8	19–40
Home	29.6	4.9	20–38
Total	94.7	11.1	78–115

Girls and boys both had averages of 91 and 94 respectively. Girls were found to have remained stable from interview 2 to interview 3 on all the subscales and the total self esteem score. Boys had significantly higher home self esteem scores and total self esteem scores at interview 3 compared to interview 2. This finding indicates that boys were responding positively to the foster care environment. Citing children's perceptions of their self esteem from the qualitative analysis, a range of views are evident. It was apparent that for some children being in care affected their self concept. The comments below provide glimpses into children's views of themselves.

- 'It's like we are second hand kids, unless that's how all kids feel who are my age' (female, 12 years).
- 'I don't really know what it's like to be a foster adult. I don't really know what it's like to be a normal child' (male, 17 years).

Many compared themselves to their non care peers for reassurance.

- 'When I see my friends with their parents I see nothing different... it just seems the same, like I've got PlayStations and Nintendos and being allowed to play and going to friends' houses as well' (male, 13 years).

When asked what they liked or disliked about themselves many commented positively.

- 'I'm a loving and caring person. And I'm hopeful' (male, 13 years).
- 'I'm creative, I'm intelligent. I don't know…I'm gentle, I'm caring, I'm nice to people' (female, 9 years).
- 'I have respect for people. I'm not as rude as I was. Sometimes I am more confident' (female, 17 years).

Analysis of self esteem scores
HSES scores were analysed according to different demographic and care variables to identify factors affecting the children's self-perceptions.

Care history: Analysis of children's HSES in relation to impact of care variables such as age at entry into care, time in care and changes in placement found that

- *Age at entry:* Age at entry to care showed relationships with home self esteem and school self esteem ($p=0.06$) suggesting that school and home self esteem is higher amongst younger children in the sample, but the findings are just outside statistical significance.
- *Number of placements:* There was a relationship between number of placements and peer self esteem ($p=0.01$); that is, the less placements, the better the peer self esteem.
- *Cohesion with current foster family:* The analyses related HSES scores to a dichotomous rating of getting on 'very well' compared with all other cohesion ratings 'quite well or less'. There was a significant correlation between the total HSES score and cohesion with the foster mother ($p=0.01$) such that children who recorded higher self esteem on this measure rated their relationship with the foster mother more positively.

Caseworker assessments of child's integration with placement and overall adjustment

Caseworkers were asked to indicate the extent to which they felt the child was integrated or settled in the placement and their perceptions of the child's overall adjustment.

Integration with the placement

Caseworkers rated the child's integration with their foster family on a five-point scale. Over half (61%) are described as being 'fully integrated and settled'. Age and gender differences are evident in the integration rating: 81 per cent of those below 12 years old were assessed as fully integrated, whereas only 31 per cent of those over 12 years were rated fully integrated ($p=0.002$). Females appear more likely to be described as fully integrated (61%, males 39%).

General adjustment

Caseworkers rated the child's adjustment over the last 24 months on a four-point scale where 1= 'poor' and 4= 'excellent'. Caseworkers rated 84 per cent of children's adjustment as 'excellent' (40%) or 'adequate' (44%). The remainder are rated as having 'mixed' (10%) or 'poor' (6%) adjustment. Younger children are rated as having better adjustment (mean = 3.5) than older children (mean = 2.7) ($p=0.002$). In terms of relationship to behavioural outcomes, lower ratings of overall adjustment are associated with CBCL ratings above the clinical threshold for total problems ($p=0.001$) and externalizing problems ($p=0.001$).

Ninety-three per cent of those who are fully integrated have been with their current carer for three years or more, compared with 63 per cent of those who are not fully integrated ($p=0.009$). Length of time with the current carer is related to several adjustment variables. Those children who have been with their carers for at least three years are rated as having, on average, better *academic progress* (<3 years = 1.5; >3 years = 2.1) ($p=0.05$), better overall *adjustment* (<3 years = 2.4; >3 years = 3.4) ($p=0.001$) and as being in a more *satisfactory* placement (<3 years = 3.7; >3 years = 4.6) ($p=0.05$).

Implications of findings for policy

The research focused on a cohort of children who retained a birth family connection but could not return home and for whom permanent foster care or adoption was the intended goal. Despite this many experienced significant instability, particularly in their initial care history. Placement moves were accompanied by change of schools and disrupted adult and peer attachments. Overall longer residence in placements were associated with better outcomes as assessed by caseworkers. Children are at risk of their psychological and social development being compromised when stability of their living environment is not maintained (Perkins-Mangulabnan and Flynn 2006; Chapters 3 and 7 of this volume). Recurrent findings on the impact of disruption must reinforce the commitment of care systems to plan proactively for placement stability through targeted support to carers and children and timely decision making.

As in the research of Chapman *et al.* (2004) and Johnson, Yoken and Voss (1995) the children rated their relationship with carers highly. The higher the cohesion at previous interviews the better were the outcomes at interview 3 suggesting the benefits of cohesion extended beyond the immediate placement. Greater cohesion with carers was associated with a stronger repertoire of pro-social behaviours, better self esteem and emotional and behavioural development outcomes. Further, high cohesion with the foster father was associated with fewer conduct problems (lower LAC conduct subscale score) and lower CBCL externalizing problem score, better peer relationship outcomes (lower LAC peer subscale) and increased relationship building skills (Fernandez 2009). This is a clinically significant finding that points to an important area of supportive foster care and accessible area for intervention. It suggests that where children received well modelled relationships in earlier placements or teaching of these skills the more likely they will develop cohesive relationships in subsequent caring arrangements. Resources and training to enable care systems to build on these strengths are to be addressed.

There has been support for maintaining links with significant members of the children's birth families. Frequency of contact was greatest with siblings followed by birth mother and then father. Contact with birth mother was negatively related to foster mother attachment. However, as children did report high attachment ratings, the lowest cohesion rating for foster mothers being 'quite well', it cannot be concluded that more frequent birth mother contact prevents cohesion with the foster/ adoptive family. While acknowledging strong attachment with foster parents children desired more contact with their birth families. The results on contact have been mixed indicating no significant impact on disruption patterns (Barth and Berry 1988) to evidence supporting beneficial contact as a protective factor (Cleaver 2000; Fratter 1991). Carers must be supported in their dual task of building attachments with their foster children and responding to their continuing need for connection with birth families.

The data suggested that children in this sample experienced high levels of psychological need as indicated in the LAC profiles and CBCL ratings. It is noted that children with externalizing problems and conduct disorders are vulnerable to the placement breakdown and to the escalation of these problems (Clausen *et al.* 1998; Newton, Litrownik and Landsvok 2000). The group showed some significant improvement at second and third assessments which in restorative programme is a positive finding. Some of this change may be attributed to the effects of foster care and specialist mental health services from which children benefited as well as the positive attachments they experienced with carers. Children also displayed resilient outcomes in the domains of family and social relationships and pro-social behaviours as they progressed through care placements overtime. Lower caseloads and supervisory support for caseworkers can facilitate consistent support and direct work with carers and children. The vulnerabilities of children based on age and gender indicate the need for differential and individualized responses from carers and caseworkers.

The children's scores on self esteem were lower than normative data initially with improvements overtime. The overall trajectory of self esteem is subject of a wide ranging literature. However, researchers and theorists have attributed changes in self esteem in childhood and adolescence to both maturational and socio-contextual changes (Harter 1993). Care variables accounted for differences in specific domains of self esteem, especially peer self esteem. In keeping with a resilience orientation, approaches to enhancing children's relationship building skills and reinforcing their self worth through opportunities for positive peer and adult attachments are to be encouraged. The role that foster/ adoptive parents can play to influence the continuum of risk factors and assets and give children a sense of relational continuity is significant to children's outcomes. Effective ways of assessing and enhancing positive foster parenting practices is a research priority.

A strength of the research is its focus on the ongoing experience of children currently in care. The perceptions of children add an important dimension to the study bringing into the research their lived experience. This underlines the importance of listening to children and respecting their capacity for self expression and their right to participate in research about them (Gilligan 2002; Kufeldt, Simard and Vaehon 2003). Eliciting data from multiple informants and longitudinally, contributed to a more comprehensive picture of outcomes. A major limitation of the study is the sample size and the heterogeneity of the group in terms of age. The analysis of outcomes is correlational, the study being non experimental. Further research with larger samples and incorporating multi informant perspectives, is needed to enhance the knowledge base on the wellbeing of children in care.

Acknowledgements

The author thanks the children and young people and carers who shared their experiences and insights in successive interviews. Thanks are also due to the caseworkers of Barnardos Find a Family Program for participating in the research.

References

Achenbach, T.M. (1991) *Manual for the Child Behaviour Checklist and 1991 Profile.* Burlington, VT: University of Vermont.

Armsden, G.C. and Greenberg, M.T. (1987) 'The inventory of parent and peer attachment: individual differences and their relationship to psychological well-being in adolescence.' *Journal of Youth and Adolescence 16,* 427–454.

Australian Institute of Health and Welfare (2009) *Child Protection Australia 2006–2007,* Child Welfare Series No 43. Canberra: AIHW.

Babbie, E. (2001) *The Practice of Social Research* (9th ed.). Belmont, CA: Wadsworth/Thomson Learning.

Burns, B.J. Phillips, S.D. Wagner, H.R. Barth, R.P. *et al.* (2004) 'Mental health need and access to mental health services by youths involved with child welfare: a national survey.' *Journal of the American Academy of Child and Adolescent Psychiatry 43,* 8, 960–970.

Cantos, A. Gries, L.T. and Slis, V. (1997) 'Behavioral correlates of parental visiting during family foster care.' *Child Welfare LXXVI,* 309–329.

Chapman, M.V. Wall, A. and Barth, R.P. (2004) 'Children's voices: the perception of children in foster care.' *American Journal of Orthopsychiatry 74,* 293–304.

Clausen, J. M. Landsverk, J. Ganger, W. Chadwick, D. and Litrownik, A. (1998) 'Mental health problems of children in foster care.' *Journal of Child and Family Studies 7,* 3, 283–296.

Cleaver, H. (2000) *Fostering Family Contact.* London: The Stationery Office.

Fanshel, D. Finch, S.J. and Grundy, J.F. (1989) 'Modes of exit from foster family care and adjustment at time of departure of children with unstable life histories.' *Child Welfare 68,* 391–402.

Farrington, D.P. (1991) 'Longitudinal research strategies: advantages, problems and prospects.' *Journal of the American Academy of Child and Adolescent Psychiatry 30,* 369–374.

Fernandez, E. (2008) 'Unravelling emotional, behavioural and educational outcomes in a longitudinal study of children in foster-care.' *British Journal of Social Work 38,* 7, 1283–1301.

Fernandez, E. (2009) 'Children's wellbeing in care: evidence from a longitudinal study of outcomes.' *Children and Youth Services Review 31,* 1092–1100.

Fratter, J. Rowe, J. Sapsford, D. and Thoburn, J. (1991) *Permanent Family Placement: A Decade of Experience.* London: BAAF.

Gilligan, R. (2002) 'The Importance of Listening to Children in Foster Care.' In G. Kelly and R. Gilligan (eds) *Issues in Foster Care: Policy, Practice and Research.* London: Jessica Kinsley Publishers.

Grodin, A.M. and Glantz, L.H. (1994) *Children as Research Subjects: Science, Ethics an Law.* New York, NY: Oxford University Press.

Hare, B.R. (1985) *The HARE General and Area-Specific Self-Esteem Scale.* Unpublished manuscript, Department of Sociology, SUNY Stony Brook, Stony Brook, NY.

Harker, R.M. Dobel-Ober, D. Berridge, D. and Sinclair, R. (2004) *Taking Care of Education.* London: National Children's Bureau.

Harter, S. (1993) 'Causes and Consequences of Low Self Esteem in Children and Adolescents.' In R.F. Baumeister (ed.) *Self Esteem: The Puzzle of Low Self-regard.* New York, NY: Plenum Press.

Howe, D. (1995) *Attachment Theory for Social Work Practice.* London: Macmillan.

James, S. (2004) 'Why do foster care placements disrupt? An investigation of reasons for placement change in foster care.' *Social Service Review 78,* 4, 601–627.

Johnson, P.R. Yoken, C. and Voss, R. (1995) 'Family foster care placement: the child's perspective.' *Child Welfare 74,* 5, 959–976.

Kufeldt, K. Simard, M. and Vachon, J. (2003) 'Improving outcomes for children in care.' *Adoption and Fostering 27,* 8–19.

Masten, A.S. and Coatsworth, J.D. (1998) 'The development of confidence in favorable and unfavorable environments: lessons from research from successful and unsuccessful children.' *American Psychologist 53,* 205–220.

Newton, R.R. Litrownik, A.J. and Landsverk, J.A. (2000) 'Children and youth in foster care: disentangling the relationship between problem behaviours and number of placements.' *Child Abuse and Neglect 24,* 10, 1363–1374.

Padgett, D.K. (1998) *Qualitative Methods in Social Work Research: Challenges and Rewards.* Thousand Oaks, CA: Sage.

Parker, R. Ward, H. Jackson, S. Aldgate, J. and Wedge, P. (1991) *Looking after Children: Assessing Outcomes in Child Care.* London: Her Majesty's Stationery Office.

Pecora, P.J. Williams, J. Kessler, R.C. Hiripi, E. O'Brien, K. and Emerson, J. (2006) 'Assessing the educational achievements of adults who were formerly placed in family foster care.' *Child and Family Social Work 11,* 3, 220–231.

Perkins-Mangulabnan, J. and Flynn, R.J. (2006) 'Foster Parenting Practices and Foster Youth Outcomes.' In R.J. Flynn, P.M. Dudding and J.G. Barber (eds) *Promoting Resilience in Child Welfare.* Ottawa, ON: University of Ottawa Press.

Quinton, D. and Murray, C. (2002) 'Assessing Emotional and Behavioural Development in Children Looked After Away From Home.' In H. Ward and W. Rose (eds) *Approaches to Needs Assessment in Children's Services.* London: Jessica Kingsley Publishers.

Rubin, D.M. Alessandrini, E.A. Feudtner, C. Mandell, D.S. Localio, A.R. and Hadley, T. (2006) 'Placement stability and mental health costs for children in foster care.' *Paediatrics 113*, 5, 1336–1341.

Rutter, M. (1990) 'Psychosocial Resilience and Protective Mechanisms.' In J. Rolf, A.S. Masten, D. Cichetti, K.H. Neuchterlain and S. Weintraub (eds) *Risk and Protective Factors in the Development of Psychopathology.* Cambridge: Cambridge University Press.

Sawyer, M.G. Arney, F.M. Baghurst, P.A. Clark, J.J. *et al.* (2001) 'The mental health of young people in Australia: key findings from the child and adolescent component of the national survey of mental health and well-being.' *Australian and New Zealand Journal of Psychiatry 35*, 6, 806–814.

Sinclair, I. Barker, C. Wilson, K. and Gibbs, I. (2005) *Foster Children: Where They Go and How They Get On.* London: Jessica Kingsley Publishers.

Strauss, A. and Corbin, J. (1998) *Basics of Qualitative Research: Techniques and Procedures for Developing Grounded Theory* (2nd ed.) Thousand Oaks, CA: Sage.

Wulczyn, F. Barth, R.P. Yuan, Y.T. Jones-Harden, B. and Landsverk, J. (2006) *Beyond Common Sense: Child Welfare Child Wellbeing and the Evidence for Policy Reform.* Piscataway, NJ: Aldine Transaction.

Commentary by Robert Flynn on:

Wellbeing in Foster Care: An Australian Longitudinal Study of Outcomes

Elizabeth Fernandez

The research described in Elisabeth Fernandez' chapter is a welcome addition to the child welfare literature, for several reasons. First, the study is longitudinal in nature, an essential attribute for research wishing to do justice to developmental processes and outcomes. Second, the study gives voice to young people in care, in line with contemporary emphases on the rights of the child. Third, Elizabeth Fernandez practises a welcome triangulation, in analysing the responses and views of the three parties at the heart of foster care – young people in care, caregivers and caseworkers – as well as the responses of the children's teachers. Fourth, the study is a good example of the utility of mixed methods, in its informative blend of quantitative results from responses to standardized instruments and qualitative data derived from answers to open-ended interview questions.

In our respective research programmes, Elizabeth Fernandez and the author of this commentary have been greatly influenced by the international Looking After Children initiative (Ward 1995). I would thus like to focus on selected parallels that I found in her findings in New South Wales, Australia and our results in Ontario, Canada (our Ontario Looking After Children project is now in its ninth year of assessing the needs and monitoring the developmental outcomes of young people in care).

The first parallel concerns our common finding that young people in care report very positive relationships with their foster mothers and foster fathers, but especially with the former. From a resilience perspective, this is good news and adds weight, from a child welfare perspective, to Ann Masten's (2006) observation that 'a close relationship with a caring and competent adult is widely considered the most important and general protective factor for human development.'

The second parallel consists of the finding that, in Australia as in Canada, the mental health of the young people in care showed encouraging signs of improvement over time. Moreover, as the Looking After Children perspective would predict, with its grounding in authoritative-parenting theory and resilience theory, the young people's improvements in mental health were positively related to the quality of their relationships with their caregivers.

A third parallel relates to findings about self esteem. Despite differences in our respective measures, Elizabeth Fernandez in Australia and we in Canada (Flynn, Beaulac and Vinograd 2006) found a robust relationship between the young people's level of self esteem and their ratings of the quality of their relationships with their foster mothers.

Fourth, Elizabeth Fernandez' research and our own (Perkins-Mangulabnan and Flynn 2006) both suggest that there are important payoffs to greater placement stability. In both countries, young people who had been with their current caregivers for a longer period of time exhibited better overall adjustment.

Finally, many of the implications for policy and practice that Elizabeth Fernandez draws from her findings have direct parallels in our Canadian data. Like her, we find that our Canadian children in care have high levels of psychological needs (Marquis and Flynn 2009). Like her, we also find that greater placement stability and better relationships with foster carers are associated with better foster child outcomes, across a range of domains.

References

Flynn, R.J. Beaulac, J. and Vinograd, J. (2006) 'Participation in Structured Voluntary Activities, Substance Use and Psychological Outcomes in Out-Of-Home Care.' In R.J. Flynn, P.M. Dudding and J.G. Barber (eds) *Promoting Resilience in Child Welfare.* Ottawa, ON: University of Ottawa Press.

Marquis, R.A. and Flynn, R.J. (2009) 'The SDQ as a mental health measurement tool in a Canadian sample of looked after young people.' *Vulnerable Children and Youth Studies 4, 2,* 114–121.

Masten, A.S. (2006) 'Promoting Resilience in Development: A General Framework for Systems of Care.' In R.J. Flynn, P.M. Dudding and J.G. Barber (eds) *Promoting Resilience in Child Welfare.* Ottawa, ON: University of Ottawa Press.

Perkins-Mangulabnan, J. and Flynn, R.J. (2006) 'Foster Parenting Practices and Foster Youth Outcomes.' In R.J. Flynn, P.M. Dudding and J.G. Barber (eds) *Promoting Resilience in Child Welfare.* Ottawa, ON: University of Ottawa Press.

Ward, H. (1995) *Looking After Children: Research into Practice.* London: HMSO.

A Synthesis of Research Findings and Direction for Policy, Practice, and Research in Foster Care

Richard P. Barth and Elizabeth Fernandez

Child welfare service programs—and their most visible component, foster care—are extraordinarily varied across the globe. Even within countries, different practices have emerged with regard to who enters foster care, how long they stay and what services they receive (this variation may be somewhat more limited in countries with highly centralized service provision but we expect that it is always substantial). The result is, inevitably, that different service careers and child welfare outcomes are likely to follow from differential selection for admission into services, type of services, and duration of services. June Thoburn more than proves this point in her chapter which is a rich compilation of some of the key differences between "foster care" programs. Indeed, she shows that foster care is a heteronym unto itself—a term that is spelled and sounds the same but has a different meaning (depending on where it occurs). The variation articulated in Thoburn's chapter immediately raises the question of whether understanding a service like "foster care" can be accomplished through international study. We hope that this volume has demonstrably and loudly exclaimed the value of international comparisons.

We endeavoured to have this comparison work at several levels. The first was to have each of the authors try to explain how foster care operates. This was an attempt to literally explain "how foster care works." We also expected that each of the studies would also provide information about "how foster care works out." Most of the chapters do provide data on outcomes of foster care, but none of them did so definitively. Nonetheless, anyone reading this volume has to be impressed with how far foster care research has come in recent years.

The chapters are rich with rigorous comparisons between outcomes for youth with different kinds of child welfare experiences. Flynn and colleagues (this volume) take the top prize for comparisons by developing one based on a randomized clinical effectiveness trial. Although the chapter does not take the story to its conclusion, the rationale for the work and the design of the intervention and preliminary findings are promising. The foster children who had received tutoring in reading and math from their foster parents during year one of the randomized field trial experienced statistically and practically important gains in the key academic skill areas of reading (i.e. Sentence Comprehension) and math (i.e. Math Calculation), compared with the foster children who had not received the foster-parent tutoring intervention.

Most of the comparisons are between similar groups or between dissimilar groups as they emerge over time. Although taking many different forms, most of these methods employ prudent classifications of children according to the type of placement they started in, or whether they are in placement at all, or the kind of reasons that they left care. The certainty with which we can interpret the importance of comparisons is always limited but the longitudinal nature of these data yields more certainty than has previously been available about how foster care works out. We know, of course, that many outcomes will be determined slowly and over a very long period of time. Feigelman's (1997) seminal study of children who have been adopted (largely by couples) shows, for example, that when compared to biological children raised by couples and to children in single-parent families, that the adopted children look more like those children raised in single parent households at 20 years of age but, by age 30, look much more like the biological children who are also raised by couples. We could certainly expect that there might be similar cross-over effects if we followed children long enough.

Barth and Lloyd's (this volume) comparison of three groups of children to estimate the relative impacts of home care, foster care, and adoption noted children returning home to biological parents and those with adopted parents had similar and positive outcomes concluding that placement stability and carer commitment are major determinants of outcomes. The authors also note that at the fith year of data collection between 80 and 90 percent were in the non-clinical range for summary scores of the Achenbach CBCL ratings. Fernandez' (this volume) prospective follow up of children in long-term care found that developing cohesion with foster carers and greater placement stability were associated with incremental gains across various domains as children progress over time in their placements.

Our longitudinal work has improved measurement, improved sample size, but, generally, still lacks sufficient longevity. An extraordinary exception, in this volume, is the work by Vinnerljung and colleagues (this volume) and that of Pecora and colleagues (this volume), respectively, who follow youth who have experienced foster care well into their twenties. The outcomes for Swedish children who had been in foster care were quite a bit worse than the comparison group on many dimensions—starkly countering the notion that if a foster youth grows up into a mature social welfare state that contributes substantially, if not completely, to providing housing, day care, higher education and health benefits, that this would be the great equalizer with youth who grew up in a more conventional household. These effects were mitigated for children who experienced foster care as a younger child. Clearly, there is more to the determinants of youth outcomes than access to social and health services as an adult. It is reasonable to think that there is selection into being in foster care as an adolescent that may involve both the conditions of the youth's family of origin and the character of the youth's behavior and that foster care during adolescence did not cause all of these problems. Nonetheless, these findings clearly indicate the need to do more and different. Vinnerljung and colleagues have suggestions and we have some, too—to develop programs for adolescents that involve intensive services (like Multi-Systemic Therapy or Multi-Dimensional Foster Care) that work with the families of those youth, for as long as is needed, to try to repair the capacity of the family members to support each other during young adulthood.

Indeed, there is a growing consensus in these international findings that foster care is not fulfilling its aspirations of helping to rehabilitate children to the point at which the negative impact of their prior experiences are largely mitigated. Part of this apparently adverse impact of foster care is artifactual because children who enter foster care are children with significant behavioral health problems that may have arisen independent of abuse and neglect (Barth, Wildfire and Green 2006; McDonald and Brook 2009) and caused the foster care placement. Nonetheless, some of the poorer outcomes experienced by foster children may result from multiple placements (Farmer, Fernandez and Delfabbro, del Valle and López, Sinclair, Strijker, Ward and Munro, Wulczyn and Chen) (this volume) and the disruption of family ties.

Several chapters contribute to the growing literature on placement disruption and its impact on relationships, emotional and behavioral health, and education. Wulczyn and Chen provide a nuanced analysis of pathways and timing of movement, identifying high rates of movement in the first six months of care episodes. Fernandez and Delfabbro extend the analysis of pathways and movements to reunification outcomes, noting most children reunify within 5–8 months and a declining rate of reunification is seen thereafter. Children with behavioral problems who are older and those who experience multiple moves and children from indigenous backgrounds, are vulnerable to longer stays in care before reunification. In common with Wulczyn they highlight the critical role of early intervention and support to parents, children and carers in the initial six months of placement, a vulnerable period when exits and placement changes are concentrated. Ward and Munro's chapter which focuses on a particularly vulnerable group, the under fives, reminds us that care planning and decision-making for infants calls for a developmentally sensitive approach that minimizes disruption considering their attachment needs in the early years.

Sinclair provides intriguing data on the diverse pathways of children and young people and extends the lens on placement stability to focus beyond absence of moves to "quality" of placements emphasizing children's subjective sense of belonging to the foster family and enacted commitment of carer and child to each other. Exploring placement breakdown in a three and half year follow up Strijker found that despite the intent of long-term care, a third of the placements ended prematurely, some children returning to residential care. Risk factors identified include age, severity of behavioral problems, and replacements confirming trends in other studies. Strijker joins Pecora *et al.* in advocating for more effective coordination of mental health and child welfare services.

Even though foster care in Spain reflects greater stability in living arrangements, many children remaining with foster carers beyond transition to adulthood. A unique characteristic of the Spanish out of home care system noted by del Valle and López (this volume) in their analysis of kinship and non-kinship care is the high utilization of kinship care (85% of placements). In the wake of increasing reliance on kinship care as an out of home care resource outcome research and developing policy have focused on this area (Maluccio, Ainsworth and Thoburn 2000). The research represented in this volume reflects positive support for kin placement (Sinclair, del Valle and López, Farmer) acknowledging the need for increased training and financial and other support to kin carers. Findings to emerge from subsequent waves of data collection from the Danish longitudinal study (Knudsen and colleagues, this volume) comparing kin and non kin care will no doubt enhance the evidence base in this important area.

The themes on placement disruption taken together speak to the need for individualizing care planning and enhancing supports and training for carers with a policy and practice emphasis endorsed by several authors in this volume. Farmer in particular draws attention to the stresses experienced by carers from challenging fostering situations and personal life stresses and their need for support.

The significant challenges in the area of mental health education and employment that confront young people transitioning from care systems to independent living is the focus of contributions by Pecora *et al.* and Daly and Gilligan (this volume). Pecora and colleagues' analysis indicates that 45 percent of fostered alumni – most of whom were placed into long term foster care as older children – were diagnosed with at least one mental health condition in the last year. Among the range of conditions identified Post-Traumatic Stress Disorder (PTSD) accounts for 20 percent. Their carefully crafted recommendations for preventative and remedial interventions are an important contribution to the evidence base.

Young people's educational and employment outcomes are the focus of the work of Daly and Gilligan. A finding of interest is that young people were significantly more likely to continue their education when they remained in care beyond the age of 18 and lived with the same carer, a finding that further underscores the importance of stability.

On the subject of contact with birth families various authors comment on the positive and negative aspects of contact. Farmer's comment on the need for a differential approach to contact decisions which supports grandparent contact and promotes children's links with extended family members merits attention. Similarly Pecora and collegues (this volume) advocate supporting fragments of the relationship that remain with the birth family noting that "youth leave foster care but their relationships—positive or negative—will always be there with the family of origin."

In our introduction we advocated a broader focus on child wellbeing moving beyond the focus on safety, survival, and permanence. The United Nations Convention on the Rights of the Child provides a normative framework for understanding child wellbeing that is multidimensional and ecological. The task is to advance the discourse and inquiry into what supports the creation of environments that can effectively nurture the wellbeing of children in care. The discourse on conceptualizing and measuring child wellbeing is constantly evolving as new theoretical and empirical developments emerge. The recognition of children and young people as a distinct group has given impetus to different understandings of child wellbeing and a more child focused approach (Ben Arieh 2009). Changing views of childhood (James and Prout 1990; Qvortrup 2004) have advanced the thinking in this area to emphasise themes of participation, rights, and provision, not merely survival; to move the focus from children's future development towards adulthood (well becoming) (Qvortrup 1999) to children's present lives (wellbeing); towards understanding of "quality of life" for children (Huebner 2004); and importantly, to emphasize children's voices apart from adult perspectives and thus be respectful of children's ability to interpret their current lives to others (Berrick, Frasch and Fox 2000; Burton and Phipps 2009; Fernandez 2007). The potential of standardized measures of achievement and competence identified by adult researchers and clinicians to capture the complexities of children's lives is a further subject of debate in the evolving discourse on child wellbeing (Folman 1998 cited in Maluccio *et al.* 2000). It challenges us to consider how we might balance adultcentric approaches to research and measurement and those that capture wellbeing in ways that are meaningful to children themselves .

The sophistication of child welfare research is increasing with evidence of more cohort studies and streamlined information systems that enable consistency in variables used. The merits of prospective longitudinal studies which enable variables of interest to be captured at several points in time and monitored for change or stability is well illustrated in major studies such as NSCAW and others in this volume. Further developments of significance include the valuable longitudinal studies assembling outcome data on samples representing the national population of children and youth (for example Longitudinal study of Australian Children (LSAC) 2006; Growing up in Canada: (NLSCY) National Longtiduninal Study of Children and Youth; Human Resources Development Canada and Statistics Canada 1996) and the growth of rigorous clinical trials in the US, UK and Sweden to test promising family preservation and foster care programs.

We hope the findings reported in this volume have the potential to increase holistic understanding of the complex interaction of factors that nurture or impede children's wellbeing and point to opportunities for outcome oriented care planning, timely provision of services and support and the development of policy and future research.

We believe that this volume will provide ideas for clarification of "foster care" types, research designs, measurement strategies and interventions that could enhance the outcomes of foster care. The authors represented here each stand atop the shoulders of pioneering child welfare scholars in their own countries and, now, with this volume and others identified by Whittaker (this volume) in his Foreword, we can begin to weave together best practices in research, policy, and practice.

References

Barth, R.P. Wildfire, J. and Green, R.L. (2006) 'Placement into foster care and the interplay of urbanicity, child behavior problems and poverty.' *American Journal of Orthopsychiatry 76*, 3, 358–366.

Ben-Arieh, A. (2009) 'From Child Welfare to Children Well-Being: The Child Indicators Perspective.' In S. Kamerman, S. Phipps and A. Ben-Arieh (eds) *From Child Welfare to Children Well-Being: An International Perspective on Knowledge in the Service of Policy Making.* New York: Springer.

Berrick, J. Frasch, K. and Fox, A. (2000) 'Assessing children's experiences of out-of-home care: methodological challenges and opportunities.' *Social Work Research 24*, 2, 119–127.

Burton, P and Phipps, S. (2009) ' In Children's Voices.' In S. Kamerman, S. Phipps and A. Ben-Arieh (eds) *From Child Welfare to Children Well-Being: An International Perspective on Knowledge in the Service of Policy Making.* New York, NY: Springer.

Feigelman, W. (1997) 'Adopted adults: comparisons with persons raised in conventional families.' *Marriage and Family Review 25*, 199–223.

Fernandez, E. (2007) 'How children experience fostering outcomes: participatory research with children.' *Child and Family Social Work 12*, 4, 349–359.

Huebner, E.S. (2004) 'Research on assessment of life satisfaction of children and adolescents.' *Social Indicators Research 66*, 3–33.

Human Resources Development Canada and Statistics Canada (1996) *Growing Up in Canada. National Longitudinal Survey of Children and Youth. Minister of Industry.* Ottawa.

James, A. and Prout, A. (1990) *Constructing and Reconstructing Childhood.* Basingstoke: Falmer Press.

Longitudinal Study of Australian Children (LSAC) (2006) *2005–2006 Annual Report.* Melbourne: Australian Institute of Family Studies.

Maluccio, N. Ainsworth, F. and Thoburn, J. (2000) *Child Welfare Outcome Research in the United States, the United Kingdom and Australia.* Washington, D.C.: CWLA Press.

McDonald, T. and Brook, J. (2009) 'Typologies of children in foster care for reasons other than abuse or neglect.' *Journal of Public Child Welfare 3*, 391–408.

Qvortrup, J. (2004) 'Childhood Matters: An Introduction.' In J. Qvortrup, M. Bardy, G. Sgritta and H. Wintersberger (eds) *Childhood Matters: Social Theory, Practice and Politics.* Aldershot: Avebury.

Contributors

Richard P. Barth (Co-Editor) Richard P. Barth is Dean and Professor, School of Social Work, University of Maryland. He has served as the Frank A. Daniels Distinguished Professor at the School of Social Work at the University of North Carolina at Chapel Hill. He was previously the Hutto Patterson Professor, School of Social Welfare, University of California at Berkeley. His books include *Adoption and Disruption* (1988), *From Child Abuse to Permanency Planning: Pathways through Child Welfare Services* (1994), *The Tender Years: Toward Developmentally-Sensitive Child Welfare Services* (1998) and *Beyond Common Sense: Child Welfare, Child-Well-Being and the Evidence for Policy Reform* (2005). He has directed more than 40 studies and, most recently, served as Co-Principal Investigator of the National Survey of Child and Adolescent Well-Being, the first national probablility study of child welfare services in the US.

Lijun Chen Lijun Chen is a senior research specialist at Chapin Hall at the University of Chicago. His research interests include the development, education and general well-being of maltreated children and children in the child welfare system and the performance evaluation of providers of child welfare services. He works on several projects, including a longitudinal analysis of NSCAW survey to understand the effect of contextual factors on developmental trajectories of children involved in the child welfare system and a cross-national study of child disciplinary practices of parents in 30 nations funded by UNICEF. He also participates in the performance evaluation of foster care agencies for several states and individual counties.

Fiona Daly Fiona Daly is currently the Research Officer in the Irish Association of Young People in Care (IAYPIC). Before joining IAYPIC, she was a Research Fellow in the Children's Research Centre, Trinity College Dublin. During her time in the Centre, she was co-author with Robbie Gilligan and lead researcher on 'Lives in Foster Care' (Children's Research Centre, Trinity College Dublin, 1995). She has a Masters in Social Policy and BA (Hons) in Economics and Sociology.

Paul Delfabbro Dr Paul Delfabbro is an Associate Professor in the School of Psychology at the University of Adelaide, where he lectures in applied methodology and statistics and learning theory. He has qualifications in economics, commerce and social science. He has authored and co-authored over 100 reports and articles and other publications in the areas of applied social research relating to gambling, foster care and other areas of social policy. He has undertaken a number of funded projects that have examined the relationship between out-of-home care outcomes and the psychological and behavioural well-being of children in the care system.

Tine Egelund Tine Egelund is programme director for research concerning Children at SFI – The Danish National Centre for Social Research in Copenhagen. Her field of research is social work with socially marginalized or excluded children and their families, within which she conducts major studies, e.g. the Danish longitudinal study of children placed in out-of-home care. Tine Egelund is, furthermore, Professor in Social Work at the University of Stockholm.

Elaine Farmer Elaine Farmer is Professor of Child and Family Studies in the School for Policy Studies at the University of Bristol in the UK. An experienced child care social worker, her research and teaching centres on child protection, foster, kinship and residential care, adoption and reunification. Seven of her studies have been in national programmes of research funded by the Department of Health or the Department for Education. Her books include *Trials and Tribulations: Returning Children from Local Authority Care to Their Families* (1991), *Child Protection Practice: Private Risks and Public Remedies* (1995), *Sexually Abused and Abusing Children in Substitute Care* (1998), *Fostering Adolescents* (2004), *Kinship Care: Fostering Effective Family and Friends Placements* (2008) and *Adoption Agency Linking and Matching: A Survey of Adoption Agency Practice in England and Wales* (2010). Her current research includes studies on informal kinship care, family finding and matching in adoption and a five year follow-up of case management and outcomes for neglected children.

Elizabeth Fernandez (Co-Editor) Dr Elizabeth Fernandez is an Associate Professor, School of Social Sciences and International Studies, University of New South Wales, Australia teaching courses in Human Behaviour: Life Span and Life Stress, Child and Family Welfare and Professional Supervision and is co-ordinator of the postgraduate research degree programme. Her current research programme focuses on outcomes for children in foster care; the impact of family based interventions on children and families; and the reunification of separated children with their families. She has collaborated with Barnardos Australia in the research and Implementation of the Looking After Children framework in Australian out-of-home care programmes. Her publications include *Significant Harm: Unravelling Protection Decisions and Substitute Care Careers* (1996) and journal articles and book chapters on foster care, child protection, family support and practice learning.

Jorge Fernandez del Valle Professor Jorge Fernandez del Valle teaches in the Faculty of Psychology at the University of Oviedo (Spain) and his research and teaching interests are closely related to child protection and programme evaluation in residential care and foster care. He is director of the Child and Family Research Group that is currently developing several projects of programme evaluation for regional authorities in the field of child and family policies. This research group has carried out the first evaluation of kinship care in Spain in 1998 and the main national evaluations of foster care in 2003 and 2008. He has published widely in this field.

Eva Franzén Dr Eva Franzén works at the Swedish Ministry of Health and Social Affairs. She is a social scientist conducting research in the fields of poverty, youth studies and welfare. Her research focuses on integration and social exclusion.

Robert J. Flynn Dr Bob Flynn is a Full Professor in the School of Psychology and the Director of the Centre for Research on Educational and Community Services at the University of Ottawa, Canada. For the past decade, he has directed the Ontario Looking After Children project, in partnership with the Ontario Association of Children's Aid Societies (OACAS) and the Ontario Ministry of Children and Youth Services (MCYS). The project involves annual evaluations of the needs and developmental outcomes of some 8000 young people in long-term care in Ontario, with the goal of continuous improvement of local and provincial decision-making and service quality.

Robbie Gilligan Robbie Gilligan is Professor of Social Work and Social Policy, Head of the School of Social Work and Social Policy and a Fellow of Trinity College Dublin. He is also Associate Director (and co-founder) of the Children's Research Centre. His publications include *Lives in Foster Care* (2005) published by the Children's Research Centre; *Promoting Resilience – Supporting Children and Young People who are in Care, Adopted or in Need* (second edition) (2009) published by British Agencies for Adoption and Fostering, London; *Child Development for Child Care and Protection Workers* (co-authored with Brigid Daniel and Sally Wassell) (2010); and 'Issues in Foster Care' (co-edited with Greg. Kelly) (2000).

Anne-Dorthe Hestbæk Anne-Dorthe Hestbæk is the Head of the Child and Family Research Department at SFI – The Danish National Centre for Social Research (Denmark's biggest research centre in the social field). For several years, she has been carrying out research at the Centre, focusing on children and families with special needs, children in out-of-home care, kinship care, the consequences of being exposed to different adversities and the characteristics of resilient children. Before taking the position as Head of Department, she was managing a large, longitudinal study on children in Denmark (DALSC95 – Danish Longitudinal Study on Children). She has been awarded the annual research prize from the Danish National Health Foundation.

Anders Hjern Anders Hjern is a medical doctor, trained as a paediatrician at the Karolinska University Hospital in Stockholm. He is an epidemiologist at the National Board of Health and Welfare and an Affiliated Professor of Paediatric Epidemiology at the Nordic School of Public Health. His research interests include adoption, health of foster children, migrant health and child public health.

Irving Hwang Irving Hwang, MA, is a statistical programmer and data analyst in the Department of Health Care Policy at Harvard Medical School. He is a data analyst for numerous large-scale projects, most notably the WHO World Mental Health Survey Initiative, the National Co-morbidity Survey and most recently, the largest study ever of suicide in the US military, the Study to Assess Risk and Resilience in Service Members. In addition to co-authoring over 15 peer-reviewed scientific publications, Hwang is one of the primary data analysts for a WHO WMH Survey Initiative five-book series to be published by Cambridge University Press.

Ronald C. Kessler Ronald C. Kessler, PhD is a Professor of Health Care Policy at Harvard Medical School. Kessler's research deals broadly with the social determinants of mental health and illness as studied from an epidemiological perspective. He is the author of over 500 publications and is a member of both the Institute of Medicine and the National Academy of Sciences. He is the PI of the National Co-morbidity Survey, the first nationally representative survey of the prevalence and correlates of mental disorders in the US and a Co-Director of the World Health Organization's World Mental Health Survey Initiative.

Lajla Knudsen Lajla Knudsen has an MSc in Political Science and a BA in Ethnography and Social Anthropology from the University of Aarhus. Since 2007 she has been working as a research assistant at SFI. She is the author of a publication comparing kinship care and ordinary foster care and she is co-author on publications about 'Children in Care – a Danish Longitudinal Study' and about alternatives to out-of-home placement for young people. The study of kinship care and the study of alternatives to out-of-home placement will be followed up with additional data collections and publications focusing on outcomes.

Christopher Lloyd E. Christopher Lloyd is an Assistant Professor of Social Work at the University of Arkansas at Little Rock. He earned his MA from the University of Chicago and his PhD from the University of North Carolina at Chapel Hill. His interests include child welfare, child development, psychotherapy, quantitative analytic methodologies and services for children. His papers appear in social work and medical journals.

Frank Lindblad Frank Lindblad is a child psychiatrist, working as a researcher at the Department of Neuroscience, Uppsala University. He is also Affiliated Professor at the Stress Research Institute, Stockholm University and Associated Professor at the Department of Clinical Neuroscience, Karolinska Institute. His research concerns childhood trauma, stress and vulnerability.

Mónica López Mónica López is a Research Assistant in the Faculty of Psychology at the University of Oviedo (Spain) and a member of the Child and Family Research Group. She has developed extensive research in foster care in Spain and has coordinated the first national evaluation of foster care in Spain funded by the Ministry of Education and Social Policy. She is currently evaluating foster care programmes for several regional child care authorities.

Robyn A. Marquis Robyn A. Marquis is a doctoral student in the clinical psychology programme at the University of Ottawa, Canada. Her thesis is on the topic of foster children's mental health gains from academic tutoring by their foster parents.

Emily R. Munro Emily Munro is Research Fellow at the Centre for Child and Family Research, Loughborough University, England. She has undertaken a number of studies funded by the Department of Health and Department for Children, Schools and Families to inform policy and social work practice and promote positive outcomes for vulnerable children and families. Her publications include *Babies and Young Children in Care: Life Pathways, Decision-making and Practice* (co-authored 2006) and *Young People's Transitions from Care to Adulthood: International Research and Practice* (co-edited 2008).

Lee Ann Murdock Lee Murdock joined Casey Family Programs when she was 15 years old after spending time in state care and as a homeless youth. With help of Casey she returned to college at 30 years old and is now a Senior Program Analyst with the Yakima County Department of Human Services working with the Homeless Network of Yakima County. At 41 she still maintains her relationship with her foster mother and frequently works with her local Casey Family Program Office.

Kirk O'Brien Kirk O'Brien, PhD is the Director of Foster Care Research at Casey Family Programs in Seattle, Washington, where he has worked since 2001. His primary responsibilities include managing, evaluating and providing consultation on studies of youth in and alumni formerly in foster care and studies evaluating strategies to help youth exit foster care by safely achieving permanence. Dr O'Brien received his BA in Psychology from Emory University and received his doctorate in Developmental Psychology (with a speciality in quantitative methods) from the University of Houston. His professional interests include the Transtheoretical Model, family systems theory and quantitative methods.

Marie-Pierre Paquet Marie-Pierre Paquet is a research assistant at the Centre for Research on Educational and Community Services at the University of Ottawa, Canada. She will soon begin doctoral studies in clinical psychology.

Peter J. Pecora Peter J. Pecora is Managing Director of Research Services at the Casey Family Programs and Professor of Social Work at the University of Washington, Seattle. He has researched and published extensively in the field of child and family outcomes. He was a line worker and later a programme coordinator in a number of child welfare service agencies in Wisconsin. He has also served as an expert witness for a number of states. He has co-authored the books *Evaluating Family Based Services* and *The Child Welfare Challenge*, journal articles and book chapters on child welfare programme design, administration and research. He has led a study of foster care alumni with the states of Oregon and Washington in conjunction with Harvard Medical School and the University of Michigan.

Catherine Roller White Catherine Roller White, MA, is a Research Analyst at Casey Family Programs, where she has worked since 2004. Ms. White coordinates studies of youth in foster care and alumni of foster care; these studies describe youth and alumni outcomes and examine how experiences in foster care can be made better to improve outcomes. In addition, she coordinates evaluations of interventions to help youth in foster care achieve permanency. She has authored and co-authored numerous journal articles and chapters related to well-being outcomes for youth and young adults who have been or are currently in foster care. Ms White's primary areas of interest are in education and mental health.

Nancy Sampson Nancy Sampson is a Senior Research Director in the Department of Health Care Policy at Harvard Medical School, where she supervises a team of ten biostatisticians in data analyses carried out for numerous projects, most notably the WHO World Mental Health Survey Initiative, the National Co-morbidity Survey and the largest study ever of suicide in the US military, the Study to Assess Risk and Resilience in Service Members. Ms Sampson has over 25 years of experience in survey research data collection, data management and data analysis, and has co-authored more than 40 peer-reviewed scientific publications.

Ian Sinclair Ian Sinclair is a Professor Emeritus at the University of York. After a first degree in philosophy and ancient history, he worked in teaching, probation, social services, counselling and industrial and social research. He has a PhD from the London School of Economics and has done work on delinquency, elderly people and adult relationships. He was Director of Research at the National Institute of Social Work and then Professor of Social Work and co-director of the Social Work Research and Development Unit at the University of York. His recent work has been on residential care and foster care for children.

Johan Strijker Johan Strijker is an Associate Professor at the Department of Special Needs Education and Child Care, University of Groningen in the Netherlands. He teaches foster care and programme evaluation. His research interest is primarily theory building for the domain of foster care and secondarily sexual abuse. Recent work includes studies on the movements of foster children, trauma and psychopathology of foster children. He has published a book, *Kennisboek pleegzorg* (2009) (Knowledge base of foster care), and is participating in different European networks for research in foster care.

June Thoburn June Thoburn is Professor Emeritus of the UEA School of Social Work and Psychology, Norwich, UK. A qualified and experienced child and family social worker, she has been teaching and researching across the field of child welfare since 1978. She was awarded a Leverhulme Emeritus Fellowship to undertake the international comparison of children in out-of-home care reported in her chapter. She has been Vice Chair of the General Social Care Council for England and was awarded the CBE in 2000 for services to social work.

Bo Vinnerljung Bo Vinnerljung works as researcher for the National Board of Health and Welfare in Stockholm. He is also Affiliated Professor of Social Work at the University of Stockholm. His current research is mostly longitudinal studies of vulnerable children, based on combinations of data from various Swedish national registers (data banks covering the entire population).

Harriet Ward Harriet Ward is Professor of Child and Family Research at Loughborough University, UK, where she directs a research centre specializing in providing the evidence base for national policy development. Her current research programme includes studies on: outcomes for looked after children and the assessment of individual and agency performance; children and young people's views of care and accommodation; the costs and consequences of delivering children's services; decision making and care experiences of very young children at risk of significant harm; transitions to adulthood from care; core reporting requirements for children's services. Much of Professor Ward's research developed from the 'Looking After Children' project, which she led from 1992 to 2003 and which has been implemented throughout the UK, in several Canadian provinces and Australian states and in parts of Eastern Europe.

James K. Whittaker James K. Whittaker is The Charles O. Cressey Endowed Professor Emeritus at the University of Washington School of Social Work, Seattle where he has served as a member of the senior faculty since 1970. His research and teaching interests encompass child and family policy and services, and the integration of evidence-based practices into contemporary child and family services. A frequent contributor to the professional literature, Dr Whittaker is author/co-author/editor of eight books and nearly 100 peer review papers and book chapters. In all, Dr Whittaker's works have been translated into eight languages and he presently serves on the editorial review boards of a number of social service journals including: *Social Service Review* (US); *Journal of Public Child Welfare* (US); *The British Journal of Social Work* (UK); *Child and Family Social Work* (UK) and *International Journal of Child and Family Welfare* (Belgium). He is a member of the International Association for Outcome-Based Evaluation and Research on Family and Children's Services (Padua, Italy) and an Associated Board member of EUSARF, the European Scientific Association for Residential and Foster Care for Children and Adolescents (Leuven, Belgium).

Fred Wulczyn Fred Wulczyn is a Research Fellow at Chapin Hall Centre for Children at the University of Chicago where he directs the Centre for State Foster Care and Adoption Data. He is the recipient of the National Association of Public Child Welfare Administrators' (NAPCWA) Peter Forsythe Award for leadership in public child welfare. Wulczyn is lead author of *Beyond Common Sense: Child Welfare, Child Well-Being and the Evidence for Policy Reform* (Aldine Transaction, 2005) and co-editor of *Child Protection: Using Research to Improve Policy and Practice* (Brookings Institution, 2007).

Subject Index

Author Index